Penn Greek Drama Series

Series Editors
David R. Slavitt
Palmer Bovie

The Penn Greek Drama Series presents fresh literary translations of the entire corpus of classical Greek drama: tragedies, comedies, and satyr plays. The only contemporary uniform series of all the surviving work of Aeschylus, Sophocles, Euripides, Aristophanes, and Menander, this collection brings together men and women of literary distinction whose versions of the plays in contemporary English poetry can be acted on the stage or in the individual reader's theater of the mind.

The aim of the series is to make this cultural treasure accessible, restoring as faithfully as possible the original luster of the plays and offering in living verse a view of what talented contemporary poets have seen in their readings of these works so fundamental a part of Western civilization.

Euripides, 4

Ion, Children of Heracles,
The Madness of Heracles,
Iphigenia in Tauris, Orestes

Edited by
David R. Slavitt *and* Palmer Bovie

PENN

University of Pennsylvania Press
Philadelphia

Copyright © 1999 University of Pennsylvania Press
The Madness of Heracles copyright © 1999 Katharine Washburn and
David Curzon

10 9 8 7 6 5 4 3 2 1

Published by
University of Pennsylvania Press
Philadelphia, Pennsylvania 19104-4011

Library of Congress Cataloging-in-Publication Data
Euripides.
   [Works. English. 1997]
   Euripides / edited by David R. Slavitt and Palmer Bovie
      p.   cm. — (Penn Greek drama series)
   Contents: 1. Medea. Hecuba. Andromache. The Bacchae—
2. Hippolytus. Suppliant women. Helen. Electra. Cyclops—3. Alcestis.
Daughters of Troy. The Phoenician Women. Iphigenia at Aulis. Rhesus—
4. Ion. Children of Heracles. The Madness of Heracles. Iphigenia in
Tauris. Orestes
      ISBN 0-8122-3415-4 (v. 1 : cloth : alk. paper). —ISBN 0-8122-1626-1
(v. 1 : pbk. : alk. paper).—ISBN 0-8122-3421-9 (v. 2 : cloth : alk. paper).—
ISBN 0-8122-1629-6 (v. 2 : pbk. : alk. paper).—ISBN 0-8122-3343-X
(v. 3 : cloth : alk. paper).—ISBN 0-8122-1650-4 (v. 3 : pbk. : alk. paper).—
ISBN 0-8122-3500-2 (v. 4 : cloth : alk. paper).—ISBN 0-8122-1697-0
(v. 4 : pbk. : alk. paper)
      1. Euripides—Translations into English.   2. Greek drama (Tragedy)—
Translations into English.   3. Mythology, Greek—Drama.   I. Series.
PA3975.A1   1997
882'.01—dc21   97-28892
                                                              CIP

Contents

Introduction

Palmer Bovie

Classical Greek tragedy, which flourished in Athens during the fifth century B.C., grew out of country festivals originating a century earlier. Three different celebrations in honor of Dionysus, known as the rural Dionysia, occurred during the winter months. One of these, the Lenaea, was also observed at Athens in the sanctuary of Dionysus. In addition to song it offered ecstatic dances and comedy. Another, the Anthesteria, lasted for three days as a carnival time of revelry and wine drinking. It also included a remembrance of the dead and was believed to be connected with Orestes' mythical return to Athens purged of guilt for killing his mother Clytemnestra.

The rural Dionysia were communal holidays observed to honor Dionysus, the god of wine, of growth and fertility, and of lightning. Free-spirited processions to an altar of Dionysus were crowned by lyrical odes to the god sung by large choruses of men and boys chanting responsively under the direction of their leader. The ritual included the sacrifice of a goat at the god's altar, from which the term "tragedy," meaning goat-song, may derive. Gradually themes of a more serious nature gained ground over the joyful, exuberant addresses to the liberating god, legends of familiar heroes, and mythological tales of divine retribution. But the undercurrent of the driving Dionysiac spirit was seldom absent, even in the sophisticated artistry of the masterful tragic poets of the fifth century.

Initially the musical texts were antiphonal exchanges between the chorus and its leader. Thespis, who won the prize of a goat for tragedy at Athens in 534 B.C., is traditionally said to have been the first to appear as an actor, separate from the chorus, speaking a prologue and making set speeches, with his face variously disguised by a linen mask. A fourth festival, the City Dionysia or the Great Dionysia, was instituted by the ruler Peisistratus, also in 534, and nine years later Aeschylus was born. It seems that the major era of Greek tragic art was destined to begin.

The Great Dionysia, an annual occasion for dramatic competitions in tragedy and comedy, was held in honor of Dionysus Eleutheros. Its five-day celebration began with a procession in which the statue of Dionysus was carried to the nearby village of Eleutherai (the site of the Eleusinian Mysteries) and then back, in a parade by torchlight, to Athens and the precincts of Dionysus on the lower slopes of the Acropolis. In the processional ranks were city officials, young men of military age leading a bull, foreign residents of Athens wearing scarlet robes, and participants in the dramatic contests, including the producers (*choregoi*), resplendent in colorful costumes. The ceremonies ended with the sacrificial slaughter of the bull and the installation of Dionysus' statue on his altar at the center of the orchestra.

For three days each of the poets chosen for the competition presented his work, three tragedies and one satyr play (a farcical comedy performed in the afternoon after an interval following the staging of tragedies). In the late afternoon comedies were offered. The other two days were marked by dithyrambic competitions, five boys' choruses on one day, five men's on the other. The dithyramb, earlier an excited dramatic dance, became in the Athenian phase a quieter performance, sung by a chorus of fifty and offering little movement.

The theater of Dionysus at Athens was an outdoor space on the southern slope of the Acropolis. A semicircular auditorium was created on the hillside from stone or marble slabs, or shaped from the natural rock with wooden seats added. Narrow stepways gave access to the seats, the front row of which could be fitted out with marble chairs for official or distinguished members of the audience. From sites visible today at Athens, Delphi, Epidaurus, and elsewhere, it is evident that the sloping amphitheater had excellent acoustic properties and that the voices of the actors and the chorus were readily heard.

The acting area began with an *orchestra*, a circular space some sixty feet in diameter where the chorus performed its dance movements, voiced its commentaries, and engaged in dialogue with the actors. In the center of the orchestra was an altar of Dionysus, and on it a statue of the god. Behind the orchestra several steps led to a stage platform in front of the *skene*, a wooden building with a central door and doors at each end and a flat roof. The actors could enter and exit through these doors or one of the sides, retiring to assume different masks and costumes for a change of role. They could also appear on the roof for special effects, as in Euripides' *Orestes* where at the end Orestes and Pylades appear, menacing Helen with death, before she is whisked away from them by Apollo. The skene's facade represented a palace or temple and could have an altar in front of it. Stage properties included the *eccyclema*, a wheeled platform that was rolled out from the central door or the side of the skene to display an interior setting or a tableau, as at the end of Aeschylus' *Agamemnon* where the murdered bodies of Agamemnon and Cassandra are proudly displayed by Clytemnestra.

Another piece of equipment occasionally brought into play was the *mechane*, a tall crane that could lift an actor or heavy objects (e.g., Medea in her chariot) high above the principals' heads. This device, also known as the *deus ex machina*, was favored by Euripides, who in the climactic scene of *Orestes* shows Apollo protecting Helen in the air high above Orestes and Pylades on the roof. Or a deity may appear above the stage to resolve a final conflict and bring the plot to a successful conclusion, as the figure of Athena does at the end of Euripides' *Iphigenia in Tauris*. Sections of background at each end of the stage could be revolved to indicate a change of scene. These *periaktoi*, triangular in shape, could be shown to the audience to indicate a change of place or, together with thunder and lightning machines, could announce the appearance of a god.

The actors wore masks that characterized their roles and could be changed offstage to allow one person to play several different parts in the same drama. In the earliest period tragedy was performed by only one actor in counterpoint with the chorus, as could be managed, for example, in Aeschylus' *Suppliants*. But Aeschylus himself introduced the role of a second actor, simultaneously present on the stage, Sophocles made use of a third, and he and Euripides probably a fourth. From such simple elements (the orchestra space for the chorus, the slightly raised stage and its scene front, the minimal cast of actors) was created the astonishingly powerful poetic drama of the fifth-century Athenian poets.

What we can read and see today is but a small fraction of the work produced by the three major poets and a host of fellow artists who presented plays in the dramatic competitions. Texts of tragedies of Aeschylus, Sophocles, and Euripides were copied and stored in public archives at Athens, along with Aristophanes' comedies. At some later point a selection was made of the surviving plays, seven by Aeschylus, seven by Sophocles, nine by Euripides, and ten others of his discovered by chance. In the late third and early second centuries B.C., this collection of thirty-three plays was conveyed to the great library of Alexandria, where scholarly commentaries, *scholia*, formed part of the canon, to be copied and transmitted to students and readers in the Greco-Roman cultural world.

Euripides (485–406 B.C.) was born near Athens, the son of prosperous middle-class parents. He spent most of his life in study and in writing his poetry "in a cave by the sea in Salamis." At Athens his associates included Archelaus, a pupil of the philosopher Anaxagoras, Protagoras, Prodicus, and Socrates. Such acquaintances, cited by early biographers, are well worth considering in view of Euripides' flair for weaving philosophical debates into many dramatic dialogues or marshaling logical principles in set speeches. During the oppressive decades of the Peloponnesian War, Euripides may have incurred the hostility of his fellow citizens by his denunciation of war and its havoc, a recurrent theme in many of his plays. For whatever reason, he withdrew into retirement, living a rather unsociable existence. For his conventional treatment of mythological figures and situations he was mercilessly mocked by the comic poets, especially Aristophanes. And his skeptical approach to standard religious conceptions may have disturbed many of his listeners. Late in life, three or four years before his death, Euripides left Athens for residence, first in Magnesia and then in Macedon at the court of King Archelaus, where he was received with great honor. There he continued writing plays, his last work being *The Bacchae*, a dramatic limning of the dire consequences of abandoning belief in Dionysus.

Euripides differs from his fellow playwrights in several ways. He adopts unusual versions from the repertory of myth, and his plots and characters are often so realistically developed as to seem new and modern rather than classical. Often we see his principals escape from their predicaments. Fate turns out to be the unexpected. The chorus may interact with the players or its lyrics may form a descant on themes quite separate from the action in progress. In the fluent and quick-witted play of ideas, skepticism can override belief and logic and challenge simple convictions.

His *Electra* varies from the versions of Aeschylus and Sophocles in its astonishing recharacterization of Electra as now married to a peasant farmer who treats her with respect and honors her chastity. Their simple country hut becomes the scene of Clytemnestra's murder. Electra summons her mother on the pretext of having borne a child and wanting her there to perform the ritual of cleansing. With this ironic, macabre embellishment on the conventional murder scene, Euripides seems to be actually increasing the guilt felt by the children. But until this point Electra's conduct as the humble helpmeet of a husband with a heart of gold outclasses her mourning. She smolders with resentment but bides her time, waiting for Orestes, hoping. That Euripides sees her in a different light is also signaled in his refuting the others' recognition tokens. A lock of hair, a scrap of child's clothing, footprints? absurd to think of such things as clues to Orestes' identity! What he can be known by is the scar on his forehead, "on his brow— where he was cut in a fall, chasing a fawn with you in his father's courtyard" (ll. 568–69). So tangible and realistic a memory convinces Electra. The fact is that Orestes is scarred for life. His identification was not just a clever bit of literary criticism.

Brother and sister are, at the end of the *Electra*, brought to the depth of sorrow by the realization of what they have done. But they are lifted out of despair by the timely appearance of their divine relatives Castor and Polydeuces, *ex machina*. The Dioscuri, the heavenly Twins, have paused as they "speed to seas off Sicily, to protect the ships in danger there" (ll. 1335–36). Athens had sent an expedition to the aid of the fleet in Sicily in 413, so it appears that Euripides is being historical as well as mythical here. Electra is to leave Argos and marry Pylades, to live in exile. Orestes must go to Athens and await trial at the Areopagus. The children's generation, marked by the ancient curse of violence on their house, has nevertheless emerged to survive. The Dioscuri (Castor and Polydeuces were the divine brothers of Helen and Clytemnestra) also report, almost casually, that Menelaus and Helen will attend to the burial rites for Clytemnestra and Aegisthus. They explain that Menelaus and Helen have recently arrived from Egypt. She, Helen, never went to Troy, they add laconically.

The year 412 saw the production of Euripides' drama *Helen*, which offers the counter-myth that Hermes had spirited Helen away to Egypt, substituting for her at Troy a phantom image. In Egypt she enjoyed the protection of the king, Proteus, during the ten years of the Trojan war, but after his death his son holds her hostage and wants to make her his wife. She fends him off by maintaining a constant vigil at Proteus' tomb, a sacred refuge. This story line, sketched in by Helen in the prologue in her play, was suggested earlier by an episode in Book II, the Egyptian book, of Herodotus' *Histories*, and poems in praise of Helen by Stesichorus and other sixth-century lyric poets in Euripides' combination. He has seized the opportunity to dramatize Helen's rescue, starting with her joyful reunion with Menelaus, who has been shipwrecked with his crew and the phantom Helen on these shores. Her meeting with him surely constitutes the most appealing recognition scene of any in the Greek drama we know, and Euripides weaves a spell of exciting suspense as husband and wife devise the strategy for eluding their Egyptian captor. Plans are made and discarded until finally Helen hits on the right tactics, saying (almost under her breath) that even a woman might have "a good suggestion" (l. 1086). Their daring plan enables husband and wife to escape from impending doom, and Helen from captivity and slander.

Another Euripidean heroine to escape from peril is found in *Iphigenia in Tauris*. Orestes and Pylades join forces with Iphigenia in devising a plan to outwit the barbarous king of Thrace and sail away to Athens. The men supply the force, the woman the strategic plan. Men may be forceful, Euripides implies, but women are more resourceful. In other female figures, like Ion's mother in the *Ion* and Alcestis in the *Alcestis*, women are rescued from tragedy. Alcestis, indeed, is wrested from the arms of Death by Heracles and restored to her husband's embrace.

Euripides explores the complex dimensions of female character from many angles. In plays from the Trojan War cycle, women are towering figures of tragic sorrow as they voice the grief that descends on the victims of war. Swept up in the grotesque futility of war, the Trojan women endure further humiliation in the senseless murders of their children in the war's catastrophic aftermath. Small wonder that we should weep for Hecuba. A later representation of Andromache finds her married to Neoptolemus, Achilles' son, and having borne a son to him. As if this irony were not insult added to injury, Andromache is now threatened with murder by the new mistress who has replaced her. She is protected by Peleus (a Trojan Woman saved by a Trojan Man), but Menelaus and Hermione, the new mistress, are still bent on doing her in. At the melodramatic moment, Orestes arrives on the scene and will despatch Neoptolemus, taking Hermione as his bride. Here Euripides has ingeniously rescued two women from imminent destruction, one Trojan and one Greek, Hermione being the daughter of Helen. He evidently found such figures as the poignant Andromache and the jealousy-ridden rival Hermione well worth close attention.

The poet's fascinating portraits of celebrated women drawn from the mythological traditions rises to the level of Aeschylean or Sophoclean theatricality. While he may not invoke the grandeur of Aeschylus' vision or the nobility of Sophocles' unerring judgment, Euripides offers his audience real life human beings, natural characters under, at times, supernatural pressures. His memorable women Medea and Phaedra become avenging forces and are demonically driven to destroy the source of their happiness. They do not gain wisdom through suffering, but plunge into darkness. Medea may fly off to Athens in a chariot drawn by dragons, but in reality her burden is her murdered children and all she and Jason once cherished. Her husband is ruined: she, almost worse, is deluded. What she said of herself turns out to be true: "My will is stronger than my reason." Phaedra's psychological burden in the *Hippolytus* is shame and guilt. Her lust humiliates her and compels her to bring disgrace on the innocent young hero. His devotion to Artemis conflicts with her subjection to Aphrodite: both Hippolytus and Phaedra are destroyed in the clash of wills. Tragedy is, of course, the truth realized too late: and too late Theseus discovers his son's innocence and his wife's aberration.

From a terrifying view of women driven to a demonic state we find, in *The Bacchae*, Euripides' last play, what can be considered a misogynist stance. But on the whole this brutal drama chiefly brings to mind the peril of denying an underlying neutral power, the life force that of necessity controls all beings. That is, Dionysus, whose cosmic energy animates life and whose passionate powers motivate the "drama," the forward motion registered by Greek tragedy.

Toward men as heroes Euripides' attitude is sometimes disparaging. The men in *Iphigenia at Aulis* are hardly impressive as they assemble to sail against Troy. Only Achilles achieves some stature, and all are far below the unblemished radiance of Iphigenia, their victim. And Orestes, in the tragedy named after him, is frantic, haunted by his guilty conscience; he plunges wildly into futile gestures of revenge. Heracles can be driven mad and returns to his senses, chastened but none the wiser. In the first play of which we have a record, the *Alcestis*, produced at Athens in 438 B.C. and winner of second prize in the contest at the Great Dionysia, Euripides plays woman against man, wife against husband. The drama itself was in fact the fourth of the group offered, in place of a satyr play. But it does not function as a satyr play; rather, it sets the stage for a reconciliation of an ordinary man and his extraordinary wife. Alcestis has offered to die in her husband's stead, and it is only when Death leads her off the stage that her husband Admetus realizes what he has lost by his wrongminded acceptance of Alcestis' sacrificial gesture. Luckily, Heracles has come to visit his friend Admetus, who, in his characteristically hospitable manner, receives him cordially and hides his knowledge of Alcestis' death. But Heracles learns the truth and it is not too late: he strides off to confront Death, wrests Alcestis from the fatal grasp, and leads back a veiled female figure. He places her in Admetus' hands, instructing his host not to raise the veil until three days have passed. The bulky hero leaves. The play ends. We realize that this well-intentioned but blundering man and his somber, self-denying wife were well worth being saved from their tragic destiny, as the chorus exits, singing:

> The Powers take on many shapes;
> the gods accomplish miracles.
> What was predicted fails to happen,
> then gods reveal their hidden design:
> and this was what took place.

Ion

Translated by
Deborah H. Roberts

Translator's Preface

Ion is one of several Euripidean tragedies that on first encounter defeat a modern reader's expectations of tragedy and that continue to complicate our understanding of the genre. When I ask my students, at the beginning of a course on the tragic tradition, what characterizes tragedy, someone is sure to reply that "everyone dies in the end." But in these plays the central characters ultimately escape misfortune with the promise of happiness to come. Death (though the thought of it plays a role in the pity and fear engendered by the drama) is a part of the past, real or imagined, or of a threatened future that never comes to be.

Ion, probably first performed between 415 and 410 B.C., tells the story of how Creusa, daughter of the king of Athens, raped in her youth by the god Apollo, bore a son, abandoned the baby out of shame, and many years later was reunited with him in Delphi, site of the most revered of Greek oracles, where the god had arranged that he be raised. The play begins as Creusa and her husband Xuthus come to Delphi in search of some remedy for their childlessness. Creusa, who has never recovered from her loss, also plans to ask in secret about her missing child. When the oracle gives Xuthus that child (now grown to manhood) as his own, and appears to refuse Creusa an answer and to deny her any children of her own, she plots to kill the boy, who has been given the name Ion. Her plot is thwarted and Ion in turn threatens her life, but the intervention, first of Apollo's prophetess, the Pythia, and then of Athena, reunites mother and child and reveals the truth to them (though not to Xuthus). Athena predicts the future glory of the Ionians descended from Ion, and all prepare rejoicing to return to Athens.

The ending of this play would have been less surprising to its fifth-century audience than to readers conditioned by the later tradition of tragedy. One of the great monuments of Athenian tragedy, Aeschylus' trilogy the *Oresteia*, also ends with escape, reconciliation, and future promise, and we find the same motifs at the conclusion of Sophocles' *Philoctetes* and of

Euripides' *Alcestis, Iphigenia in Tauris, Helen,* and *Orestes.* It is in Aristotle's *Poetics* (a fourth-century treatise whose surviving first book is largely concerned with tragedy) that we first find the change from happiness to misfortune identified as particularly tragic, and Aristotle recognizes that this outcome is not the favorite of spectators and does not necessarily represent the best type of plot in other regards.

What ancient audiences did expect, as a general rule, was the use in tragedy of traditional myth, seriously treated, with largely familiar characters. In *Ion* (as in the other plays mentioned above) Euripides challenges and plays on that expectation by his use of less well-known stories and variant or invented versions and by his inclusion of comic and parodic elements. He further disconcerts his audience by his manipulation of our sympathies and by shifting and questioning the grounds for our judgments.

The story of Ion is a relatively late addition to the body of Greek myth and does not always include the divine parentage that is clearly a compliment to Athens. Euripides dramatizes and elaborates this complimentary version of the myth, but complicates our response both by playing parts of the story out in a comic register and by taking seriously, as the stuff of tragedy, the familiar mythic situation of the woman who bears a child to a god. He grants the solemnity of tragedy not so much to the divine all-knowing father (whose comic misjudgment of human behavior the play makes plain) as to the sorrowful short-sighted mother and son and their shared but competing experiences of irremediable loss—a loss that, in the play's final comedic turn, is in fact remedied.

Hints of the comic regularly intrude on or modulate conventional tragic scenes in *Ion.* The initial entry of a tragic chorus is generally a moment of solemnity or heightened emotion. But in *Ion* the chorus express themselves neither in heartfelt grief nor in meditative pronouncement on divine or human affairs; they speak instead as a group of awestruck sightseers new to the wonders of Delphi. In the encounter between Ion and Xuthus—a version of the conventional recognition scene—the humor is located in the initial misunderstanding and the disparate responses of the two men. Xuthus believes he is greeting his son and exhibits a pompous and self-conscious enthusiasm; Ion is apparently afraid he is being propositioned and, even when he learns the truth, he is never more than reluctantly accepting. The Servant's account of the feast in Ion's honor takes the form of a conventional messenger's speech, the usual locus for tragedy's narration of all that is most appalling and unfit for representation on stage; here, however, the single pathetically described death is that of a bird. And finally, in the play's conclusion, Apollo's reluctance to show himself can be read not only as a dignified divine withdrawal from mere human recrimination but also as the cowardice of a god who knows he is to blame and who is too anthropomorphic to escape such reproach easily.[1]

At the same time, the play is hardly comic in the story it tells, a story not only of private grief but also of the destruction of civic continuity. Creusa's apparent childlessness is the greatest of misfortunes both for herself and for her royal line, and the drama confronts us repeatedly with that childlessness and its past cause, as Creusa's rape by Apollo and the loss of her child are narrated over and over in the course of the play. Hermes lays out the facts in the prologue with divine dispassion, and when Creusa first meets Ion she hesitantly gives him a brief account of what happened to "a friend." After she finally despairs of either learning her child's fate or bearing another, Creusa retells the story to her old servant and the chorus, first in song and then in dialogue, this time with every detail of fact and feeling. The end of the play brings two more brief narratives of the same events, as Creusa assures Ion that Apollo is in fact his father and Athena assures everyone that Apollo's actions were for the best.

These repeated tellings are not, however, merely cumulative in their effect, but serve to make difficult any final judgment of what happened. The divine versions of the tale and Creusa's concluding version emphasize the helpful role of Apollo, something the gods have always known and Creusa has come to accept. Apollo has, in Athena's words, "managed everything quite neatly." But Creusa's suffering from the rape itself and from the presumed death of her only child has been so eloquently expressed in the middle of the play as to give the lie to Athena's words. We have heard how she screamed for her mother and how the baby reached out for her as she left it to die; we have heard her rage at the god, her "cruel, wicked lover." Nor has her child's own life been one of unmixed happiness. Ion ostensibly delights in his life as a glorified temple servant, but he also describes this

---

[1]On comic elements in *Ion* and in other plays of Euripides see especially Bernard M. W. Knox, "Euripidean Comedy," in his *Word and Action: Essays on the Ancient Theater* (Baltimore: Johns Hopkins University Press, 1979), 250–74.

service as slavery, and he is preoccupied with his unknown parents and his lost childhood. His loss, like Creusa's, has both private and public implications: he still regrets the never-experienced comfort of being a baby in his mother's arms, and at the same time hopes desperately that she may prove to be a free woman and an Athenian so that his status as a citizen will be assured.

Euripides shows us how judgment yields to experience, to self-interest, and to changing concerns. When Ion first hears Creusa's story as the story of an anonymous woman's rape he is shocked at the god's behavior, but when he hears it again as the story of his own conception he is delighted. Similarly, when Ion first suggests to Creusa that Apollo may have saved the baby and raised him, she is struck by the injustice of such a proceeding, since the child belongs to them both. By the end of the play, however, she is willing to justify the god's pretenses to Ion, on the grounds that only by this subterfuge could Ion gain his rightful position in Athens. Will the audience's experience of the play's happy ending similarly erase or correct their earlier judgment of Apollo's actions? Euripides challenges our understanding of the play and involves us in a kind of balancing act by making Creusa's wretchedness so central and so vivid and then seeming to write it off in the relief of the conclusion.

That conclusion provides not only a prediction of happiness for Ion, Creusa, and Xuthus but a promise of extended power and glory for the city of Athens. But neither this final promise nor the myth of divine paternity make of Athens any simple object of admiration or civic pride. The Athenian audience could find in this play—located in Delphi but preoccupied with Athens—repeated praises of its city. Ion calls it famous; the chorus dwells lovingly on its places, its rituals, and its royal house; and everyone comments on the fact that its citizens are not immigrants but (through the founding myth of Erichthonius' birth) literally rooted in the soil. But Euripides gives Ion a speech that by its very matter-of-factness vividly conjures up the less pleasant civic realities of the Athenian democracy of the playwright's own day—the power struggles, the climate of suspicion and blame. And the chorus' attitude confirms the city's frank and sometimes disquieting hostility to outsiders. Euripides thus sets a mythic past and future against the audience's own present experience, and fractures our vision of Athens.

The playwright also makes it difficult for us to maintain a consistent judgment even of the play's generally sympathetic human characters. The Creusa we pitied as a bereaved mother becomes a vengeful stepmother, plotting against an innocent boy. That innocent boy, raised in the purity and decency of the Delphic shrine, contemplates violating the sanctity of an altar in order to take vengeance. The trajectory of our sympathies in this drama is characteristically Euripidean. In play after play, we are asked to feel for the character that suffers, but as soon as that character acts our sympathy is shaken or even replaced by horror. The Medea who has been abandoned by Jason wrings our hearts; the Medea who takes her own fortunes in her hand and kills her rival, her rival's father, and her own children appalls us. Conversely, the very characters whose actions and words have revealed their callousness and cruelty become objects of pity and even of sympathy when they in turn meet with suffering or destruction. The suspicious and tyrannical Pentheus of *The Bacchae* dies a pathetic death and is fondly remembered as an affectionate grandson. A desolate vision of human possibility emerges, one in which we may be good-hearted and just only in passivity (often while suffering at the hands of others) but put our justice and humanity at risk as soon as we take action.

Unlike *Medea* and *The Bacchae*, this play ends not with a scene of desolation but with fair prospects for the future and with reconciliation, both among mortals and between gods and mortals. The happiness its characters attain seems genuine, even if for Xuthus it is based in part on an illusion and for Creusa and Ion it requires forgetfulness. But in spite of its happy ending, *Ion* like most Greek tragedies confronts us with the limits and failings of human knowledge and action and with the mysteries of the human encounter with the divine; and the very juxtaposition of these issues with the happy ending is one of the ways this drama, like many other Euripidean tragedies, engages in a process of questioning and self-questioning.

It is not only at the end that the drama questions its own terms. Throughout the play, Euripides reminds us that we are story-telling creatures, that this play and the myths on which it is based are instances of stories, and that stories can always be called into question. Characters in this play regularly make up stories for themselves that are plausible but at odds with the facts. Creusa says over and over, in spite of the absence of evidence, that birds or wild animals killed her child. Xuthus and Ion construct a plausible but quite untrue story of Ion's conception during Dionysiac revels. The Old Man invents a deliberate plot by Xuthus, and the chorus declare that such male treachery—rather than the conventional stories of women's misbehavior—should from now on be the topic of poetry. The greatest storyteller in the play is of course the absent Apollo, who as prophetic god can narrate the future as well as the past, but whose story is no more true to the detail of actual events as they unfold than the ones the mortals make up.

Even the myths that form a kind of historical background to the play are stories and open to question. The chorus' words remind us that the adventures of Heracles and the love of gods for mortal women are tales they have heard told. Is the earth's navel really at Delphi, they ask Ion; and he in turn asks Creusa whether it is true that her grandfather Erichthonius was born from the earth. She confirms the story, but when Ion later wonders whether he himself might have been earth-born, Xuthus brusquely declares such a thing impossible. Euripides thus embeds in his play a denial of the autochthony that is both a foundation myth of Athens and a fundamental theme of the tragedy itself.[2]

In translating *Ion* I have tried both to engage the reader in the story and to maintain the uncertainties and contradictions that further engage us even as they distance and disconcert us. A given work will be realized differently in translations made at different times and for different purposes. I have tried to write a translation I would like to teach: one that the reader will experience as poetry and as drama, and one that insofar as is possible represents fairly where it cannot replicate the verbal texture of Euripides' play.

But misrepresentation is inherent in translation; not only translators' interpretations but their idiosyncratic solutions to problems will come between the reader and the text. I have in places been more concise than Euripides, usually in choral passages where I felt I could not be as elaborate as the poet and make the lyric work. In other places I have been more expan-

---

[2]On the theme of autochthony, see especially Nicole Loraux, "Kreousa the Autochthon: A Study of Euripides' *Ion*," in *Nothing to Do with Dionysos? Athenian Drama in Its Social Context*, ed. John J. Winkler and Froma I. Zeitlin (Princeton, N.J.: Princeton University Press, 1990), 168–206 and Arlene W. Saxonhouse, "Myths and the Origins of Cities: Reflections on the Autochthony Theme in Euripides' *Ion*," in *Greek Tragedy and Political Theory*, ed. J. Peter Euben (Berkeley: University of California Press, 1986), 252–73.

sive, sometimes for clarity's sake and sometimes because I wanted to include in my translation both readings of an ambiguous phrase or a disputed text. Where modern English lacks good equivalents for the Greek, as for example with exclamations of horror or grief, I have freely used substitution or periphrasis. Sometimes a literal rendering of the Greek might mislead or confuse a reader; where Euripides describes a lyre as *horn* I have written *wood*. I have found particularly helpful Michael Riffaterre's reminder that in translating poetry the translator is engaged in what he calls "transposing presuppositions": connotations that cannot be directly carried over in the translation of a word or a phrase may be suggested elsewhere or otherwise.[3]

The semantic and cultural presuppositions that complicate translation may be exemplified in the case of *Ion* by the difficulties that the translator encounters in rendering the various references to Apollo's rape of Creusa. In Hermes' opening speech, the act is described (lines 10–11 in the Greek text; my lines 12–13) as follows:

> . . . paid' Erechtheos Phoibos ezeuxen gamois
> biai Kreousan
>
> Phoebus yoked the child of Erechtheus,
> Creusa, in *gamos* by force.

In most of the contexts in which it occurs, *gamos* may be reasonably translated by "wedding" or "marriage." It refers to the sexual or procreative aspect of marriage, that is, legally speaking, to its consummation rather than to any prior commitment or solemnization; and this is borne out by the fact that the word may be used in contexts where the relationship is not one of marriage. *Gamos* doesn't, then, simply mean marriage, but the association with marriage remains primary, and the word does not simply signify sexual intercourse, though it may always entail it.

The phrase in line 10, "to yoke in *gamos*," is a standard expression for marriage; the addition of "by force" (*biai*) makes plain that this was rape. But to translate the expression simply by "rape" would be to ignore the way

---

[3]Michael Riffaterre, "Transposing Presuppositions on the Semiotics of Literary Translation," in *Theories of Translation: An Anthology of Essays from Dryden to Derrida*, ed. Rainer Schulte and John Biguenet (Chicago: University of Chicago Press, 1992), 204–17.

Euripides has ordered his sentence. The language of marriage only reveals itself as the language of rape as we move from one line to the next; we thus read briefly as marriage what then proves to be rape. The gods stand outside human law (as Ion recognizes when he briefly imagines them as— an impossibility!—subject to legal penalties). What they impose on mortal women is therefore neither marriage nor rape, and yet it is both. I have tried by my somewhat oxymoronic and self-conscious rendering ("wed Erechtheus' daughter—by force, that is") to suggest the contradiction Euripides conveys, both here and throughout the drama, by his mixture of modes of reference in common usage.[4]

The word "rape" itself, a word whose force in English we should be wary of diminishing, I have reserved for two contexts: the passage in which Ion imagines the gods as legally liable for their behavior and the passage in which Creusa declares that she will no longer conceal what happened to her. In the first of these, Euripides uses the same pair of words as in his prologue, speaking of the act of forced *gamos* and the penalty for it; I have used the word "rape" here because Ion's fantasy of gods subject to human law seemed to me to call for a legal term in English. In the second (one of a number of references in Creusa's song) the word is simply *lechos*, whose literal meaning is "bed" but which refers most often to the marriage bed, and thus like *gamos* to the sexual realization of marriage. And here, though I am clearly in a sense misrepresenting the Greek, I have used the word "rape" because Creusa's deliberate breaking of silence and her refusal to be shamed out of her painful revelation seemed to me to demand it; I needed a strong word to convey the transgressive force of Creusa's speech, especially given the silence expected of decent women in fifth-century Athens.

The translation of poetry into poetry invites the translator to try to represent rhythm. Greek meter cannot really be duplicated in English; it is based on length of syllable rather than on stress, and the metric patterns of lyric in particular are hard for a foreign ear to grasp. I have used a loose

---

[4]For a sense of the larger literary and linguistic context of these issues, see Adele C. Scafuro, "Discourses of Sexual Violation in Mythic Accounts and Dramatic Versions of 'The Girl's Tragedy,'" *differences* 2 (1990): 127–59; Froma I. Zeitlin, "Configurations of Rape in Greek Myth," in *Rape*, ed. Silvana Tomaselli and Roy Porter (Oxford: Oxford University Press, 1986), 122–51. Scafuro argues that in *Ion* and elsewhere Euripides creates a distinctive voice to express women's perspective on rape; for a different reading, see Nancy Sorkin Rabinowitz, *Anxiety Veiled: Euripides and the Traffic in Women* (Ithaca, N.Y.: Cornell University Press, 1995).

iambic pentameter for dialogue, to represent the somewhat similar iambic line of the Greek. For choral lyric, lyric dialogue, and monody, I have for the most part used a variety of shorter lines, usually iambic but with an occasional suggestion of different Greek meters. These lyric passages would, I think, repay being set to music in actual production.

Euripides occasionally makes use in this play's dialogue of a longer metric line, one that seems to have been common in early tragedy and recurs sporadically in our extant plays. Since longer trochaic or iambic lines tend to be used primarily for outright humor in English verse (consider "I am the very model of a modern major general"), I have avoided them here—except at the very end of the play, where I have also added rhyming couplets. My aim in doing this is to express formally what I take to be the inescapably comedic sense of artifice in Euripides' ending, whose happy resolution declares itself to be the gift of the gods and hints as well that it is the gift of the author, a being whose ordering of things we experience as almost equally capricious.

This translation is one of three very recent versions in English, all quite different. For another contemporary rendering of *Ion* as poetry, see W. S. Di Piero's translation, with introduction and notes by Peter Burian; Kevin Lee's literal prose translation, with introduction and extensive notes, will give the reader a more exact idea of the vocabulary and phrasing of Euripides' Greek. Among earlier translations, one is a work of literature in its own right: H. D.'s imagist version, eloquent in its compression. The humility I felt each time I returned to Euripides' Greek was equaled by the humility I felt in reading H. D.'s English.[5]

My understanding of *Ion* is indebted to the many fine interpretative studies of the past decades. I have mentioned only a few of these in my notes; further readings (on tragedy, on Euripides, and on *Ion*) may be found in Kevin Lee's very useful bibliography.[6] I have for the most part followed J. Diggle's Oxford Classical Text, but have also departed from it freely and

---

[5]Euripides, *Ion*, trans. W. S. Di Piero, with introduction, notes, and commentary by Peter Burian (New York: Oxford University Press, 1996); Euripides, *Ion*, with introduction, translation, and commentary by Kevin Lee (Warminster: Aris and Phillips, 1997); H. D., *Ion: A Play After Euripides* (Redding Ridge, Conn.: Black Swan Books, 1986).

[6]Good places to start include Lee's and Burian's introductions and C. Wolff's "The Design and Myth in Euripides' *Ion*," *Harvard Studies in Classical Philology* 69 (1965): 169–94.

usually in the direction of greater conservatism. In particular, of the passages Diggle considers inauthentic, I have omitted only two: line 1117 and lines 1364–68 (following lines 1110 and 1351 of the present translation). I have also adopted Gilbert Murray's omission, in his earlier Oxford text, of the end of line 389 (whose first words appear here at the beginning of line 386).[7]

Kevin Lee kindly shared his translation with me while it was still in manuscript, and I have benefited from his lucid exposition. I am grateful to him and to Helen Bacon, Richard Hamilton, Aryeh Kosman, Sheila Murnaghan, and David Slavitt for helpful comments and suggestions, thankfully received if not always followed. I would also like to thank Haverford College for support from the Whitehead Faculty Development Fund, and Rachel Hadas for getting me into this. The translation is dedicated to the memory of John Herington, with whom I first read *Ion*.

[7]*Euripidis Fabulae*, 3 vols., ed. James Diggle (Oxford: Oxford University Press, 1981–94); *Euripidis Fabulae*, 3 vols., ed. Gilbert Murray (Oxford: Oxford University Press, 1901–13). For a commentary on the Greek text, see Euripides, *Ion*, ed. A. S. Owen (Oxford: Oxford University Press, 1939).

*(The area before Apollo's temple at Delphi, a little before sunrise. In
the background we see the front facade and entry of the temple,
with the beginnings of a grove of laurel to one side. At the other
side, and toward the front, stands an altar to Apollo. Enter the
god Hermes.)*

HERMES

Atlas, who on his brazen shoulders wears
the sky, the ancient household of the gods,
fathered my mother Maia with a goddess,
and she in turn bore me to greatest Zeus.
I am Hermes, servant to divinities.
I have come to Delphi, navel of the earth,
Apollo's home, from which he sings to mortals
what is and will be, ever the prophet god.
Why am I here? The story begins with a city,
a city of Greeks, not without some reputation,
named for Athena of the golden spear.

10

There once Apollo wed Erechtheus' child—
by force, that is; Creusa was her name.
And this was at the place called the Long Rocks
in Athens, the northern side of Pallas' hill.
Without her father's knowledge—so the god chose—
she carried her burden; then, when it was time,
she had the child at home, and brought him out
to the cave in which the god had slept with her.
There, in the hollow of a covered basket,   20
Creusa set her baby out to die.
She kept the custom of her ancestors
and of the earth-born Erichthonius,
to whom Athena gave two guardian snakes
before she brought him to Aglaurus' daughters
to keep him safe; from this has come the custom
by which Athenian mothers raise their children
with gold snake-amulets. Well, Creusa too
fastened upon her child what finery
a girl could offer, and left him there to die.   30
        Then Phoebus, as my brother, asked me this:
"Please" (he said) "brother, go to glorious Athens,
whose people's roots are in the earth itself.
You know Athena's city; nearby you'll find
a baby in a cave. Please pick him up,
and with his cradle and his coverings carry
the child to my oracle at Delphi. Set him
right at the entry to my house. The rest—
and you should know he's mine—is my concern."
I did my brother the favor he had asked,   40
took up the woven cradle, brought it here,
and set the child down on these temple steps,
opening the basket so that he might be seen.
And it happened that at sunrise the Pythia
was going up to the oracle of the god,
and caught sight of the infant. She was amazed
that any girl of Delphi could have dared

cast off her bastard in the house of god.
She was ready to banish the baby from the temple,
but out of pity relinquished that cruel plan,   50
and the god was with the child, and kept him there.
The priestess raised him, but never knew Apollo
was his father, never knew his mother's name;
nor does the boy know who his parents are.
    As a child, he played here and there around the altars
that fostered him, and when he was a man,
the Delphians made him keeper of god's gold,
and trusted steward; among Apollo's shrines
he has lived till now a celebrant's honored life.
As for Creusa his mother, she married Xuthus.   60
Here is how that happened: Athens was at war
with Chalcodon's heirs, the rulers of Euboea.
Xuthus fought for the city, saved it by his spear,
and got as reward this marriage with Creusa
even though he was no native, being Achaean,
son of Aeolus, the son of Zeus. Many years
he has shared her bed, but they are childless still.
This is why they have come to Apollo's oracle:
they long for children. It was the god himself
who brought this fate on them, and he has not   70
been forgetful after all, though it might seem so.
When Xuthus enters this oracular shrine
Apollo will give him his own son, and declare
it is Xuthus' child. This way, the boy will come
to his mother's house and be made known to Creusa;
her marriage to Phoebus stays secret, and her child
will have the benefits of his position.
The god will establish a name for him: all Greece
will call him Ion, founder of Asian cities.
    But I will go in among these laurel trees,   80
and watch to see how the child's fate is fulfilled:
for now Apollo's son is coming out
to sweep the gateway clean before the temple

with laurel boughs. The name he will be known by,
Ion, I am the first of the gods to use.
(*Exit Hermes, as Ion emerges from the temple. He wears a garland on his
head and a bow and arrows on his back; he carries
a laurel branch he will use as a broom. A small
group of temple servants enter from another
direction, carrying various golden pitchers and jars,
and pause by the altar. Ion turns to the East, where
the sun is rising.*)

ION

Now the sun's four-horsed chariot
shines down on earth, and by its fire
the stars are banished into night.
And now Parnassus' gleaming peaks,
where none can walk, receive the light   90
of day's bright wheel for mortals.

The smoke of myrrh's dry incense rises
up to the roof of Phoebus' shrine.
The Delphian woman takes her seat
upon god's tripod; to the Greeks
she sings out loud Apollo's song.
(*He turns toward the attendants.*)
Come, Delphians who attend the god,
go to Castalia's silver streams,
in her pure water bathe yourselves,
then make your way to the temple.   100
Watch your words, or keep silence here;
be sure to show yourselves well-spoken
to those who seek the oracle.

But as I've done since I was small
with brooms of holy laurel branch
I'll sweep Apollo's entry-way,
and wet the ground with water-drops;

and with my bow I'll put to flight
the flocks of birds that settle here
to spoil the sacred offerings.   110
Since I am motherless from birth,
and have no father, I tend these shrines,
Apollo's shrines that raised me.

(He begins to sweep the area around the altar and the temple steps.)

Come, fresh leaves of laurel,
fairest laurel, do service,
sweeping the hearth
of Apollo's temple;
come from the gardens,
undying gardens,
where sacred waters   120
flow ever in,
all among the myrtle
and laurel leaves,
with which, dawn to dark
as the sun wings its way,
I sweep the god's ground:
his day-laborer.

Paean, healer:
blessed and blessing
may you be ever,   130
Leto's child.

This labor is finest,
to serve in your household,
and honor your shrine.
My labor's my glory:
I am slave not to mortals,
but to the undying.
Of these sacred labors
I never grow weary.
Apollo's my father,   140

for I praise him who feeds me,
and the god's constant help to me
makes me his son.

Paean, healer:
blessed and blessing
may you be ever,
Leto's child.

(He lays aside his laurel broom, picks up one of the golden jars by the
*   altar, and begins to sprinkle the area he has swept.)*

Now ends my work with laurel boughs;
It's time to toss from golden jars
the water Castalia's spring spills forth.   150
In purity I pour it here,
and this is my wish: that my servitude
to Phoebus may never end—unless
it ends in some good fortune.

(Ion quickly puts down the jar and wheels to look toward the top of the
*   temple; he takes his bow from his back and aims,*
*   but does not shoot his arrow.)*

What's this?
The birds have come to visit us,
leaving their nests on Parnassus.
Stay away from these golden roofs,
or my bow will bring you down, even you,
great eagle, messenger of Zeus,   160
whose beak has given you mastery
among the birds.
And now a swan sails toward the shrine.
Set your red feet some other place!
The harmonies of Apollo's lyre
bring you no help against my arrows.
Fly back to Delos, back to your lake;
do as I say, or end your sweet-voiced
song in pain.
And look!   170

What new bird comes to make its nest
of straw beneath the temple eaves?
My bow will stop such building here.
Won't you do as I say, and go
to raise your family near the stream
of Alpheus, in Zeus' temple, or
Poseidon's Isthmian grove—
so that the offerings here stay safe,
and Phoebus' shrines unspoiled.
I would be ashamed to kill you, creatures   180
who tell us what the gods intend.
But I do the work I have to do,
as Apollo's slave, and I will not cease
to care for those who feed me.

(*Ion continues his interrupted work with the water jars as the chorus
                enters. Its members are women servants of Creusa,
                on their first visit to Delphi, looking at everything
                around them, particularly the temple sculptures. In
                the first part of their song, individual members take
                separate parts as marked.*)

CHORUS
        —Not just in Athens, then, god-favored city,
        are fine tall-pillared temples found,
        and offerings to the god that guards the ways,
        but here with Phoebus too, the son of Leto,
        I see the lovely glancing beauty
        of statues on the temple's double face.   190

        —Look! You can see the Hydra here,
        and Heracles is killing it
        with a golden sickle—come and look!

        —I see; by his side there's someone else,
        holding up a fiery torch.
        Is it the one we have heard about in stories,

told as we work the loom?
Iolaus the fighter, comrade of Heracles,
who takes upon himself and shares the troubles
that burden the son of Zeus?   200

—Now look at this one over here,
riding the winged horse! He's killing
the three-bodied beast with its fiery breath.

—I see. I'm looking at everything.
There, carved in stone, the giants in retreat!

—Yes, we can see it too.

—You see her shake her Gorgon shield
right at Enceladus?

                    —Yes. My Athena!

—And what about this? The thunderbolt,
flame upon flame, in the hands of Zeus   210
who hurls it from afar.

                    —I see;
he's burning up the ferocious Mimas.

—And Bromius too, the Bacchants' god,
with his ivy staff not meant for war
kills another of earth's children.
(They catch sight of Ion, standing back near the temple.)

CHORUS
    You there by the temple: may I walk in?
    Is it lawful to set foot within the shrine?

ION
    It isn't allowed.

CHORUS

Then would you please tell us—

ION

Tell you what?

CHORUS

Is it true that earth's navel is here?
Right here in the house of Apollo?   220

ION

Yes, wreathed in wool, with Gorgons round it.

CHORUS

It's true, then, just as people say.

ION

If you offered a cake in front of the temple,
and if you are here to consult the god,
you can come to the altar; the inner shrine
requires a sheep-sacrifice too.

CHORUS

I understand, I won't break the god's law.
What is outside is pleasure enough.

ION

Go ahead, look at all that's allowed.

CHORUS

My master and mistress gave me leave   230
to see the temple.

ION

What household is yours?

CHORUS

My mistress' home is Pallas' home—
you ask, and here she comes herself.
(Enter Creusa, accompanied by an attendant; Ion goes forward to
meet her.)

ION

Your looks bear witness to nobility
and gentle ways, whoever you may be.
And as a general rule, a person's looks
will tell you right away if she's well-born.
What's this?
You startled me: why did you close your eyes,
why did your cheeks grow wet with tears, my lady,   240
when you saw the holy shrine? Why does the sight
that makes all others happy make you sad?

CREUSA

I cannot, stranger, think you impolite
to wonder at my tears. But when I saw
Apollo's house, I measured once again
the depths of an old memory of mine.
My thoughts were there though I am standing here.
Poor women. Shameless acts the gods commit.
Where can we look for justice, if our rulers
themselves destroy us by their injuries?   250

ION

I can't interpret this: what caused your grief?

CREUSA

Nothing. I've let my arrows fly. I'll say
no more of this, so feel no more concern.

ION

Who are you? From what country have you come?
Who are your people, and what name should I give you?

CREUSA

    Creusa is my name, Erechtheus' daughter,
    and Athens is the city of my fathers.

ION

    A famous city and a noble family!
    You have my admiration and respect.

CREUSA

    My good luck goes so far. It goes no farther.   260

ION

    And is the story true that people tell?

CREUSA

    What story, stranger? What are you asking me?

ION

    The one about the earth-born ancestor.

CREUSA

    Erichthonius? It's true. It hasn't helped me.

ION

    And did Athena take him from the earth?

CREUSA

    Yes, in her virgin's hands; he was not hers.

ION

    And did she give him, just as in the paintings—

CREUSA

    To Cecrops' girls, to guard, but not to see.

ION

    I've heard they opened the box the goddess gave.

CREUSA

That's why they died, bleeding on rocks below.   270

ION

I see.
And is that other story true or false—

CREUSA

Which one? Go on: I have the time to answer.

ION

Your father Erechtheus sacrificed your sisters?

CREUSA

He forced himself. It was for Athens' sake.

ION

And how did it happen that you alone were saved?

CREUSA

I was new born and in my mother's arms.

ION

And is it true a chasm conceals your father?

CREUSA

The Sea-god's trident killed and buried him.

ION

Is there a place in Athens called the Long Rocks?   280

CREUSA

Why do you bring that up? Your words remind me . . .

ION

The Pythian and his lightning honor it.

CREUSA

Honor? I wish I'd never seen the place.

ION

Why do you hate what's dearest to the god?

CREUSA

Never mind. Those caves and I share shameful knowledge.

ION

And what Athenian is your husband, lady?

CREUSA

No citizen; he comes from another country.

ION

Who is he? I presume he's nobly born.

CREUSA

Xuthus, the son of Aeolus son of Zeus.

ION

How did a stranger come to marry you?   290

CREUSA

A city named Euboea is our neighbor—

ION

Across the water? Yes, I've heard of it.

CREUSA

He sacked that city in a joint campaign.

ION

I see: as ally? And then married you?

CREUSA

My dowry was his spear-prize, won in battle.

ION

Have you come to the oracle with him, or alone?

CREUSA

With him. He turned aside at Trophonius' shrine.

ION

Sightseeing, or in search of prophecy?

CREUSA

We have the same request for god and hero.

ION

Is this about the harvest, or for children?   300

CREUSA

We are still childless, after years of marriage.

ION

You've never given birth at all? No children?

CREUSA

Apollo knows about my childlessness.

ION

Poor woman. Your luck in other things is no luck.

CREUSA

And who are you? Your mother's a happy woman.

ION

I am called the god's slave; that is who I am.

CREUSA

A city's offering, or bought from someone?

ION

I only know that I am called Apollo's.

CREUSA

Then, stranger, I may pity you in turn.

ION

Because my parents are unknown to me.   310

CREUSA

Do you live in the temple here, or have you a home?

ION

The god's home's mine, wherever I fall asleep.

CREUSA

Did you come here as a child or as a young man?

ION

Those who seem to know say I was still a baby.

CREUSA

And which of the Delphian women gave you milk?

ION

I never knew the breast. The one who raised me—

CREUSA

Who was she, poor boy? My pain discovers pain.

ION

I count Apollo's prophetess as my mother.

CREUSA

And how did you support yourself till manhood?

ION

The altars fed me, and their visitors.   320

CREUSA

You seem well off enough: your clothes are fine.

ION

I wear the finery of the god I serve.

CREUSA

And have you never tried to find your parents?

ION

No, since I have no evidence at all.

CREUSA

What sorrow for your mother, whoever she was.

ION

Perhaps my birth was a wrong done to some woman.

CREUSA

Ah . . .
Another woman suffered like your mother.

ION

Who? If she shared my pain I would be glad.

CREUSA

The one for whose sake I've come without my husband.   330

ION

With what request? You may count on my support.

CREUSA

I want a secret oracle from Phoebus.

ION

Tell me, and I will be your sponsor here.

CREUSA

Here is the story—no—I'm too ashamed.

ION

Then you'll do nothing. Shame's a lazy goddess.

CREUSA

One of my friends says that she slept with Phoebus.

ION

A mortal woman with Phoebus? It can't be so.

CREUSA

And had his child without her father's knowing.

ION

No! Some man did this to her, and she's ashamed.

CREUSA

She says not. She has suffered terribly.   340

ION

And she slept with a god? What did she do to suffer?

CREUSA

She abandoned the child to whom she'd given birth.

ION

This child she abandoned: is it still alive?

CREUSA

    Nobody knows. That's what my question is.

ION

    If it is dead, how did it come to die?

CREUSA

    Wild animals, she thinks, killed the poor thing.

ION

    Does she have any evidence for this?

CREUSA

    When she came back to find him he was gone.

ION

    And were there drops of blood along the track?

CREUSA

    She says not, though she searched it thoroughly.   350

ION

    How long ago was this—the baby's death?

CREUSA

    He would be about your age, if he had lived.

ION

    The god does wrong. I pity that poor mother.

CREUSA

    She has not borne another child since then.

ION

    But what if Phoebus took the child, to raise him?

CREUSA

  To enjoy alone what they should share? Unjust!

ION

  A painful story. Her fate's in tune with mine.

CREUSA

  Your mother too must long for her lost child.

ION

  Don't make me grieve for what I had forgotten.

CREUSA

  I will say no more. Accomplish what I ask.   360

ION

  Do you see the difficulty for your plea?

CREUSA

  What is not difficult for my poor friend?

ION

  How will the god declare what he wants hidden?

CREUSA

  If he sits on the tripod all Greece shares, he will.

ION

  He feels ashamed. You must not question him.

CREUSA

  And she feels pain—the woman he mistreated.

ION

  No one will give this prophecy to you.
  If he were made to seem as base as this,

in his own house, the god would rightly punish
the one who spoke the answer. Let it go.   370
We can't divine a truth the god opposes.
It would be foolishness to force the gods
unwillingly to say what they refuse us
by sacrifices or the flights of birds.
The things we seek by force, with the gods unwilling,
we get as goods that bring no benefit.
But what they give us gladly is our gain.

CHORUS

Most mortals meet disaster on disaster;
only the shape is new. Try as you may
you will find no life completely fortunate.   380

CREUSA

Phoebus, both in Athens and here you prove unfair
to the woman who is present only in these words.
You did not save your own child, as was right,
nor will you speak as prophet to his mother,
so that, if dead, he might at least be buried,
and if he lives—but I must let this go,
if the god prevents our learning what I want.
Now, stranger, since I see my noble husband
has left Trophonius' shrine and joins me here,
don't tell him what I've said: I'd be ashamed   390
of doing secret favors, and the story
might turn out otherwise than we intended.
For men find fault with much that women do,
and we good women, mixed in with the bad,
are hated: such is the sorrow we are born to.

(Enter Xuthus. He turns toward the altar first, then toward Creusa.)

XUTHUS

Let the god be the first to receive the greeting
I offer here; and wife, I greet you too.
But have I frightened you by my delay?

CREUSA
    No.
    As I began to worry, you arrived.   400
    But tell me what Trophonius had to say;
    what must we do to have a child together?

XUTHUS
    He did not think it right to anticipate
    the Delphic god's response, but told me this:
    I won't return home childless, nor will you.

CREUSA
    Mother of Phoebus, grant that our return
    be fortunate, and may our former dealings
    with your son be changed now into something better.

XUTHUS
    They will. Now, who here represents the god?
(Ion steps forward.)

ION
    I am in charge outside; what happens inside   410
    others will see to, noble Delphians,
    chosen by lot to sit beside the tripod.

XUTHUS
    That's good. Then I have everything I need.
    I'll go in, since I hear the sacrifice
    for visitors has fallen by the temple;
    today is a lucky day to seek my answer.
    You, wife, place laurel branches round the altars,
    and pray that I may bring from Apollo's house
    predictions of our happiness in children.
(Xuthus goes into the temple.)

CREUSA
    I will. I will. And if Apollo wishes   420
    at last now to repair the wrong he did,

he will not altogether be a friend,
but what he wants I accept. He is a god.
(*Exit Creusa and attendant.*)

ION

Why does this foreigner with her hidden words
reproach the god always in riddling terms?
Out of love for the woman on whose behalf she comes?
Or to keep quiet a thing she must not speak of?
But why should I concern myself with her,
Erechtheus' daughter? She's nothing to do with me.
I'm off to pour pure water from golden pitchers   430
into the sacred vessels. Yes, but Phoebus—
he needs my advice. What is he up to now?
Forcing girls into his bed, betraying them,
conceiving children that he leaves to die?
No! Since you rule us, you should practice virtue.
A wicked mortal is punished by the gods,
so how can it be just that you who write
the laws for mortals live without the law?
But if—it will not happen, but supposing
you paid the penalty assigned for rape—   440
you, and Poseidon, and world-ruling Zeus—
in paying you would empty all the temples.
Eager for pleasure, and incautious with it,
you do great wrong. It can't be fair to blame us
for imitating what the gods delight in:
the fault is yours for teaching us such things.
(*Exit Ion, pitchers in hand, bow on back. The chorus moves into center
stage.*)

CHORUS

My lady Athena,
born without pain,
by Prometheus delivered
from the head of great Zeus,   450
blessed Victory, come

to the house of Apollo.
From Olympus the golden
fly down to these streets,
where the altar of Phoebus,
his hearth at earth's center
by the tripod we dance round
foretells and fulfills.
Leto's daughter, come too.
Two maidens, two goddesses,   460
sisters of Phoebus,
intercede for us now,
and pray that this family,
the house of Erechtheus,
ancient of days,
meet the plainest of prophecies:
children at last.

What can be happier for mortals,
What surer gain in life is there
than that a father's halls be bright   470
with the young children of his line,
fruitful in turn to receive his wealth
for children of their own?
They are his strength in evil times,
his dear delight when times are good,
in war his land's protection.
Better than wealth I say it is,
better than royal palaces,
to love and care for children.
I hate the childless life, and those   480
who choose it I think wrong.
I wish for a life of moderate means,
my happiness in children.

O place Pan loves,
close by the caves
they call the Long Rocks,

where Aglaurus' daughters
step in the dance,
on the grassy place
before Pallas' shrine,   490
to the wavering cry
of the pipes you play,
O Pan,
in your sunless caves;
where a girl once gave birth
(poor girl) to a child,
Apollo's own son,
and then set it out
for the feasting of birds,
bloody meal for wild beasts,   500
born of the violence
of that bitter mating.
No tale at the loom,
no story I've heard,
gives a god's mortal child
good fortune.
(Enter Ion.)

ION

Serving women, who wait here and keep watch
for your mistress by this house of sacrifice,
has Xuthus left the holy tripod yet,
done with the oracle, or is he still inside,   510
asking the god about his childlessness?

CHORUS

He is still inside, and has not left the temple.
But he must be coming out; I hear the sound
of closing doors—and here my master is.
*(Xuthus comes out of the temple, looks about, sees Ion, and after a brief
                    pause walks up to him and greets him effusively.)*

XUTHUS

    How are you, dear child? Yes, this is the right beginning.
(He tries to embrace Ion, who backs away.)

ION

    I am well; act sensibly, and we'll both do well.

XUTHUS

    Give me your hand to kiss and let me hold you.

ION

    Are you in your right mind? Have you gone mad?

XUTHUS

    Not mad: I have found what I love best of all,
    and long to embrace it.

ION

                Stop; you must not touch me!   520
    You'll break the sacred garland of the god.

XUTHUS

    I will take hold of you. This is no theft:
    I have found and I will keep what belongs to me.
(Ion backs away again, and fits an arrow to his bow.)

ION

    Let me go, or take my arrow in your heart.

XUTHUS

    Why do you refuse to know me as your own?

ION

    I don't teach lessons to uncouth crazy strangers.

XUTHUS

    Kill me, burn me; you will be your father's killer.

ION

How can you be my father? Is this a joke?

XUTHUS

No. Listen now: my story won't take long.

ION

What are you going to tell me?

XUTHUS

I am your father,   530

and you my child.

ION

Who says so?

XUTHUS

Loxias,

the one who raised you.

ION

That's as *you* bear witness!

XUTHUS

Yes, but informed by the god's own oracle.

ION

You must have failed to read his riddles rightly.

XUTHUS

Then I heard wrong.

ION

What were his actual words?

XUTHUS

The person I encountered—

ION

Encountered when?

XUTHUS

in leaving the god's house—

ION

Would meet what fate?

XUTHUS

is my own son.

ION

By birth, or as a gift?

XUTHUS

A gift, but mine.

ION

And I'm the first you met?

XUTHUS

No other, my child.

ION

How did this come about?   540

XUTHUS

I am as amazed as you.

ION

And who is my mother?

XUTHUS

I couldn't say.

ION

Did Phoebus?

XUTHUS

I was so happy
I didn't ask.

ION

Perhaps I was born from the earth.

XUTHUS

The ground does not bear children.

ION

But how can I
be yours?

XUTHUS

I don't know. But the god must know.

ION

Let's try some other explanations.

XUTHUS

Good.

ION

Were there other women?

XUTHUS

Yes, in my foolish youth.

ION

Before you married Erechtheus' daughter?

XUTHUS

Yes—

not after, certainly!

ION

Well, was it then

you fathered me?

XUTHUS

Let's see. The time works out.   550

ION

Then how did I come to Delphi—

XUTHUS

I'm at a loss.

ION

—such a long way?

XUTHUS

That puzzles me as well.

ION

Have you visited the Delphic rock before?

XUTHUS

I came once to the Bacchic torch-procession.

ION

Did you stay with one of the sponsors as a guest?

XUTHUS

Someone who . . . ah, yes, with the Delphian girls . . .

ION

He initiated you?

XUTHUS

Yes—with the Bacchic Maenads.

ION

Sober or drunk?

XUTHUS

I indulged in Bacchic pleasures.

ION

That explains my birth.

XUTHUS

Fate has found you out, my child.

ION

And I came to this shrine—how?

XUTHUS

Left by a girl, perhaps?   560

ION

My slavery has ended.

XUTHUS

Come to your father's arms.

ION

I must not disbelieve the god.

XUTHUS

That's right.

ION

What more could I want—

XUTHUS

You see things as you should.

ION

than to be Zeus' grandson?

XUTHUS

Exactly as has happened!

ION

Should I touch my father?

XUTHUS

Yes, as the god commands.

(They embrace.)

ION

My greetings, father.

XUTHUS

I receive them gladly,

ION

And greetings to this day.

XUTHUS

It has made me happy.

ION

Dear mother, will I some day find you too?
Now more than ever do I long to see you,
whoever you may be. But perhaps, perhaps   570
you are dead, and I will never have my wish.

CHORUS

>   The household's happiness is ours as well.
>   But still I could have wished the same good fortune
>   in children for our mistress and her line.

XUTHUS

>   My child, the god has rightly brought about
>   my finding you, and joined us to each other.
>   You have found your closest kin, unknown before.
>   And you are right to want to find your mother;
>   I want that too, for you and for myself—
>   to know what sort of woman you were born from.   580
>   If we give the matter time, perhaps we'll find her.
>   But leave the god's house, leave your homelessness,
>   feel as I do, and come with me to Athens.
>   A father's prosperous power awaits you there,
>   and his great wealth as well. No disadvantage
>   will let them call you poor or of bad family;
>   you will be known as well-born, and as rich.
>   No answer? You stand there with your eyes cast down,
>   worried now, where you were glad before?
>   This change puts fear into your father's heart.   590

ION

>   Things do not look the same when close at hand
>   as what you supposed, observing from a distance.
>   It's true, I am glad at this new turn of fortune,
>   glad to have found you, father. But father, listen
>   to what I think. They say the Athenians
>   take pride in being native to their soil.
>   I will arrive there twice disabled, born
>   of a foreign father and myself a bastard.
>   With this against me, if my position's weak,
>   I will be called a nobody, a nothing.   600
>   And if I try for prominence in the city,
>   and seek to be someone, those who have no power

will hate me: for what's stronger always rankles.
While those who are capable and worthy sorts,
but wisely don't rush into politics
will laugh at me and take me for a fool
who won't keep quiet in a city prone to blame.
And if I somehow gain a reputation
beyond that of the men who run the city,
they will make sure the voting is against me.   610
Yes, father, this is how things tend to go.
Those who rule cities and hold office in them
are fiercely hostile to a rival's claims.

  Then, entering your house as an outsider,
I meet a childless woman, who has shared
with you a common sorrow up till now,
but with my coming will find herself alone
to endure in bitterness her separate lot.
How will she not quite reasonably hate me,
when she sees me at your side? She has no children,   620
and will look with bitter pain on what you love.
Then you will either give me up for her,
or honor me and so disrupt your household.
How many wives have stabbed or drugged their husbands!
Besides this, father, I pity your poor wife,
growing old childless. She comes of a noble family,
and should not have to suffer in this way.

  The power of a king receives much empty praise;
it may seem sweet to others, but in private
brings only pain. How can anyone be happy   630
who must be always fearful, on the lookout
for violence as he drags out his days?
I would rather live as an ordinary person,
in decent comfort, than be a land's sole ruler,
who enjoys the company of worthless friends
and hates the good because he fears his death.
You may say wealth will overwhelm such cautions,
delightful wealth; but I can take no pleasure

in hearing men's censure as I save my money.
A plain untroubled life is what I want. 640
Let me tell you what good things were mine here, father.
First, I had leisure, best of all possessions,
and just the right amount of bother, no more;
no worthless person forced me from his path—
and that's a thing I could not tolerate,
to give way to inferiors. I prayed to gods,
and talked with mortals, and the ones I served,
mortals and gods, were happy, not sorrowful.
I sent some on their way, and others came,
and I was welcome as I welcomed them. 650
What people pray for, even if reluctantly,
that is, to be just, both nature and law together
have granted me, for the god. Considering this,
I think what I have is better than what you offer.
Let me stay here, please: happiness in small things
brings the same joy as pleasure in what's great.

CHORUS

I like your words—as long as those I love
may find the happiness your friends enjoy.

XUTHUS

Stop making speeches. Learn to be fortunate.
I want to give a feast here where I found you, 660
a public feast, and offer sacrifices—
the ones I did not make when you were born.
I'll treat you as a family friend for now,
and give you dinner; then we're off to Athens.
We will pretend you came to see the place,
and not let on at first that you're my son,
because I would not want my own good luck
to hurt my childless wife. As time goes by,
I'll find the right occasion to persuade her
that you should govern Athens after me. 670

I name you Ion, a name that suits your fate,
since we first met as I was moving on
from the god's shrine. Now gather all your friends,
and ask them to a sacrifice, and after it
a farewell feast, since you are leaving Delphi.
Slave women, I command you to keep silent:
to tell my wife what happened means your death.

ION

    I'll go; but still one piece of luck is lacking:
for if I cannot find the one who bore me,
life's not worth living. If I may pray for this,   680
only let my mother be Athenian born
so that from her I gain the right to speak.
When a foreigner comes to a city of pure blood,
he may be a citizen in name but still
his mouth's a slave's mouth and he can't speak out.

(Xuthus and Ion go off together.)

CHORUS

    I can foresee the tears and the cries of grief
when my queen knows
her husband is happy in his son, and she
stays childless still.

    What oracle is this you sang, Apollo?   690
Who is this boy,
this foster-child of your prophetic shrine?
Who is his mother?

    This oracle of yours does not appease me:
I am not fooled.
I sense some trickery. I fear the outcome,
whatever it may be.

    Uncanny the god's word, uncanny the news it brings:
all know this foreign boy contrives some trick.

Friends, shall we tell our mistress how her husband,   700
with whom she shared
all of her hopes, poor thing, has what he wants,
while she has failed,

and now grows old, and now her husband brings
dishonor on her too?
Worthless outsider, to whom her house gave all
and he gives no return.

Death to him for deceiving my dear mistress;
let him find in the flame
of sacrifice no favor from the gods.   710
Now he will learn

how dear to us is our queen, whom grief awaits,
while they go feast, new father with new son.

Hills of Parnassus, stony crag, heaven's lofty seat,
where Bacchus, swift of foot
with a torch in either hand goes leaping,
leading his Bacchants, his night-wandering women—
never to my city, never may that boy come,

but let him depart his life and his youth and die.
My city has good reason   720
to defend itself against interlopers,
foreign intruders. Call on our ancient leader:
Erechtheus, king, come lead us once again!
(Enter Creusa and an old man, a long-time family servant. They move
          slowly; he leans on his stick and she guides him.)

CREUSA
     Old man, who tended my father long ago
     when he was still alive and saw the light,

come up now to Apollo's oracle
so you may learn with me if Loxias
has prophecies for us concerning children.
It's good to have friends near when things go well,
and if—may this not happen!—things go badly,   730
then too it's good to see a friend's kind face.
Though I am your mistress, still I care for you
as for the father to whom you gave such care.

OLD MAN

Daughter, you act as your parents would have acted,
worthy as they were, and you have not shamed
your family and their ancient earth-born house.
Come, take me up to the oracular shrine.
This is steep going. Help me walk, and so
provide some remedy for my old age.

CREUSA

Follow me, then; watch where you set your foot.   740

OLD MAN

Look:
My step is slow, my mind as quick as ever.

CREUSA

And use your staff: the path's a winding one.

OLD MAN

My staff's as blind as now my sight is poor.

CREUSA

Still, don't be overcome by weariness.

OLD MAN

On purpose, no; but what I lack, I lack.

CREUSA

> Women who work my loom, servants I trust:
> when my husband left, had things gone well with him?
> Did the god grant the children that we came for?
> Tell me! And if you have good news for me,   750
> I will not be ungrateful in my joy.

CHORUS

> O god!

CREUSA

> This is not the prelude to a happy story.

CHORUS

> Poor thing!

CREUSA

> Does the oracle bring trouble on your masters?

CHORUS

> What shall we do? We risk death if we speak.

CREUSA

> What song is this? And why are you afraid?

CHORUS

> What should we do? Tell her, or keep it quiet?

CREUSA

> Tell me: I see you have bad news for me.

CHORUS

> I *will* speak, if it means I die twice over.   760
> You will not hold a baby in your arms,
> mistress, nor put him ever to your breast.

CREUSA
    If only I could die.

OLD MAN
    Daughter—

CREUSA
                I'm so unhappy.
    I cannot bear the grief.
    I cannot live with the grief.

OLD MAN
    My child—

CREUSA
                No, stay away.
    The pain's like a knife.
    It stabs me through the heart.

OLD MAN
    Don't yet give way to sorrow—

CREUSA

                        Sorrow's here.   770

OLD MAN
    Until we learn—

CREUSA

                    What new report could matter?

OLD MAN
    Whether your husband shares in this disaster
    and suffers too, or you are quite alone.

CHORUS

>   To him, old man, Apollo gave a son,
>   and privately he celebrates his fortune.

CREUSA

>   This is the worst of all:
>   you bring me grief upon grief.

OLD MAN

>   The child you speak of: is he still to be born,
>   or did Apollo mean a child now living?

CHORUS

>   Apollo gave a child already born,   780
>   a young man grown. And I was there to see it.

CREUSA

>   What do you mean? Don't say it!
>   I cannot bear to hear.

OLD MAN

>   Nor I. How did the god fulfill his word?
>   Tell me more clearly. Who is the son he spoke of?

CHORUS

>   The first your husband met as he was leaving,
>   whoever it was, the god gave as his son.

CREUSA

>   No. No. Then did he declare
>   my life childless still?
>   My house forever bereft?   790

OLD MAN

>   Who was the child foretold? Who met the husband
>   of this poor woman? How and where did they meet?

CHORUS

Do you remember, mistress, the young man
who swept the temple grounds? He is the child.

CREUSA

If only I could fly
through the misty air from Greece
as far as the western stars.
Friends, what pain I have felt.

OLD MAN

What was the name his father gave to him?
Do you know, or is this still a private matter?   800

CHORUS

Ion, since he first met him moving on.
And who his mother is I cannot say.
But so you may know all I know, old man,
her husband's gone to make the sacrifices
of birth and welcome on the boy's behalf.
In the sacred tent, without Creusa's knowledge,
he holds a public feast for his new son.

OLD MAN

Mistress, we are betrayed—yes, we: I share it—
by your husband, and he has most cleverly
insulted us and cast us from our home,   810
Erechtheus' home. It's not that I dislike
the man, but you of course mean more to me.
He came to us a stranger, married you,
received your household and inheritance,
and turns out secretly to have had children
with another woman. I will tell you how.
He knew you childless and he was not willing
to share your fate and put up with that loss.
So taking a slave girl to his bed in secret

he got this child. Then, sending him abroad,   820
he gave him to some Delphian to raise.
In the god's house, in order to stay hidden,
the boy was brought up as a creature of the shrine.
And when your husband knew he was full grown,
he urged you to come here to ask for children.
The god spoke truth; it was the man that lied,
who had this child long since, and wove such plots,
and meant, if he were caught, to blame Apollo.
To fortify himself against time's passing,
he planned to pass his kingship to this boy,   830
for whom he has now made up a new name, Ion,
to suit the way they met—or seemed to meet.

CHORUS

How I hate men who do such wicked harm.
First they contrive to wrong you, then they hide it
with clever tricks, and make it all look fine.
I'd rather have a decent fool as friend
than someone clever but to no good purpose.

OLD MAN

And you will suffer what is worst of all:
this boy without a mother, worthless boy,
child of a slave, now master of your house.   840
Oh, yes—I would not call it quite so bad,
if the child's mother were of noble birth,
and Xuthus had persuaded you to this,
because of your long-standing childlessness.
Or if that would have made you too unhappy,
he could have married one of his own folk.
But given what he has done, act like a woman:
take up a sword, or by some trickery—
poison would do—kill Xuthus and the boy
before death comes to you from them instead.   850
For if you let go this chance, your life is over:

when two who hate each other share a house,
one or the other must do badly there.
I'm willing to assist you in this struggle
and help to kill the child. I'll go to where
the feast is being held, and to my masters
repay what I owe them, whether I die or live.
Only one thing brings shame upon a slave:
the name of slave. And if he acts with honor,
in all the rest he is as good as free.   860

CHORUS

   I too, dear mistress, wish to share your fate,
   and die or live with honor at your side.

CREUSA

   O my soul, how be silent?
   But how can I bring to light what lay in shadow
   and feel no shame? What stops me now from speaking?
   With whom do I compete for virtue now,
   since my own husband has betrayed me here?
   I have no house, no children of my own.
   My hopes are gone, and all I tried to gain
   by keeping quiet about that other marriage,   870
   quiet about the child that I so mourn for.
   No; by the starry home of Zeus above,
   and by the goddess of our own high places,
   and by the sacred headland of her lake,
   I will no longer hide my rape, but speak—
   and with that burden gone I will rest easy.
   The tears fall from my eyes, my heart's in pain,
   brought to this sorrow by the wicked plans
   of men and gods: whom I will show to be
   ungrateful traitors to the ones they've loved.   880

   You whose playing
   calls forth the voice

of the seven stringed lyre's
once-living wood,
sweet-singer of songs
the Muses know,
      you, child of Leto, I blame to this bright day.

You came to me, gleaming
and golden-haired,
as I gathered up   890
in the folds of my cloak
the flowers that blossomed
with yellow light;
      you grasped my pale wrists, took me to that cave.

As I screamed for my mother
you lay with me,
a god, without shame,
and you pleased Aphrodite.
But I, unhappy,
gave birth to your son,   900
      and fearful for his sake, as mothers are,

still cast him out,
in your bed, that place
where you made me suffer
and suffer again.
   .   And now he's dead, my child, a meal for birds.

My child and yours,
hard-hearted god.
And still you play and sing.

Yes, it is you I call on, son of Leto: 910
you who speak oracles to those who come
to the golden halls, the navel of the earth.
I cry it in your ear: cruel, wicked lover.

What had my husband ever done for you
that you should settle children in his house?
And my son, your son—do you even notice?
The birds stole him away and he is gone,
taken from the baby clothes his mother gave him.

Delos hates you,
your sacred island,   920
the laurels hate you
by the leafy palm,
where Leto bore you
in sacred labor,
the child of Zeus
in the gardens of Zeus.

CHORUS

The treasury of sorrow she unlocks
makes us all weep. I cannot bear to hear it.

OLD MAN

Dear girl, I cannot take my eyes from you,
and feel such pity I am robbed of judgment.   930
One wave of troubles all but drowned me; another,
rising at your words, engulfs my mind.
In telling me this you turn from present evils
to walk on evil paths of other pain.
What are you saying? What is this charge you bring
against Apollo? What child did you bear?
Where in our city did you set him out,
a burial to beasts' liking? Tell me again.

CREUSA

I am ashamed, old man, but still I'll tell you.

OLD MAN

Do; I can share your sorrow like one well-born.   940

CREUSA

Then listen. You know the cave that faces north
from Cecrops' hill at the place we call the Long Rocks?

OLD MAN

Yes; Pan's shrine and his altars are nearby.

CREUSA

That's where I fought him in a dreadful contest.

OLD MAN

What contest? Your words have brought me close to tears.

CREUSA

My wretched unwanted wedding with Apollo.

OLD MAN

Daughter, was that the time I knew about?

CREUSA

I don't know. I will say if you are right.

OLD MAN

You grieved in secret for some hidden illness.

CREUSA

That was the sorrow I now speak openly.   950

OLD MAN

You slept with the god; how did you hide what happened?

CREUSA

I had the child—try to bear what I tell you now—

OLD MAN

Where? Who was midwife? Or were you alone?

CREUSA

    Alone in the cave where I was yoked in marriage.

OLD MAN

    Where is the child? At least you would have a child!

CREUSA

    He's dead, old man, abandoned, food for wild beasts.

OLD MAN

    Dead? And that coward Apollo did not save him?

CREUSA

    He did not help. The child grows up in Hades.

OLD MAN

    Who was it set out the child to die? Not you?

CREUSA

    Yes, after I wrapped him closely, in the darkness.   960

OLD MAN

    And no one knew you had abandoned a child?

CREUSA

    Only my sorrow and my secrecy.

OLD MAN

    How could you bear to leave him in the cave?

CREUSA

    How? Crying out pitiful words I could not stop.

OLD MAN

    Poor girl.
    You were hard-hearted, but the god was worse.

CREUSA

If you had seen the baby stretch out its hands—

OLD MAN

Wanting the breast or wanting to be held?

CREUSA

Wanting what I was wrong to keep from him.

OLD MAN

What did you think would happen when you left him?   970

CREUSA

I thought the god would surely save his own.

OLD MAN

Winter has come to our once prosperous house!

CREUSA

Why do you hide your head and weep, old man?

OLD MAN

I look on your misfortunes, and your father's.

CREUSA

That's being mortal. Nothing stays the same.

OLD MAN

Then let's not cling to lamentation, daughter.

CREUSA

What should I do? Misfortune makes me helpless.

OLD MAN

Pay back the god who first mistreated you.

CREUSA
How can I, a mortal, surpass what is so strong?

OLD MAN
With fire. Burn down his sacred oracle.   980

CREUSA
I'm afraid. My present suffering's enough.

OLD MAN
Then dare what can be done, and kill your husband.

CREUSA
I respect our marriage and his former goodness.

OLD MAN
Well, kill the boy at least—your new-found rival.

CREUSA
How? If only I could, that's what I want.

OLD MAN
Arm your own servants: make of us your swordsmen.

CREUSA
I would. But where could we accomplish this?

OLD MAN
In the sacred tent, where Xuthus feasts his friends.

CREUSA
Murder makes itself known, and slaves are weak.

OLD MAN
You're losing courage. Have you a better plan?   990

CREUSA

    I do, a trick that can be carried out.

OLD MAN

    I'll help you with the trick and with the doing.

CREUSA

    Then listen: do you recall the giants' fight?

OLD MAN

    When they made war at Phlegra with the gods?

CREUSA

    And Earth bore the Gorgon, terrifying monster.

OLD MAN

    As an ally for her children against the gods?

CREUSA

    Yes, and Zeus' daughter, Pallas, killed it.

OLD MAN

    Is this the story I heard when I was young?

CREUSA

    Athena wears its skin upon her breast.

OLD MAN

    The thing they call the aegis, Athena's armor?   1000

CREUSA

    So named from her eagerness in that great battle.

OLD MAN

    What is the shape of this ferocious thing?

CREUSA

It is a breastplate, armed with snaky coils.

OLD MAN

How, daughter, can it harm your enemies?

CREUSA

You know the story of Erichthonius?

OLD MAN

First of your fathers, to whom the ground gave birth?

CREUSA

When he was born Athena gave him a gift . . .

OLD MAN

What gift? You seem to be hesitant to say.

CREUSA

Two drops of blood. The blood was from the Gorgon.

OLD MAN

And these have some effect on human beings?   1010

CREUSA

One is deadly, one protects against disease.

OLD MAN

How did she give them to the newborn child?

CREUSA

In a golden bracelet, passed down to my father.

OLD MAN

And when he died the poison came to you?

CREUSA

Yes, and I wear it here upon my wrist.

OLD MAN

How does it work—the goddess' double gift?

CREUSA

The drop that fell from the creature's hollow vein—

OLD MAN

How do you use it? What power does it have?

CREUSA

It keeps off illness and it nurtures life.

OLD MAN

And the second you spoke of? What does that drop do?   1020

CREUSA

It kills. It is venom from the Gorgon's snakes.

OLD MAN

Do you wear them mixed together or apart?

CREUSA

Apart; for good cannot be mixed with bad.

OLD MAN

Dearest child—then you have everything you need.

CREUSA

The boy will die of this; you will be the killer.

OLD MAN

Where? What shall I do? You speak, and I will act.

CREUSA

In Athens, after the boy comes to my house.

OLD MAN

No good; remember the flaw you found in my plan.

CREUSA

What do you mean? Do you suspect, as I do—

OLD MAN

They will think you killed him even if you didn't.   1030

CREUSA

Yes, it's proverbial: stepmothers hate their children.

OLD MAN

Then kill him here, where you may deny the killing.

CREUSA

So much the sooner will I have the pleasure.

OLD MAN

And keep from Xuthus what he would keep from you.

CREUSA

You know what you have to do. Take from my hand
Athena's golden bracelet, this ancient work.
(She hands the bracelet to the old man.)
Go to my husband's secret sacrifice,
and when they have finished eating, and are ready
to make libations—take the poison, hidden
in your robes, and pour it in the young man's drink.   1040
Not everyone's: keep separate from the rest
the one for the destined master of my house.
And if he swallows it, he will never come
to glorious Athens, but will stay here, dead.

OLD MAN

> Go back now to the household of your hosts,
> and I will carry out my given task.

(Exit Creusa.)

> Come on, old feet, grow young again in action,
> even if time has taken speed and strength.
> Go fight against the foe beside your mistress
> and with her kill him, rid the house of him.   1050
> It's fine to respect what's right when you're well off,
> but when you have enemies you wish to harm,
> I say there is no law to keep you from it.

(Exit the old man.)

CHORUS

> Demeter's daughter, goddess of the ways,
> you who govern attacks by night,
> now, though by day my mistress brings to bear
> the Gorgon's throat-cut blood,
> still guide the deadly cup
> against this threat to the Erechtheids' house.
> Never may any other rule my city: 1060
> only that noble race.

> If, having tried so hard, she cannot kill him—
> no second chance for this bold act
> that gives her hope—she will take a sword
> to her throat, or put a noose around her neck,
> and end her suffering with more suffering,
> going down to a different world.
> She won't see daylight and still tolerate
> foreign rule in her house, born as she is
> of a noble line of fathers.   1070

> I feel shame before Bacchus, the god of many songs,
> if by the sacred streams of Callichorus
> a stranger, unsleeping, sees

the torch that burns
all night to celebrate the mysteries,
when the starry sky of Zeus
is leader in the dance,
and the moon is dancing too,
and Nereus' fifty daughters
by the sea and the running rivers   1080
do reverence in dance
to the gold-crowned maiden and her holy mother.
This is where he hopes to rule,
taking what others have worked for,
Apollo's vagrant boy.

Look, all you poets who sing in such harsh strains
of our unholy loves, our couplings governed
by lawless Aphrodite:
see how much more respect to the gods
we show than men do ever   1090
in their unjust breeding of children.
Let song reverse itself:
sing harshly of *men's* loves.
For Xuthus, grandson of Zeus,
forgetful of his marriage,
did not get children at home, and share his luck
with my mistress; instead he favored
a foreign Aphrodite,
and acquired a bastard boy.

(Enter a slave, one of Creusa's menservants.)

SERVANT

Women, where is the daughter of Erechtheus,   1100
our royal mistress? I have searched and searched
throughout the city, but I cannot find her.

CHORUS

What is it, fellow-servant? Why do you hurry?
What is the news you bring us in such haste?

SERVANT

    We are hunted. And the rulers of this place
    are seeking her so she may die by stoning.

CHORUS

    You frighten me. What are you telling us?
    Our scheme to kill the boy: has it been found out?

SERVANT

    It has. You too will share the punishment.

CHORUS LEADER

    How were the secret plans she made discovered?   1110

SERVANT

    The god revealed them: he would not be defiled.

CHORUS LEADER

    How? I am begging you: please tell me this.
    I will die, or live, more happily if I know.

SERVANT

    After Creusa's husband left the oracle,
    taking along his just-discovered son
    to feast and sacrifice in celebration,
    he himself went to the place where Bacchic fire
    leaps up, to wet the double peaks with blood,
    in place of the usual offering for a birth.
    He said to the boy, "Son, you stay here, and set   1120
    the tents up carefully with the workmen's help.
    If I am delayed in making sacrifice
    to the birth gods, let our friends begin their feast."
    He took the cattle and left. Then the young man,
    very serious, started putting up the tent,
    carefully watching the sun's rays, to make sure
    no one would face mid-day or sunset glare.

He made the sides one hundred by one hundred,
and rectilinear, as the experts say,
the area within ten thousand square,   1130
so he could invite all Delphi to the feast.
Taking some sacred hangings from the shrine,
he made a shade for people to marvel at.
First, as a covering, a roof of robes,
Amazon plunder offered to the god
by Heracles, the son of Zeus. Among them
were woven pictures such as these: the Sky
was gathering stars within his lofty circle;
Sun drove his horses to the fiery finish,
drawing behind him the bright Evening Star.   1140
Night in black cloak swung round her chariot
and pair; the stars came following the goddess.
The Pleiades journeyed through the middle air,
and Orion, sword in hand; above, the Bear
turned at the pole her gleaming golden tail.
The full moon that divides the month in two
shot her light upward, with the Hyades,
clearest of signs for sailors, while the Daystar
put other stars to flight. Around the sides
he put up more of these barbarian weavings: 1150
ships with stout oars meeting Greek ships in battle,
creatures half beast, half human, and great hunts
on horseback after deer and savage lions.
And by the entrance, Cecrops near his daughters,
spiraling snaky coils, an Athenian's gift.
In the middle of the dining place he'd made,
the boy set golden bowls for wine; the herald
drew himself up and called all citizens
who wished to feast. And as the place grew crowded,
with garlands on their heads guests took their fill   1160
of the fine food set before them. When they were done,
an old man came and stood there, right in the middle,
and made the diners laugh at his busy ways.

He kept on taking water from the pitchers
for ritual washing, and he burnt the myrrh,
and passed round to the guests the golden cups,
taking this unassigned task upon himself.
When it was time for flutes and the common wine-bowl,
the old man said, "Now you must take away
the little wine cups, and bring in the large,   1170
so that these guests may sooner lift their spirits."
The servants set to work, then, bringing in
goblets of gold and silver. He picked one out
with special care, as if to please his new master,
filled it, and gave it to him, after putting in
a powerful poison his mistress had supplied,
(they say) because she wanted the boy to die.
And no one knew it. This late-appearing son
was ready to make libation with the others
when one of the servants spoke unlucky words.   1180
Well, the boy was raised in a shrine, among its seers:
he took this as an omen and gave orders
to fill a new bowl. The libation he had ready
he poured on the ground, and ordered all to do so.
A silence followed. We filled the sacred bowls
again with water and with wine from Biblos.
And while we were at this task, a flock of doves
flew in (for in the house of Loxias
they live unfearing), and where the wine was poured,
they put their beaks to it, thirsty for a drink,   1190
and drew it in with their fair-feathered throats.
The libation did no harm to the other birds,
but the one that settled where the new-found son
had spilled his wine, and tasted it, straightway
shook her feathered body in a Bacchic frenzy,
and screamed in a way we could not understand,
giving an uncanny cry. The crowd of diners
was astonished at the poor bird's sufferings.
It died then, gasping for air, letting go limp

its red-clawed legs. The boy from the oracle   1200
shook back his cloak, set his hands on the table
and shouted: "Who is the one who planned to kill me?
Tell me, old man. For you were so attentive,
and it was from your hand I took my drink."
He took the old man by the arm and searched him,
so as to catch him with the evidence.
He was caught; but it took force to make him tell
of Creusa's bold deception with the drink.
The boy foretold by Apollo's oracle
straightway ran out, taking some guests along,   1210
and standing among the Delphian leaders said
"O sacred land, do you hear? I almost died
by the drugs of Erechtheus' child, a foreign woman."
And the lords of Delphi, voting with one voice,
decreed that my mistress should be stoned to death
for plotting the murder of one consecrated,
and in the shrine itself. The whole city seeks
for the one who in sadness took to this sad course.
She came to Phoebus because she longed for children,
and has put an end to those children and to herself.   1220
(The servant makes a gesture of farewell and leaves in haste.)

CHORUS
No turning aside this death
for me in my sorrow; none.
It is clear now, clear that venom
was mixed with the wine-god's grapes
in a deadly libation; clear
that an offering to those below must follow:
disaster for me, my mistress' death by stoning.
Can I take wing, or burrow
in darkness beneath the earth,
to escape stones, death, and destruction?   1230
Can I mount the swiftest chariot, or take ship?

There is no hiding without a willing god to help.
What is there left, my poor mistress, for you to suffer?
Is this what will be? We wanted to harm those near us,
and will suffer harm ourselves, and this is justice.
(Enter Creusa, running.)

CREUSA

Servants, I'm being hunted down for slaughter,
condemned by the Delphians' vote and given up.

CHORUS

We know, poor thing, the calamity you face.

CREUSA

Where can I run to? I barely escaped the house
with my life, and I have evaded my enemies   1240
by stealth. Now I am here; where can I turn?

CHORUS

Where else but the altar?

CREUSA

What good is that to me?

CHORUS

It is wrong to kill suppliants.

CREUSA

The law itself is my death.

CHORUS

Only if caught—

CREUSA

And now my bitter opponents
are here, with sword in hand.
(Enter Ion, followed by a group of armed Delphian men.)

CHORUS LEADER

Sit upon the altar,
and if you die, you will put blood guilt on those
who killed you. But what comes you must endure.
(*Creusa climbs up on the altar steps and clings to the altar, as Ion runs
toward her.*)

ION

Bull-horned Cephisus, river god of Athens,
ancestor of Creusa, what a viper
you sired in her—or should I say a snake   1250
that gazes with a look of deadly flame?
She would do anything—no less poisonous
than the Gorgon's blood with which she planned to kill me.
(*He addresses his followers, who move forward, but hesitate to approach
the altar.*)
Get hold of her; let the uplands of Parnassus
comb out for her those untouched locks of hair
when she is tossed down on the rocks below.
(*He turns to Creusa.*)
What a piece of good luck this happened here,
before I came into your power at Athens!
Still among friends I measured your intentions,
saw how you hated me, what harm you meant.   1260
For if you once had trapped me in your home,
you would have sent me—no escape—to Hades.
But neither Apollo's altar nor his shrine
will save you, and the pity you might expect
belongs by rights to me and to my mother—
whom I can name although she is not here.
Look at this criminal, how she contrives
trick upon trick: she's cowering at the altar
to escape the punishment for what she's done.

CREUSA

You cannot kill me. In this I speak for myself   1270
and for the god with whom I am taking refuge.

ION

And what do you and Phoebus have in common?

CREUSA

My body is his, a consecrated gift.

ION

And so you tried to kill what's his with poison?

CREUSA

You were no longer his: you were your father's.

ION

I became my father's; I say I *am* the god's.

CREUSA

You were once the god's: now I am his, not you.

ION

Where is your piety? My life was pious.

CREUSA

I wanted to kill the enemy of my house.

ION

I did not come in arms against your land.   1280

CREUSA

You did. You were trying to burn Erechtheus' house.

ION

Yes? With what torches? With what fiery flames?

CREUSA

You meant to rob me and rule what had been mine.

ION

    And you tried to kill me, fearing my intentions?

CREUSA

    So as not to be killed, if you went beyond intending.

ION

    Childless, you resent my father's finding me?

CREUSA

    I am childless: and will you take my home from me?

ION

    Yes, since my father gave me what was his.

CREUSA

    How do Aeolus' heirs share in Athena's land?

ION

    He saved your land with weapons, not mere words.   1290

CREUSA

    An ally's never a true inhabitant.

ION

    Do I not have a share in what is my father's?

CREUSA

    As much as shield and spear can get. That's all.

ION

    Now leave the altar and Apollo's seat.

CREUSA

    Give your own mother orders, wherever she is.

ION

You tried to kill me. Will you not pay the price?

CREUSA

If you're willing to slaughter me within the shrine.

ION

What pleasure is it to die in a sacred place?

CREUSA

I will give pain to those who have given me pain.

ION

Ah!   1300
How terrible that the gods showed such bad judgment
in the laws they made for mortals. It's not right
that criminals cling to altars: drive them out!
Only the righteous ought to touch what's holy.
Victims of injustice should seek sanctuary,
but the good and the bad, though both may take this course,
must not receive like treatment from the gods.

(At this threat to her sanctuary Creusa retreats behind the altar. Enter
the Pythia from the temple, with a basket in her
arms. She stands in front of Ion; Creusa's view of
what she holds is thus obstructed.)

PYTHIA

Stop, child. See: I have left my oracle
to cross this threshold—I, Apollo's prophet,
who keep the sacred tripod's ancient law,   1310
the chosen one of all of Delphi's women.

ION

Welcome, dear mother, my own though not by birth.

PYTHIA

I don't dislike your giving me that name.

ION

Have you heard? This woman schemed to murder me.

PYTHIA

I have heard. But you are wrong to be so savage.

ION

Should I not kill those who have tried to kill me?

PYTHIA

To their stepsons, wives are always enemies.

ION

And we to stepmothers—when they treat us badly.

PYTHIA

Let that be. Leave the temple, go to your homeland—

ION

What is it you are advising me to do?   1320

PYTHIA

Come with clean hands to Athens, and good omens.

ION

A person's clean who kills his enemies.

PYTHIA

You must not do it: hear what I have to say.

ION

Tell me, then, since I know you mean it kindly.

PYTHIA

You see this basket I'm holding in my arms?

ION

I see an ancient cradle, hung with garlands.

PYTHIA

In this I found you as a newborn child.

ION

What do you mean? The story you tell is new.

PYTHIA

Yes; I kept quiet the facts I now reveal.

ION

Why hide them when you found me long ago?   1330

PYTHIA

The god desired your service in his house.

ION

And does not want me now? How can I tell?

PYTHIA

Because he gives you a father and sends you forth.

ION

And was it at his command you saved these things?

PYTHIA

Back then Apollo put it in my heart.

ION

To do what? Tell me, and complete the story.

PYTHIA

To keep what I had found until today.

ION

What good or harm does this thing hold for me?

PYTHIA

In it are hidden the baby clothes you wore.

ION

You are bringing me a way to find my mother?   1340

PYTHIA

Since the god now wills it—as he did not before.

ION

O excellent day that brings these things to light!

PYTHIA

Take them, then, and go searching for your mother.

ION

Through all of Asia, all of Europe's lands!

PYTHIA

As you decide. By the god's will, child, I raised you,
and by his will I give these things to you.
He wanted me, without being told, to take them
and keep them; why this was so I cannot say.
No mortal being ever knew I had them
or where I kept them hidden. So, farewell.   1350
As if I were your mother I embrace you.
(She embraces Ion, and goes into the temple. Ion stands, holding the
basket; his back is still to Creusa and to the altar.)

ION

I can't help weeping when I think of this:
my mother loved in secret, hid me, sold me,
never gave me the breast. And I was nameless,

and lived as a servant in Apollo's house.
God's ways are good, but fate is hard to bear.
For when I should have lived in softest comfort,
my days all pleasure, held in my mother's arms,
I was deprived of that dear mother's care.
She too deserves my pity, since she suffered   1360
as I did, losing childhood's happiness.
(He turns and moves toward the temple steps.)
And now I will offer this cradle to the god
and not risk finding what I do not want.
For if some slave turns out to be my mother,
finding is worse than leaving her in silence.
To your shrine, O Phoebus, I dedicate this thing—
But what am I doing? I war with the god's desire,
which has saved for me these tokens of my mother.
I must open the cradle and bear with what I find;
I cannot transgress the limits fate has set.   1370
*(He turns in the direction of the altar, sets the basket down, and prepares
to open it. Creusa, who has come round to the
front of the altar in the course of his last speech,
now sees the basket.)*
You holy garlands, what have you hidden here,
guardians holding fast what once was mine?
But look: the cover on this woven cradle
is by the god's hand somehow as good as new;
the wicker is free of mildew, though much time
has passed since someone stored her treasures here.

CREUSA

What do I see? Something I had no hope of.

ION

Be quiet! You tried to destroy me before, and now—

CREUSA

Silence is not my part. Don't reprimand me.
I see the cradle in which I once abandoned—   1380

you, my own child, when you were just a baby,
at the cave of Cecrops, where the Long Rocks rise.
I will leave this altar, even if I must die.
*(She jumps down from the altar steps and starts toward the basket; in the
        course of the next speech, she reaches it and takes
        hold of it.)*

ION

Catch her! Some god has made her lose her mind:
she has leapt down from the altar. Tie her arms!

CREUSA

Yes, go on, kill me: I will still hold on
to this cradle, and you, and all that's hidden here.

ION

Strange! I am claimed by her; what theft is this?

CREUSA

Not claimed, but discovered as my very own.

ION

Your own? You did your best by stealth to kill me.   1390

CREUSA

My child, if a child is what's dearest to its parents.

ION

Stop weaving webs of trickery—or be caught!

CREUSA

If only I could be; that is the mark I aim for.

ION

Is the cradle empty, or is there something in it?

CREUSA

The things you wore when I abandoned you.

ION

And can you name them before seeing them?

CREUSA

If I cannot do so, I consent to die.
(She stands up and turns her back on the basket.)

ION

Speak. Your strange daring somehow frightens me.

CREUSA

Look for the weaving I made when I was a girl.

ION

What is it like? Girls do a great deal of weaving.   1400

CREUSA

Unfinished, like a piece of practice-work.

ION

What is its pattern? This is no way to catch me.

CREUSA

In the center of the cloth is set the Gorgon.

ION

O Zeus, what fate is this that tracks me down?

CREUSA

And the border is fringed with serpents, like the aegis.
(Ion holds up a piece of woven cloth.)

ION

Look!
Here is the weaving: its web fulfills your words.

CREUSA

O girl's work, done at my loom, so long ago.

ION

Is there more? Was that one just a lucky guess?

CREUSA

Two snakes with gleaming golden jaws, the gift   1410
of Athena, who has us put them on our children
to mime the tale of Erichthonius.

ION

What do you do with the gold? How is it used?

CREUSA

Worn as a necklace by the newborn baby.
(Ion looks in the basket.)

ION

It is here. But there is a third I need to know.

CREUSA

I put around you then a wreath of the olive
that first grew from Athena's rocky hill.
If this is that wreath, it has not ever withered,
but still is green, sprung from the maiden's tree.
*(As she speaks the last words, Ion takes the wreath from the basket and
                holds it up; then, still kneeling by the basket, he
                reaches up to touch Creusa's face as she turns to
                look at him.)*

ION

Mother. Dear mother. What happiness to see you.   1420
What happiness to touch your happy face.
(He stands and Creusa embraces him.)

CREUSA

My child, light brighter than the sun to me
(the god will forgive me), I hold you in my arms.
Unhoped-for you are here: not in the earth,
with Persephone and the dead, as I imagined.

ION

I am here before your eyes and in your arms,
dear mother, like one who died but did not die.

CREUSA

O field of shining sky,
What shall I say, what shout aloud?
Where did it come from, this unlooked-for gladness?   1430
Where did I find this joy?

ION

I would have thought that anything might happen
rather than this, mother: that I am yours.

CREUSA

I am shaking still with fear.

ION

That although you hold me here, you do not have me?

CREUSA

Yes: I had put all hope far, far from me.
(She turns to the temple, addressing the absent Pythia.)
But tell me, woman: tell me,
how did it come about
that you took my son in your arms?
By what hand did he come to Phoebus' house?   1440

ION

This was god's doing. I hope that what's to come
brings happiness to match what we have suffered.

CREUSA

    I wept when I gave birth to you
    I screamed with sorrow when I let you go.
    Now with my cheek to yours I can draw breath
    and say: what blessed happiness I have found.

ION

    In what you say you tell my story too.

CREUSA

    I am no longer childless, without heirs.
    Our home has its hearth, our land its line of kings,
    Erechtheus is young again.   1450
    The earth-born house no longer walks in darkness
    but sees with sun's full light.

ION

    Mother, my father should come and share the joy
    I've given to you both.

CREUSA

    My child, what are you saying?
    How it puts me in the wrong.

ION

    What do you mean?

CREUSA

                  Someone else—
    your father was someone else.

ION

    Then—you were unmarried, I your bastard child?

CREUSA

    There were no torchlit dances at the wedding   1460
    that gave you birth.

ION

It hurts to hear it.
Am I low-born, then, mother? Who was the man?

CREUSA

I take Athena Gorgon-slayer as witness—

ION

Why do you say this?

CREUSA

the goddess whose olives crown my rocky hill—

ION

You speak to me in twists and turns, not plainly.

CREUSA

that by the nightingales' rock, with Phoebus—

ION

Phoebus? Why do you speak of him?

CREUSA

I went to bed with him, in secret.   1470

ION

Tell me, since what you will say is my good fortune.

CREUSA

In the tenth month, my hidden pain,
you were born: the god was your father.

ION

If this is true, you tell me what I long for.

CREUSA

I wrapped you in some weaving I had done,
while still a girl—my efforts at the loom—

but did not tend you as a mother does;
I did not nurse you and I did not wash you.
In a lonely cave, a feast
for the beaks of birds to tear at,   1480
you were given up to Hades.

ION

A dreadful thing to dare.
And you endured it, mother.

CREUSA

Dear child, I was terribly frightened,
and in my fear let go your life.
I did not want to kill you.

ION

I nearly caused your death.

CREUSA

Gods, gods. What happened long ago was terrible,
and terrible what we have done here too.
We are tossed from this to that as fortune turns   1490
and good luck follows bad: the wind keeps changing.
Let things stay as they are. Enough of sorrow.
Now let there be fair weather for us, child.

CHORUS

No one could watch this happen and imagine
that anything's past human expectation.

ION

Chance, you who change the lives of countless mortals,
so bad luck follows good and good luck bad,
how close I came to murdering my mother
and suffering undeservedly myself.
But oh,   1500
as the days pass, in the sun's encircling light,

do we not come to learn of things like this?
I found you, mother—dearest discovery;
my ancestry, I take it, brings no blame.
The rest I want to say to you alone.
Come here; I want to whisper in your ear,
and wrap in darkness what I think has happened.
Be careful, mother, that having made some slip,
as happens to girls, a secret love affair,
you not lay blame for this upon the god,   1510
and trying to avoid disgrace for me,
say Phoebus is my father, when he is not.

CREUSA

No! by Athena Victory who carried her shield
beside Zeus' chariot against earth's children
you have no father among mortal men,
but Loxias who raised you fathered you.

ION

Why, then, did he give his child to someone else,
and declare I was by birth the son of Xuthus?

CREUSA

He did not call you Xuthus' son by birth.
You were a gift; as friend might to a friend,   1520
he gave his son to be our household's master.

ION

Is Apollo truthful, or an empty prophet?
It's reasonable that this should trouble me.

CREUSA

Listen then, and I'll tell you what I think.
Apollo helps you by giving you a place
in a noble house. If you were called his son,
you would have no rights as heir in your own home,
no father's name. How could you, since I hid

my marriage, and in secret tried to kill you?
He has done you good in giving you away.   1530

ION

I can't approach this matter quite so lightly.
No; I will question Phoebus in his house,
and ask if am his son or a mortal's.
(He moves toward the temple, then pauses, as the goddess Athena
appears on the roof.)
Wait—who is this that appears above the temple
with face turned toward the light; what god is this?
Run, mother: for we must not see the gods—
unless, perhaps, this is our time to see them.

ATHENA

Do not run from me: I am not your enemy.
Here as at Athens I look kindly on you;
I am Pallas Athena, for whom your city was named.   1540
I have come with an urgent message from Apollo,
who did not feel he should appear before you,
because there might have been some talk of blame
for the past; and so he sent me to explain.
This woman is your mother, Apollo your father.
He gave you away, not to your parents by birth,
but so as to bring you to your noble home.
And when the matter came out in the open,
he feared you might be killed by your mother's plots,
and she by you, and so he contrived to save you.   1550
Lord Apollo meant to keep the whole thing quiet,
then make you known, in Athens, to your mother,
and tell you that you were her child and his.
But so I may finish the matter and fulfill
Apollo's oracles—since this is why
my chariot brought me here—listen to me.
Take your son with you to the land of Cecrops,
Creusa; establish him on the royal throne.
Since he is of Erechtheus' blood, it's fitting

that he will be the ruler of my land;   1560
and Greece as well will hear of him. His children,
four of them from one stock, will give their names
to the land itself and the people of the land,
the tribes that live upon my rocky hill.
The eldest, Geleon, names the Geleontes;
then come the Hopletes and the Argades,
and those who take their tribe's name from my aegis,
the Aegicores. The sons born of your sons
at the fated time will settle the island cities
of the Cyclades, and the land along the coasts;   1570
these settlements will give my country strength.
In Asia and in Europe, the parts of both
that face the strait between, Ionians will be found:
named after Ion, they will gain great glory.
      And you and Xuthus will have children now:
Dorus, whose Dorian city will be sung
throughout the Peloponnese. A second son,
Achaeus, will be king in sea-side Rhium,
and those named after him will know fame too.
Apollo has managed everything quite neatly.   1580
He gave you a safe delivery, so no one knew;
and when you bore this boy and set him out
in baby clothes, the god commanded Hermes
to take him in his arms and bring him here.
He nourished the child and did not let him die.
Therefore keep quiet the fact that he's your son,
so Xuthus may delight in his belief,
and you may take the good that's yours, and go.
Farewell; now that you've met with this relief,
I promise happiness is all you'll know.   1590

ION

Daughter of Zeus, I hear your words, and do not disbelieve
                        them now.
I am Apollo's son, and hers: I might have known it long ago.

CREUSA

    Now hear my side. I give the god what once I could not give:
                respect,
    because he gives me back the child whom then he treated with
                neglect.
    These temple gates, this oracle, look on me now with
                friendly face,
    that were my enemies before. And so in gladness, with good
                grace,
    I grasp the gates and speak to them in parting as I leave this
                place.

ATHENA

    I praise the change that makes you speak more kindly of the
                gods: it's true
    that what we do takes time, but still we do what we set out to do.

CREUSA

    Child, let's go home.

ATHENA

                And I will follow.

ION

                      Worthy guide!

CREUSA

                          Our city's friend!   1600

ATHENA

    Come, take your seat upon the ancient throne.

ION

                        Now mine, a fitting end.
(Creusa and Ion leave, followed by the Delphians, and Athena leaves the
temple roof.)

CHORUS

> O Son of Zeus and Leto, hail! A house that is misfortune-bound
> must pay the gods all due respect, and so take courage. I
> > have found
> that in the end the good will meet a fate deserved, all
> > trouble past,
> while ne'er-do-wells, as suits their nature, never will do well
> > at last.

(Exit the chorus.)

Children of Heracles

Translated by
J. T. Barbarese

Translator's Preface

For W. S. Di Piero

When I began this version of *Children of Heracles*, of the extant translations some (Arthur S. Way's) were out of print and available only through libraries; others, like David Kovacs' 1997 Loeb Classical Library volume, were expensive or difficult to obtain.[1] But in general these editions were competing only in the sense that somewhere they fight for shelf space. None I came across, with the possible exception of the new Kovacs (itself not available until early in the fall of 1996, well after I began) and the Oxford edition of the early 1980s,[2] are capable of being performed.

> I hold it truth, and long have held:—the just
> Lives for his brother men; but he whose soul
> Uncurbed hunts gain alone, unto the state
> Useless, in dealings hard, is but to himself
> A friend—nor know this by report alone . . .

This is A. S. Way's handling of the play's opening in the 1909 Loeb edition. What went through this translator's mind? Did anyone in 1909 still *use* "hold it truth"? Metrically, and except for the choruses, Way's translation attempts to gain and keep the Miltonic high ground. The third line is noisy and breaks the metrical expectations set by the second and first, is given no help by the succession of long U's ("unto," "useless"), and surrenders whatever majesty it may have in line four, when the unspeakable yields to the incredible ("is but to himself / A friend"). At what price the pentameter? Not speech but Morse code. No matter the lexical accuracy of his rendering, it argues that the cost of precision is unintentional farce and a well-intentioned flatfootedness.

---

[1] *Euripides*, trans. Arthur S. Way, vol. 3 (London: W. Heinemann, 1912); *Euripides*, vol. 2, ed. and trans. David Kovacs, vol. 2 (Cambridge, Mass.: Harvard University Press, 1997).

[2] Euripides, *The Children of Heracles*, trans. Henry Taylor and Robert A. Brooks (New York: Oxford University Press, 1981).

Relieved of the primary role of the translator, I worked toward a text that was readable, if not actually speakable, and if not on Broadway then in those venues where plays are read. Where several dependable classicists had sought for dictionary accuracy, I took as my goal the elucidation of character, and building on those dependable translations tried for the direct ring of spoken English:

> If a lifetime of trouble has taught me a thing,
> it's this, this alone: the just have just offspring.
> And those whose wills are lawless
> are to their community worthless
> political nulls. Life has taught me this.

If not as accurate as the versions whose unspeakability makes them useless as scripts, this one is founded on indebtedness to good scholarship and a humility before strugglers against different odds—and, I gather, toward different goals—as well as an equally warm admiration for Euripides.

I began with Liddell and Scott and Garzya's (1972)[3] edition of the text and crawled through the first two hundred lines. I had lost the feel of Euripides' rhythm, the strangely excitable quality of his language, so I recorded Iolaus' opening speech and played it while driving. From the outset it seemed that the play's meaning, and perhaps its irony, were kerneled in line two and in the belief that some people are *by nature* just and therefore beget justice as naturally as they do children. Only after I had been through nearly a quarter of the text did it begin to rhyme itself out for me, at first in those places where the language seemed most naturally to hook toward parataxis. The result is a version rhymed (perfect-, slant-, and all variants in between) almost completely in couplets, but still, I hope, consistently and confidently speakable. The rhythms come from a variety of sources—from my own declaiming of the Greek to my reading of and in environing translations (Way, Kovacs, Ralph Gladstone, Louis Meridier). Finally, though, my line owes as much to the range of tetrameters one grows up hearing—Pound, Browning, Gilbert and Sullivan, Dr. Seuss' *The Five Hundred Hats*—as it does to whatever my own ear knows of rhythm.

---

[3] *Heraclidae*, ed. Antonius Garzya (Leipzig: Teubner, 1972).

The fates of Heracles and Eurystheus of Argos were tangled from the outset and a cautionary fable of how the gods can do us nothing but harm. In *Iliad* XIX, where Agamemnon welcomes Achilles back to battle and apologizes for his past behavior, to excuse himself he refers to the story of Heracles' birth and how it was vexed by Zeus' boastfulness and Hera's jealousy. Zeus, who had conceived the child on the mortal Alcmene, on the day of the child's arrival announced:

> "Today the goddess of birth pangs and labor
> will bring to light a human child, a man-child
> born of the stock of men who spring from *my* blood,
> one who will lord it over all who dwell around him . . ."[4]

Hera, meanwhile, muttering "You will prove a liar" under her breath, tricks her husband into swearing an oath on his boast. Naturally, Zeus complies. Hera then speeds to Argos, home of king Sthenelus, and induces labor in his wife Nicippe, still two months shy of term; the result is Eurystheus—who as the grandson of Perseus is *also* of immortal stock. So the vow is fulfilled and destiny takes hold of the wrong child. When Eurystheus succeeds his father, he becomes Heracles' taskmaster. It is for him that Heracles undertakes his twelve labors.

Heracleidae, as our play is often titled in the scholarly literature, is officially a Greek tragedy, yet from the outset I had difficulty naturalizing the designation with what the play actually does. Surmise has it that Euripides composed the play early in the Peloponnesian War, as a tribute to the liberality of Athenian political culture and cultural memory. Yet it seems far from tragic. In fact, it struck me as comedy in Dante's sense—a story with a foul beginning and a prosperous conclusion—as well as in less elusive modern senses. Iolaus' opening speech lays out the issues. Iolaus and the children of his boss, Heracles, have since the death of the children's father been in flight from Eurystheus. On Heracles' death, Eurystheus had begun to fear the vengeance of his mostly male offspring and sought to kill them, but they escape with Iolaus, the family's surviving *capo* (there is really no other word for the familial and professional roles Iolaus fills), and their

---

[4]Homer, *The Iliad*, trans. Robert Fagles (New York: Viking, 1990).

grandmother, Alcmene, and wander throughout Greece seeking sanctuary. (Only Trachis has welcomed them, for which Trachis was cruelly punished—an event alluded to in Iolaus' opening speech.) The play finds the exiles outside Athens, which is prepared to take them in and protect them until an oracle is produced that raises the play's central complication. It is the Athenian king, Demophon, who announces the problem: a virgin must be sacrificed before the Athenians can take the field against Eurystheus.

Iolaus' reaction is noble but muddleheaded: "Let me die instead. Give me to the Argives." Demophon correctly reminds him that his offer is "high-minded but pointless": Eurystheus is interested only in the children themselves, who will grow up knowing that their duty is to avenge their father. The complication is apparently insoluble until Makaria appears near the middle of the play ("Strangers, impute not for my coming forth / Boldness to me," as Way would have it) and offers herself up as the demanded sacrifice. Yet from here the dramatic arc subtends. Once in possession of the facts from Iolaus, whose yelling draws her from the sanctuary into the open, Makaria's thinking is clearheaded. It is she who resolves Demophon's dilemma by stepping up to face the music. "I am prepared / for the fillets and hood. Let them sacrifice me / or abuse us to all for abusing their city." So lucid is her argument that it lends to the whole a nobility (and a logic) that seems to belong to another play. Makaria sounds as if she alone has actually understood the full import of Iolaus' opening lines: "If a lifetime of trouble has taught me a thing, / it's this, this alone: the just have just offspring." The high-born are *fatally*—we would say naturally—responsible for the moral upkeep of the rest of the human race. For the first of two times in the play it is a woman, and here a young one, who sees and solves the problem.

Soon after Makaria has made her entrance the comic elements begin to accumulate. She makes only one request—that Iolaus stand by her as she dies. But witnessing her death, he whines, "would kill me too." From here, Iolaus' character quickly shrinks to the proportions of farce and predicts the fairytale fate the gods spring on him late in the play, when his youth is momentarily restored to him. Simultaneously, Alcmene's stature grows by grim physical contrast. She enters nearly on the heels of Makaria's exit and from her opening lines stands out as exactly the foil Iolaus' character demanded. He is all high rhetoric and bombast; she is shrill, earthy, shrewd, and pragmatic, with only one goal—to protect her grandchildren. She is always the complete Mediterranean grandmother, and when her grandson Hyllus arrives but fails to stop by to see her, her reaction is refreshingly candid and slightly vulgar. When she learns that Iolaus has plans to join the battle against Eurystheus, she comes right to the point: "You can't be serious. Leave the children with me / to go off and get killed? Have you gone crazy?"

Alcmene seems perfectly suited, therefore, to uncover the solution to the play's second dilemma, when the protocols of diplomacy and of the vendetta coalesce in the capture of Eurystheus. Her recommendation is ruthless, cold-blooded, and, for reasons Euripides avoids going into, satisfies the Athenians. It is interesting that a more ancient version of the story has Eurystheus slain by Hyllus, who carries his head to his grandmother for her to mutilate. Euripides' maturing interest in the old woman parallels his departure from tradition in making her Eurystheus' killer. When Eurystheus is brought on stage in restraints near the end, he, like Agamemnon, uses Hera's baleful influence to excuse his awful behavior to a great warrior (in this case Heracles), but it is clear that the only person he actually fears is the ruthless Alcmene. The text is too incontestably lacunose to be reliable, but once again a woman bails out the men with a timely suggestion.

What is the play then about? We can hardly imagine it written by that great religious apologist Aeschylus, or by Sophocles, the grand finesser of moral and philosophical differences who wrote characters of such unnerving moral ambivalence. In Aeschylus' hands this could have been, like *Seven Against Thebes*, another pious documentary about divine wisdom. One wonders how Sophocles' terrible insight into fate's undoing of human designs would have reshaped Makaria's sacrifice and this play. But Euripides, far more than his older contemporaries, is fascinated not only by how Fate shapes character but by how character occasionally misleads Fate into the production of monstrosity. Fate, in Euripides far more than his older contemporaries, is irreligious, even nihilistic. The result here is a dark but pervasive wackiness in the way the principals are shaped by situations. An old man returns to battle, prays for rejuvenation, and is rejuvenated. A young girl offers herself as a sacrifice and is led off stage and never heard of again. When the bad guys get their due, the moralizing chorus limits itself to a four-line jingle about neither morality nor politics but spiritual expediency: a swift mopping of the brow and a "Thank god that's over with." It all seems to amount to a statement, if it can be called that, that life in all its raw inexplicability is reflected in but never really clarified by our behavior, no matter what Iolaus says.

A Euripidean Polonius, Iolaus fails to see consequences, and his opening words make a sentimental point but miss the story's scariest but thoroughly Euripidean possibility: that, just or not, human beings are inconsequential until luck forces them to act and in action to affect someone else's life, usually to ruin it. From the drama of Sophocles Euripides takes only the implicit despair and the muted nihilism that Sophocles transforms into heroic humanism. He comes to the material itself with a cool disregard for anything supernatural. His gods are big, empty blanks that our dreams doodle in. His incurable obsession is with monstrosity. Thus the difference between the world's self-regarding geniuses and its fatuous time-servers, between a Jason, say, and an Iolaus, is not personality, that Shakespearean discovery, but personal luck. But both the genius and the fool are monstrosities, and one no more wants a Jason and Medea to make a visit than an Iolaus and Copreus, who are and who bring nothing but trouble.

If there is such a thing as canonical tragedy, and if a nonspecialist is allowed to say so, in *Heracleidae* Euripides made a play as anti-canonical as one can imagine. And in that spirit I approached the play, which admittedly is neither the most polished nor the most textually dependable in the Euripidean repertoire. Were it not for the death of Makaria, *Heracleidae* would be nearly a fifth-century *Twelfth Night*, with Copreus and Eurystheus combining as Malvolio. The comic elements impressed me as the most palpable and pointed me toward a prosody of rhymed tetrameter couplets for the main dialogue and crisscrossed rhyming dimeters for the chorus. The persistent lightness of the whole (including my interpolated pun on Demophon's name) is therefore interpretive and not an attempt at parody. Finally, I have avoided the play's problematic textual condition in these remarks out of candid and rational self-interest. My first encounter with the bare Greek text left me with a clear and chastening recollection of variant-crowded footnotes and several braces of lines of poetry in editorial brackets. I cannot and therefore do not take a useful position on any of the play's several cruxes, and at just about every fork have taken the road more traveled.

Cast

IOLAUS, nephew of Heracles
COPREUS, lawyer representing Eurystheus
CHORUS of Athenians
DEMOPHON, king of Athens
MAKARIA, daughter of Heracles
SERVANT, lieutenant of Heracles' son Hyllus
ALCMENE, mother of Heracles
MESSENGER, an Athenian soldier
EURYSTHEUS, king of Argos
NONSPEAKING
    Heracles' two young sons
    Acamas, brother of Demophon

*(The play opens in front of the temple of Zeus in the Athenian
    suburbs of Marathon. Iolaus is seen on the lower steps of the
    temple, leaning against one of its two stone railings, while two
    preadolescent boys play quietly at the very foot of the steps.
    Iolaus is old and, if slow, still a large physical presence on the
    stage. It is clear that he has been watching the boys play for
    some time and is skittish about their safety.)*

IOLAUS
    If a lifetime of trouble has taught me a thing,
    it's principally this: the just have just offspring.
    And those whose wills are lawless
    are to their community worthless
    political nulls. Life has taught me this.
    Respected, at peace, I might have had
    a comfortable life in Argos. Instead,
    Heracles' nephew and his foremost man,
    I took on his discomfort. Now he is in Heaven
    and I gather his children under these wings,   10
    no hen with her chicks. No, a savior who needs saving.

Once their father had gone to alleged bliss
down from his perch spiraled Eurystheus,
hot after us. And we fled—we still flee,
our homes forfeited, but alive, legally
exiled from Argos, though his lawyers maintain
we *escaped*. He adds mental to physical pain,
outraging the outraged. He never relents—
dispatches his posses the very instant
his spies give us up. Then the posse shows up,   20
demands extradition, that our hosts yield us up
to Argos, always Argos, because he *is* Argos
and his friendship is worth a whole mainland of us.
And why not? It makes sense: I'm one old has-been
with nothing to trade but some noble orphans
and one noble grandmother. With no hesitation,
gnawed by worms of self-preservation
our hosts—would-be hosts—sympathetically wring
their hands and then ours. So on we go, fleeing,
and with me in the lead, headlong in reverse.   30
And should I spurn them, my name would be dirt.
"You see how it is? These boys had no father
but old Iolaus. And now he can't be bothered."
We are damned twice, in fact—we're cut off from cities
and from our kin, too. And pleading for sanctuary.
on our bellies or bottoms. Our last hope is here,
in liberal Athens. One more strange altar!
Now, two of Theseus' children rule here,
through Pandion's line, by legal succession,
a distant hope, these two distant cousins.   40
Alcmene, meanwhile, and the two younger girls,
her virgin granddaughters, are safely squirreled
away in the temple while I make my appeal.
And if, God help us, we are shown the way out,
Hyllus is off with his brother to scout
our next port of call, the next candidate.
(From the left enters Copreus, a representative of Argos. He is well
dressed and appears otherwise well mannered—in

*fact, he looks every inch a lawyer. He might even be
carrying a briefcase.)*
Boys, leave your game, *now*, do not hesitate.
It's Eurystheus' own special prosecutor.
His whole purpose in life is slandering us
with pretentious claims and bribed witnesses.   50

COPREUS

Come on down, Iolaus. Do you think you'll evade
our justice in Athens, or that Athens will aid
you and ignore us? You're a fool if you do,
but you're fooling yourself. Get what's coming to you,
come down from those steps. I will take you to Argos
and the public stoning, your measure of justice.

IOLAUS

You know the gods' altars are sanctuary.
How dare you pollute them by threatening me?

COPREUS

This is trouble for you and more work for me.
(Copreus approaches and mounts the steps, reaching for Iolaus.)

IOLAUS

You would dare pull me down!

COPREUS

                                   You're no seer, but you see.   60

IOLAUS

You blaspheme the temple!

COPREUS

                         Then that's how it will be.
*(Copreus lays his hands on Iolaus and the two struggle. The children
                  run up the steps toward the temple door. Copreus
                  lunges for them. Iolaus restrains him by his
                  clothing while the children bat him with their fists.)*

Get your hands off my clothing. You belong to Argos!
I claim you for Argos and Eurystheus.
(A brief struggle in which both Copreus and Iolaus end up flat on their
backs. Copreus is the first to rise. Tableau: Iolaus
stretched flat on the steps, Copreus standing above
him, and the children running back up the steps,
cowering at the doors of the temple.)

IOLAUS

Athens! Help! Help, someone, anyone—
We are homeless suppliants, abused and alone,
don't allow this! We are kinsmen—yours!

CHORUS *(entering from stage left)*

Who's crying out here? Who are you, mister?
Are you sick? Are you drunk? This is God's temple!

IOLAUS

This barbarian pushed me. I am not ill,
and I did not fall. And that man is a liar!   70

CHORUS

He has said nothing yet. Do you know where you are?
Where do you come from? The islands, maybe?

IOLAUS

I come from Mycenae, no islander me.

CHORUS

And your name in Mycenae?

IOLAUS

                                            I once made the news.
I was Battling Iolaus. Great Heracles' nephew.

CHORUS

I remember that name. And those children—are
they in your charge or are you in their care?

IOLAUS
> Ladies and gentleman, Heracles' children.
> They come to Athens requesting safe haven.

CHORUS
> You are telling us things that our king needs to hear.   80

IOLAUS
> I am asking, not telling. Do not send us from here.
> Argos is death—

COPREUS *(stepping in and reaching for Iolaus)*
> No, that will not do.
> We own you and claim you—the whole lot of you.
> *(The chorus leader steps in at this juncture and blocks Copreus' access
> to Iolaus. Though it would violate historical
> propriety, the chorus leader could be a woman.)*

CHORUS
> This is God's house, mister. It is God's own place
> and above human law. Anywhere in Greece
> suppliants belong to God. It's tradition.

COPREUS
> The hell with tradition. Heard of *ex*tradition?
> You are meddling here in political matters.
> You amateur diplomats provoke the disasters.   90

CHORUS
> But extradite them? Who are under the protection
> of Zeus? It should be out of the question.

COPREUS
> Along with death and disease. You sound like children.
> What is morally right may be legal rot.

CHORUS
What *would* be is man's. What *should* be is not.
The gods set the limits—

COPREUS
But don't live by *our* laws.

CHORUS
But *we* do. And to break the oldest of laws?
You must speak to our king, produce your just cause,
make your petition.   100

COPREUS
His name?

CHORUS
                        Demophon.

COPREUS
Then I'll argue with him. This conversation
is getting me nowhere. Where is Demophon?

CHORUS
Here is himself. Out of breath. Right behind
is his brother, Acamas. You won't change his mind.
(Demophon enters, Acamas behind him. Both are sturdy, well-built
soldierly types, and neither is very old. Demophon
is the larger, cheerier presence and the one clearly
in charge.)

DEMOPHON *(to the chorus leader)*
Nice work, old friend. It belies your years
that you beat out us youngsters who came running here
when we heard there was trouble. Who's troubling Zeus?

CHORUS
>   Your majesty, the children of Heracles,
>   dressed for worship. They request sanctuary.   110
>   Standing behind them is old Iolaus.

DEMOPHON *(acknowledging Iolaus)*
>   But why all the shouting? This is God's house.

CHORUS
>   This stranger apparently pulled old Iolaus
>   down the temple steps. He was raising a ruckus,
>   on his back, cowering, and that stranger
>   was standing above him. That man did it. There.

DEMOPHON
>   He looks like a lawyer. Dresses so, too.
> *(Copreus turns his back.)*
>   Has vile manners. Sir, I am speaking to you.
>   Identify yourself. Who are you?

COPREUS *(civil, barely deferential)*
>   From Argos,   120
>   sent here by my king, the great Eurystheus.
>   Surely you know him. I represent
>   his interests here. He demands these "suppliants"
>   be surrendered to us. We contest their claim
>   to be exiles. Their real legal status
>   is covered in this writ of habeas corpus.
> *(producing a writ and handing it to Demophon)*
>   It's real and it's legal. There's a bounty on them.
>   Their claim to be suppliant exiles is a sham.
>   They were smuggled from Argos by this old fool
>   and eluded their punishment. Unless it's unusual   130
>   to assume that a state can punish criminals,

make tenable laws, and enforce them, if necessary,
we expect cooperation. This lunacy
he will try on you he has peddled around
all over the mainland, and so far he has found
no buyer. For what? What sane ruler would forgo
his peace for theirs? None that I know.
Still, folly's like candy. It's hard to decline.
So they come here to Athens, the near end of the line,
out of panicked self-interest. Or maybe they see   140
a buyer here for their delicacy?
The motives of lunatics may be complex.
Though perhaps not so loony if Athens elects—
out of all Greece—to give them protection. Athens must choose. It can welcome them in
or hand them to me. I present you these options.
If you grant us custody, I can assure
you of Eurystheus' lasting support.
If not, if you shield them, I am charged equally
to give you this warning.   150
(in a lower voice)
                    A grant of sanctuary
will muddle your fortunes.
(circles Demophon conspiratorially)
                          Will you people accept
a conflict with us taken up to protect
two old farts and their brats? When you number your dead
what gains will you count? These brats and their half-dead
ancient bodyguards? Will your citizenry
see the growth in their moral personality
as worth all the bloodshed? Or will they believe
that these boys will mature to be just as naive
as their leaders and take up this quarrel with us?
What's in it for them? Accommodate us.   160
That is all I ask: give us what is ours,
reap the advantages. Our friendship is yours.

CHORUS
> Only a fool is prepared to decide
> before hearing all witnesses.
(to Iolaus, who is still on the steps)
>   What is your side?
(Throughout this speech Iolaus should be lower than Demophon but at
> *a higher elevation than Copreus or the chorus.*
> *Only when he kneels and takes Demophon's knees*
> *should they occupy the same step. The opening of*
> *Iolaus' address to Demophon should be played*
> *lightly, particularly through his muddled laying*
> *out of the lineage of Heracles.)*

IOLAUS
> My lord, in your country the law permits men
> to hear and respond to accusers—
(to Copreus, who is attempting to interrupt)
>   When
> I am done you can shush me! But not until then.
(to Demophon)
> He is nothing to us. He is excrement!
> Sir, all these allegations, all these fancy statements
> are just legalese that some court handed down   170
> to further destroy us.
(to Copreus)
>   We were *forced* out of town,
> by an *earlier* court and a *prior* decree.
> Kicked out. We were banished. Consequently,
> exiles, we fled. Now explain, this to me—
> how stripped of our citizenship we could possibly be
> punished as citizens? We are strangers to Argos
> because Argos so wants it. *You* banished *us*.
> But Argos is certainly not the whole planet,
> so Argos can't legislate everywhere, can it?
> Athens, don't acquiesce. Do not stand   180

for these children and me to be made contraband
and Athens tricked like those jerkwater cities
impressed by his writs and "respectability."
This is not Trachis. No hicks live here,
no unlettered farmers who will wither in fear
when you come with subpoenas before God's own altar,
disputing, polluting, using big words,
quoting the law with a hand on your sword.
This is Athens. And if it should ever occur
that Athens is swayed into handing us over   190
then Athens would clearly be Athens no more—
Athens the *free.* But no: Athens endures.
It surrounds me here in these citizens
who would give up their lives before trading in
their ideals, their conscience, for expediency.
I've said the truth. What *you've* said is the lunacy.
(turning to Demophon)
As for you, king, let me attempt to explain
why it might be your *duty* to take these boys in.
Here's the long and the short: you are blood relations,
back to your grandfathers, you all are cousins.   200
First Pelops, then Pittheus, then Pittheus' daughter,
Aethra, herself being Theseus' mother,
Lord Theseus being, for the record, your father,
and their father, Heracles, Alcmene's son,
which means that he is, or was, the great-grandson
of Pelops, whose granddaughter, Alcmene, was mother
of your own grandfather's first cousin's first grandson.
(The chorus and Demophon look confused. Iolaus takes no notice.)
Then there is this: it is known wherever
they speak of Heracles and your great forebear,
that Heracles—and I saw this first-hand—   210
sailed with your father to the Amazon land
for the belt of Hippolyta. And each man of us
knows how lord Heracles rescued lord Theseus
who had gone, for Pirithous, into Hell itself

to kidnap Persephone but got caught himself
by the lord of that blank dark—it was Heracles
who rescued your father. My heart says you should
act toward these boys here as Heracles would
if the tables were turned. Do not surrender
to litigious snakes who trouble your altars   220
and make heavy claims. I'll kneel if I must.
(approaching Demophon and kneeling)
  Lord Demophon, it would hardly be just,
  it would be a mistake, a calamity,
  to surrender the children of Heracles.
(He reaches for Demophon's chin while embracing his knees—the
                    traditional posture of the suppliant. The chorus
                    should hold still as though registering the gravity
                    of the moment.)
They are your blood kin.
You *must* take them in.
You must be their friend, their father, protector.
But go back to Argos? Death would be better.

CHORUS

  Excuse us, sir, now that we hear this
  it moves us to pity. Of itself it's outrageous   230
  when the high-born are humbled by bad circumstance—
  but when they are children!
(Demophon raises Iolaus to his feet.)

DEMOPHON
                              Enough. I'm convinced
that Iolaus' claims are thrice-warranted.
One warrant is God, whose altar this is.
Then come those links of blood obligation,
a debt to a royal kinsman whose sons
should gain some good from the great good he did;
and third, my good name, which I, God forbid,
should lose carelessly. And lose it I would

if, like a lunatic, panicked, I should   240
invite into God's own sanctuary
bounty-hunters and abet blasphemy
just to sleep through the night. The word *blaspheme* would be
a code word for *Athens*, and to foreigners only
would Athens seem free. No, you do not surrender
the old and displaced and expect to engender
the world's admiration. That's cultural suicide,
not intelligent statecraft. And as much as I'd
prefer that this whole mess were avoidable,
neither you nor these boys will be further troubled   250
and forced to come down. You stay where you are.
(to Copreus)
Whereas you, counselor, must deliver my answer
to your king. Say this is a city of laws,
that we are prepared to give an ear to his cause,
but that justice is justice. The children will stay.

COPREUS
    Justice is founded in sound argument.

DEMOPHON
    So there's justice in kidnapping suppliants?

COPREUS
    If we're both disgraced, which of us wins?

DEMOPHON
    The disgrace is all mine if I were to give in.

COPREUS
    Then expel them from Athens! Let us do the rest.   260

DEMOPHON
    Only fools would test god with so transparent a test.

COPREUS
  It is uncommon wisdom to let criminals go free.

DEMOPHON
  It is common wisdom—gods' altars are free.

COPREUS
  Have you considered the cost in Athenian lives?

DEMOPHON
  Athenians rule Athens. Not you Argives.

COPREUS
  Not yet. Not so long as Athens complies.

DEMOPHON
  Play loose with man's laws, but not with the gods'.

COPREUS
  The idea sickens me. Go to war over this?

DEMOPHON
  I too dislike war. I like blasphemy less.

COPREUS
  They belong to Argos. They must accompany me.   270

DEMOPHON
  Please, don't. You'll never make it past me.

COPREUS
  Something tells me that all this is a bluff.
  *(Copreus attempts to seize one of the children and Demophon steps in
  and grabs him by the shoulder.)*

DEMOPHON
  Lay a finger on them, you'll know soon enough.

CHORUS *(stepping between the two)*
>For God's sake, he's a herald, sir! With immunity!

DEMOPHON
>Not if the ass tangles with me.

CHORUS *(to Copreus)*
>You should probably leave.
(to Demophon)
>>My lord, let him be.

COPREUS *(brushing himself off)*
>I'm going, I'm going. I came here alone,
>I'll return with company. As legions and legions
>of fully armed soldiers in the command
>of general Eurystheus. As we speak he stands   280
>poised on your borders. Ten thousand men
>stand battle-hungry, filled with battle-tension
>and awaiting the order to launch the invasion
>my message will trigger. Then an iron ocean
>will flood the countryside surrounding Athens
>right up to its walls. It is the way of great nations.
>Who would marshal and train and arm so many men
>and not commit them to combat?
(dismissively)
>>Probably Athens.

DEMOPHON
>Find your way out. You do not scare me.
>My good name and their welfare are infinitely   290
>weightier matters. No, no more debate.
>Athens is free, not some satellite state.
*(As Copreus exits, the chorus crowds excitedly around Demophon, who
>>>has helped Iolaus to his feet. Iolaus paces the steps
>>>with the pride of an owner as the children of
>>>Heracles descend the steps and resume their earlier*

game. Demophon is seen discussing something
with a member of the chorus. A general bustle
of activity.)

CHORUS

We'd better get ready, we had better prepare
and plan critically. What a total nightmare!
And how quickly it happened! The clearest decisions
are shaky in even the best of conditions.
But drop in the habit of lawyers to lie
and take what is bad and then magnify
it—imagine this mess once that liar is done!
What won't he say, what "information"   300
feed to his leader? I can just hear him now—
He will swear we abused him and barely allowed
him to leave with his life. More I don't want to know.

IOLAUS

Do high-born children realize ever
how lucky they are to have noble fathers?
What can they know of those duped by sex
into marrying badly and dooming the next
generation to worse? Wealth, reputation
are bad-luck repellents. Our situation
is proof that the high-born have hidden spies   310
where high birth is valued and kinship is prized
as it is here. Boys, show them your love,
let them embrace you, you them, for we have
arrived! Free at last! If you someday return
to your country of birth you can brag that you learned
who your friends were the hard way—though perhaps it was best
to have suffered the worst before enjoying the best.
No wars against Athens, boys, our second home.
When Argos misprized you, Athens alone
treated you lovingly. The rest shriveled up   320
like slugs in salt water when Argos showed up.

Only Athens alone stepped in and cried *stop*
and protected the helpless. What did *we* have to show,
what give them but grief? Dear god, when I go
to the land of the dead, as the god is my judge,
I'll be looking for Theseus—I give you my pledge—
when I die I will scout him and stand by his side
and tell him of this. It will fill him with pride
that his heirs proved themselves after all to be his
by protecting the children of Heracles.   330

CHORUS *(approaching Iolaus)*
    Our custom—

IOLAUS
                    I'll tell your father the good name you made
    for Athens in helping these unlucky lads.

CHORUS
    Our custom—

IOLAUS
                    proving yourself to be Theseus'
    as these are the children—

CHORUS
                            of Heracles, yes,
    but it's a custom with us—

IOLAUS
                            Contradicting the claim
    that no son in a dozen lives up to the name
    of the father that made him—

CHORUS
                                it's the custom with us
    to succor the helpless, no matter the cost.
    Your case is no different.

DEMOPHON *(dispatching a man with a message and turning to Iolaus)*
      Old words but true.
 These boys will not disappoint us — or you.   340
 Nor will I. That man has just left with my order
 to dispatch reconnaissance teams to our borders:
 we won't be caught sleeping — and it's easy to be
 when you're dealing with Argives, who swarm like bees
 to the honey of slaughter. I have summoned my priests
 to ready the god-price, the blood sacrifice.
 So into the house, then. The palace is my home,
 do treat it as yours. I want you to come
 and rest there. To the palace, out of harm's way.

IOLAUS
 I won't budge from here.
(sits)
         I'll stay here and pray.   350
 For the good of the city, a war prayer. Only when
 Argos is beaten down will I descend
 and accept hospitality. Are your gods less than theirs?
 Aren't yours better? Or is someone here scared
 that bright-eyed Pallas pales in compare
 to Hera? Is Pallas a second-rate goddess?
 Their gods have them, but our gods have *us*.
 And Pallas Athena is the perfect sidekick
 in matters of warfare and tricky logistics.   360
(The following choral ode is addressed directly to the Argives but
    reacts indirectly to Iolaus and his last oration.
    As it progresses it becomes nearly an Athenian
    fight song.)

CHORUS
 Does every Argive
 think boasts are impressive?
 They are not. In Athens
 like wind against mountains

boasts flutter and fail.
Our strength is principle.
So you're an Argive.
Is that so impressive?
Is your king such a genius?
Can he really be serious
to think he'll coerce us   370
into trading in these
god-blessed refugees
for his damned good will?
You're an Argive. Big deal.
We have our ideals.
What's more, aren't kings
charged with protecting
God's shrines and altars?
No, he sends us his lawyer—
a true bottom-feeder—   380
a low-class, ill-mannered
scum-bird whose groundless
boasts nearly cost
him his life when he crossed
King Demophon. Still,
though we are liberals
we're not total fools.
We may lack expertise
in slaughter, but we
will take him to school   390
and teach him to rule
himself among us
liberal democrats,
who love right, know limits,
and never forget
where men end, god begins.

(Demophon has reentered before the chorus concludes—perhaps when
*   the chorus names him. He seems obviously less*
*   enthusiastic than he did on parting. He approaches*
*   Iolaus tentatively.)*

IOLAUS *(to Demophon)*

> My boy, you seem gloomy, depressed suddenly.
> This has something to do with the enemy!
> Can you share it with me? Has the action begun?
> They have high-tailed it home! You had quite a tongue   400
> not ten minutes ago. It wagged at both ends
> at that fat-talking lawyer. Use it again.
> Eurystheus is a pragmatist.
> He won't dilly-dally, believe it. He'll hit,
> and to hell with guest-friendship and mandates of Zeus.

DEMOPHON

> Oh, he's out there. In number. Grand Eurystheus.
> With my own eyes I saw him, and in a real crisis
> no leader trusts anyone's but his own eyes,
> not those of point men, observers, or spies.
> No, he leans from his chariot, looking far and wide,   410
> vulturing over the countryside.
> Just over there, this side of Marathon,
> my own boys are red hot to take him on.
> Inside the walls, our plans go ahead
> for the doomed victims. The altars are scrubbed,
> the priests sacrifice in the open streets
> to a clean victory and the Argives' defeat,
> and I've charged a committee of prophets to re-
> search precedents and all prodigies
> to make sure nothing's missed—
> > but there is *one* thing . . .   420
> I want to do right, but each informs me—
> I mean each oracle, no two quite agree
> except in this detail—that if we are to prevail
> we must offer a virgin to Demeter. A girl
> high-born, of a father high-born. You do see
> the position this puts us all in, and puts *me*?
> I have nothing but good will for you and their line,
> but I can't save your kin if it means hurting mine
> or some kin of my kin, even distant relations.

Tough choices everywhere. And name me the man   430
with a heart so hard he would ransom his own
to pay the blood price on a neighbor's young?
So the temples are filled and the side streets are filling
with the sullen and outraged devout who are milling
about and calling me a true blunderer,
and making up riddles and asking each other,
"What kind of help renders helpless the helper,
estranges one's kin and makes kin of a stranger?
Whose foreign aid bankrupts his own
and enriches the Argive? King Dumbophon's."   440
You see how it is. Give the gods an appetizer
or bring hell to my house and risk civil war,
and I won't. You must help me. How do I proceed
to ensure that our mutual interests succeed?
And with minimal risk to one's popular image
among one's constituents? Kings here are slaves
to the people, to laws, to the wider consensus
and general will. This is Athens, not Argos.

CHORUS

Do we break with good form and hand over the lost
or ignore guest-friendship and incur *that* cost?   450

IOLAUS *(pacing back and forth)*

Poor boys. My shipmates. Thought we were free
of the storm! Heading landward and only to be
an arm's length from safety and the harbor and then
spun around by the storm and knocked stormward again!
That's us. This temple's the receding beach,
but how close we were! Just within reach.
Damn it, damn hope, that touches disaster
to touch up, not fix it, that cools but can't cure
wounds that we learn over time to endure!
No, Demophon, for all your intentions   460
you cannot surrender one of your own.

I cannot condemn anything you have done.
God willing, my gratitude someday will show.
But until then, who knows? My boys, what now?
And *where*? And before which new god crack this knee?
What town should we crawl to, again refugees?
I see extradition. Then execution.
Death is no bother—only that portion
of pleasure my death sets aside for my foes.
My death, it's nothing. But I'm heartsick for you   470
and your noble grandmother, Lady Alcmene, who
was born luckless, lived luckless, and luckless will die,
as beaten and hopeless and luckless as I.
We are done for, *were* done for when black fate first planned
bleak lives for us and worse lives for our children.
O sir, can't you work with me now? For I
cannot allow hope of their rescue to die.
Let me die instead. Give *me* to the Argives.
That way the boys live, they go on with their lives.
For me to continue to live would be gross.   480
Life is existence, not living, a mere dross
of years. Give me up, let them enjoy
the surrender of me instead of these boys,
to the scum that they are. Can you negotiate
or parlay with scum? It would humiliate
you and your city to drop to its knees
to parlay with *that*. Go with dogs and get fleas.

CHORUS

Old man, how quickly you slander our city.
Have we turned on you yet ? That is unfair, really,
it's libelous too. Either wounds equally.   490

DEMOPHON

Your offer is high-minded but pointless, too.
Argos is looking for them—*not for you*.
From Eurystheus' vantage, it would not make sense.

One old man's death? It is them that he wants.
He knows that the sons of high-born foes
grow up eating and sleeping revenge, and he knows
the typical outcome. It's mere commonsense,
a business decision. No intrigue, no suspense,
no double-think here. But I do remain
open to any plan you entertain,   500
and I welcome advice. I am at my wit's end,
pressured, desperate, and a little frightened.

(Enter Makaria from the temple doors. She is an adolescent, well-coifed,
plainly dressed, and clearly still a child; she poses
in the doorway and from there begins speaking,
continuing as she proceeds down the steps to take
a spot directly between Iolaus and Demophon.)

MAKARIA

Excuse me, uncle, for coming out here.
I was in midway into my morning prayers
when I heard you yowling. It distracted me,
and drew me outside though forbidden expressly
to come out the temple. You have taught me it's best
to be invisibly good and transparently modest,
to "bear yourself modestly in- or outside,
but especially out. Up to men to provide.   510
Women shut up and stay shut up inside."
I know you're in charge of our destiny,
yet without my brothers there would be no *me*.
Without them I am as impalpable
as a seawind lacking a sail to fill.
My brothers are me, my brothers are all,
without them I am inconsequential.
I know you are expert in minding our business
but there's trouble, I feel it.

(touching his sleeve)

                    What is wrong, Iolaus?

IOLAUS

> Puppet, forgive me, if I have forgotten   520
> that you are the best of Heracles' children.
> Just as things seemed to be going so well,
> going better at least, this new mess befell—
> worse than before. Now it's oracles.
> The gods want gore. Not a bird's or cattle's
> but human gore. Of one high-born,
> and not a male. Kore wants a maiden,
> a blood appetizer, if we're to survive.
> The king will not yield up his kin or the lives
> of his people—not wholly unreasonably—   530
> therefore we are stuck. He has just told me,
> in so many words, that we either conceive
> of a way out for him or pack up and leave.
> He has no outs; he must save his own.
> A way out of this or we have to leave town.

MAKARIA

> Between us and freedom stands one oracle?

IOLAUS

> Only one. Otherwise, all would be well.

MAKARIA

> If that's all it is, you need no longer fear
> Argos or exile. I am prepared
> for the fillets and hood. Let them sacrifice me   540
> or abuse us to all for abusing their city.
> Athens rose to defend us. Should it be penalized
> in return for its good faith and blood sacrifice
> with the gross spectacle of us saving our lives?
> What an impression to leave among men!
> "Heracles' children were spoiled rotten,"
> people would say, "all that supplication
> and they broke our hearts." What reputations

would dog us forever! Much better to end
our careers as captives, slain among kinsmen   550
in the city's defeat than live on with no fame,
no honor, *dis*honoring my father's good name.
What choice between honor and lifetimes of shame?
Of living as permanent squatters and drifters,
always dropping our eyes when they meet another's,
hearing, "You with your symbols that say you are pious,
your grip on your safety is awfully tenacious.
Move on. You are cowards. No help from us."
And if the boys were to die for my sisters and me,
my life would be death. What man would wed me,   560
have children with me, with no money, no dowry?
So isn't death better than an unmerited
and foul living-on? Get some other-directed
girl, some nobody's daughter, is fill
such a typical role, but for me, it's too dismal.
If in between shame and a lifetime of glory
stands one oracle, let the victim be me.
Take me to the dying place, do me as you would
a typical victim—with the garlands, the hood.
Sacrifice properly, sacrifice me,   570
then murder those swine. I voluntarily
and fully possessed of my life and my wits
trade my life for my brothers'. Athens, do it.
All that I want is this epitaph:
useless in life, priceless in death.

CHORUS

She will die for her brothers. This silences all.
Her words are too weighty for such a small girl.
None will believe that a child could utter
or act on such sentiments. Has anyone, ever?

IOLAUS

You're a true hero's child. I said so earlier—   580
the just have just offspring. You *are* Heracles' daughter.

Your words lift my hopes and yet leave me heartbroken—
though one thing alone still remains to be done.
We must do this correctly, which means we must summon
your sisters, brief them, draw lots, and apprise
our Athenian hosts who will be sacrificed.
Not to draw lots would be highly irregular.

MAKARIA

Draw lots all you want. I *still* volunteer.
Where's the glory in luck? No, don't even try
to be subtle with me. I will go knowing why   590
I die for my brothers. You should fulfill the laws
however you must, but I will not draw straws.

IOLAUS

Your words crack my will before crushing it, child.
Your courage keeps topping itself, each reply
surpassing the last in nobility.
I neither mandate nor forbid you to die.
Amen. If you die then your brothers survive.

MAKARIA

You acquiesce wisely. Do not be afraid
that you'll be condemned for the choice that I've made—
it is mine. You are free. I have one request only.   600

IOLAUS

Anything, child.

MAKARIA

         Be there beside me,
hold me as they bleed me, then cover my body.
I'm Heracles' daughter.

IOLAUS *(turns away)*

         And I'm an old man.
Bearing witness would kill me.

MAKARIA *(to Demophon)*

                                    Then give me permission
        to die in a party of women, not men.

DEMOPHON
        Anything, child. What an embarrassment
        to allow you to die then withhold my consent
        to your last will and testament. So many things—
        your courage, your commonsense—are too compelling,
        tell me that you will be called a great woman   610
        after your death. Now, embrace the old man,
        kiss your brothers goodbye, and let us move on.

MAKARIA *(approaching Iolaus)*
        Goodbye, uncle Iolaus. Give my brothers good lessons—
        to be just as apt as the moment demands
        and not a bit more. Help them understand.
        You are their tutor. Teach them to be men.
(She embraces him. He is limp.)
        Now, watch me walk to the altar to die—
        but not to get married—so they'll live happily,
        these brothers of mine, enjoying the things
        that are passing to them with my passing.   620
        Make sure they respect both you and grandmother
        there in the temple, that they're good to each other,
        and when your luck turns and your fortunes thrive
        and you're finally settled, remember whose lives
        were saved, whose not, and perform the old rites,
        recover my body and ship it back home,
        then bury me honorably. What others have known—
        children, a future—I have traded for fame,
        a glorious death, renown, a good name,
        and an after-life? Maybe. I hope there is none.   630
        If we live after, our cares may live on
        and what good are cares? Oblivion's fine.
        Oblivion is the best anodyne.
(Makaria exits slowly and with a light but genuine dignity.)

IOLAUS *(shouting after her)*
>   Dying like this, you will enter the ranks
>   of the holiest women. You die with our thanks
>   and will live on in death a near-sacred presence,
>   a near-goddess, even. Only reverence
>   for the daughter of Demeter holds my tongue.

(As Makaria disappears from the stage, Iolaus sits on the steps and drops his head. The Chorus approaches and surrounds him. The children should huddle at his knee.)

>   Children, I'm done. Dead, overwhelmed.
>   Help me to the altar, take hold of my arms,   640
>   get me a blanket. For if this oracle
>   turns out to be wrong and this child is killed
>   for nothing, then nothing can ever be well.

CHORUS
>   Like it or not,
>   whether bad luck or good,
>   behind it's a god.
>   What city is sure
>   its luck will endure?
>   Like sunlight on shadow
>   our destines follow,   650
>   fate swallows fate,
>   evicting the great,
>   mansioning vagrants
>   in major estates,
>   foreclosing on the mighty,
>   raising the small,
>   for like it or not,
>   there's a god in control.
>   Who escapes fortune,
>   good or bad? Or dictates   660
>   his fatal portion?
>   Whose art mitigates
>   the inevitable?
>   No mortal's.

Who even attempts
is beneath contempt.
So why drop to your knees
in despair and declare
that the gods hate your life?
The gods are too busy.   670
Consider the trifle
her life *might* have been
given the givens.
Who would not redeem
a life without fame
for death and a name?
Got a name, saved her kin,
got a house in the bargain,
and even helped us.
She's instantly famous!   680
In the doom she elects
people will see
her father's perfect-
ion and her pedigree,
they will claim that her acts
were just like Heracles'.
So come to your senses,
let's celebrate her,
no bitter laments
for Heracles' daughter.   690

(Enter a servant, one of Hyllus' men, from the right, upstage. He begins
speaking to the children blocked by the stone rail
leading up to the temple, and therefore doesn't
immediately see Iolaus, who is still seated and
deep in thought.)

SERVANT *(cheerfully)*
Excuse me, kids, but I'm here looking for
old Iolaus. Is he minding the altar?

IOLAUS
    I'm minding my business. Beneath you. Down here.

SERVANT
    Time to get up. There is joy in the air.

IOLAUS
    And none in my life. I am in despair.

SERVANT
    Well, get up and get happy. Time to be proud.

IOLAUS
    The spunk is all out of me, boy. I'm all out.

SERVANT
    That's why I come. I'm the man with good news.

IOLAUS
    I can use some of that. But—do I know you?

SERVANT
    I work for Hyllus. You don't recognize me?   700

IOLAUS
    My apologies, yes. It's the light, it must be.

SERVANT
    Forget it. I've news.
    (Iolaus reacts.)
                        Good news all around.

IOLAUS
    No, wait—
    (shouting up the steps)

Alcmene! Mother of Heracles!
Alcmene, come out and listen to this!
She's starved for good news, and she has had none,
and she's especially heartsick over her grandsons.
*(Alcmene appears at the door. She is an older version of Makaria and
in fact might be played by the same actor. She
is aggressive, smart, even a touch vulgar. The
audience should sense that the refugees' survival
is partly owing to her toughness.)*

ALCMENE

Iolaus, shush! So loud near the temple!
You are worse than the children. What is wrong?
(sees the servant)

Who's this?

Another lawyer from Eurystheus?
(approaching the servant threateningly)
Old as I am, I'm still Heracles' mother.   710
Who touches these children, deals with their grandmother
and this wild old man—and then with dishonor.

IOLAUS

Alcmene, calm down. He is from *Hyllus.*
He hasn't come to annoy or harass us.

ALCMENE

So why all the shouting?

IOLAUS

To get your attention.

ALCMENE

And all of Athens'?
(to the servant)

So, what of my grandson?

IOLAUS
> He comes with news of Hyllus' arrival.

ALCMENE
> Then God bless your life. Arrival, you say?
> But he did not stop by. That is not his way.
> Did something prevent him coming in person?   720

SERVANT
> The rest of his army. He's just outside Athens.

ALCMENE *(to Iolaus, in a loud whisper)*
> What's he talking about? What army? Explain.
> You told me that Hyllus was upland, was looking
> around just in case—

IOLAUS *(puts his finger over his lips)*
> Let me do the talking.

SERVANT
> Hyllus is minutes away. With an army.

IOLAUS
> And this army, how big?

SERVANT
> Enormous, believe me.

IOLAUS
> And Athens knows this—that it's here?

SERVANT
> Absolutely.
> He guards their left flank. They are elbow to elbow.

IOLAUS
> And he's armed.

SERVANT

A huge force. They are ready to go
but wait on the priests. There are victims to bleed.   730

IOLAUS

And the Argives, how far?

SERVANT

Close enough you can read
their general's lips.

IOLAUS

Is he making speeches?

SERVANT *(mockingly)*

"Never give in!" We kept hearing snatches.
But I must get back or the general will move
to attack without me.

IOLAUS

Wait. I'm going, too.
You and I think alike. We want the same thing—
to fight in hot battle.

SERVANT

You must be kidding.
Not that you're a kid.

IOLAUS

I wouldn't be me
if I didn't join in. My companions need me.

SERVANT

Your companions are dead. You're not young anymore.   740

IOLAUS

Ah, you add up the years but subtract the warrior!

SERVANT
    And the danger? Can you do *any*thing?

IOLAUS
    I can outstare the bastards.

SERVANT
                      What harm in staring?
(flexes his arm)
    It's the arm does the harm.

IOLAUS *(flexing his own arm)*
                    I've one just like that.
    I can hit a man still.

SERVANT
                And then land flat
  on your ass from the recoil.

IOLAUS
             I am ready to go.

SERVANT
    A thought's not an act. You only think so.

IOLAUS
    You talk too much. While you talk we're still here.

SERVANT
    And your weapons? Where are they? Your armor and spear?

IOLAUS *(points to the temple)*
    There are trophies stored there. Captured from the field.   750
    They will suit me just fine. If I am not killed
    I'll carry them back no worse for the wear
    and if I am killed, well, the gods won't care.

Get in there. Quickly. Haul me some armor.
This sitting and talking is a dismal mission.
Real men have battles, not conversations.
(The servant enters the temple. Iolaus begins a quick jog around the
temple, only for as long as it takes for the chorus
to conclude, then takes up a position for the first
time at center stage.)

CHORUS *(choreographed as a gossipy exchange among its members)*
Young heart, old bones!
Your body grew old
but your spirit did not!
In a way, it's wonderful!   760
In another, it's not.
At your age, Pop,
the real foe is here,
(pointing to their heads)
the irrational will
that nothing can stop,
won't settle its business
but runs up a bill
for the next generation
to reconcile.
At your age, Pop,   770
an unchecked spirit
can produce havoc.
Learn to limit it.
Your body is gone.
Relent, release it.

ALCMENE
You can't be serious. Leave these children with me
to go off and get killed? Have you gone crazy?

IOLAUS *(doing stretching exercises, jumping-jacks, etc.)*
Men make wars, the women the beds.

ALCMENE
> But how will I cope? Suppose you end up dead?

IOLAUS
> Your grandsons will help you.

ALCMENE
>   And what if they can't?   780

IOLAUS
> Have faith in Athens. Be confident.

ALCMENE
> So that's all there is? You decide, and you're gone?

IOLAUS
> Have faith in Zeus and you're never alone.

ALCMENE
> Leave Zeus out of this. I do not gripe to Zeus
> though at times his priorities leave me confused.
> *(The servant reenters from the temple laden with armor, much of it*
> *tattered and several pieces covered with what*
> *appear to be children's doodlings.)*

SERVANT
> Here's what I found. It's all there. Take a look.
> We don't have much time, so dress and let's move.
> "When war comes knocking," they tell us, "best answer
> or he'll knock the door down." If that's too much armor,
> too much weight, keep it off till you get to our lines   790
> and wear only the colors. I will follow behind.

IOLAUS *(arming himself with the spear and donning the helmet)*
> What a good idea. Put the spear in my left,
> you hold the armor, then give me a lift,

my left on your right. And walk steadily.
We're off.

SERVANT *(laden with the rest of the armor)*
Off your rocker. This is leading a baby!

IOLAUS *(descending the steps, the metal clanging loudly against the
stone)*
Just watch I don't slip. Bad luck to fall!

SERVANT
You should do this alone or not do this at all.

IOLAUS
Move! At this rate we will miss the campaign.

SERVANT
I'm not the slow one. Your speed's in your brain.

IOLAUS
Look there, at those feet.
(hopping)
                                    That's what I call speed.   800

SERVANT *(to the audience)*
The speed of dementia, not the speed of the feet.

IOLAUS
We'll see who laughs last. Wait until we arrive—

SERVANT
You mean *if*. At this rate we will never survive—

IOLAUS
—and you see me in *action*!

SERVANT
                    I would settle for *motion*.

IOLAUS *(as they prepare to leave the stage, he stops)*
      Now then, right arm, a good fight will revive
      you and your strength. You saved my life once
      when Heracles and I took on the Spartans.
      I could use you today against their general,
      Eurystheus, the bully, the shy-of-battle
      Eurystheus, whose reputation   810
      is bloated by his association
      with the high-born and the truly courageous.
      Fame, like justice, is often contagious.
      People assume that the well-to-do
      do everything well, whatever they do.

CHORUS
      Brilliant sleepless messenger Moon
      traveling all night over our weary
      and worried city, I call on you
      to pick up and make a delivery—
      take my petition up to the bar   820
      of God himself, rouse him with shouts,
      argue my case before that supreme court,
      then whistle gray-eyed Athena out
      of her white bunker. If our destiny
      is to risk our treasury and our blood
      to succor these noble refugees,
      it rests in bright metal—ours and a god's.

      It's outrageous that a city the size
      of Argos would stoop to pettiness
      and get so lost in the exercise   830
      of a dead generation's vendettas!
      But how much the worse for Athens to yield
      to the spiteful its rights and traditions

and surrender the lost and displaced of the world
to avoid a confrontation.

God is our lawyer. He represents us,
the advocate of all advocates
of principled action, of righteousness,
and only God adjudicates.
No mortal's reach reaches Heaven,   840
not Eurystheus' even.

But to you, Pallas, Athens belongs,
our mother, defender, and genius,
you will drive the law-breaking bully (along
with his lawyers) right back to Argos.
Illegally, he
troubles sanctuary.
But we're not so self-righteous to stand by and aloof,
waiting for you while he carries them off.

We have paid the god-price.   850
The fires of sacrifice
the hottest, as always,
burn for you, gray-eyes,
ever and always.
We remember your feast days,
perform all the rites,
sing the scheduled liturgies
with passion and pride.
Have we done it correctly?
As we circle the hill   860
our bodies are windbreaks
surrounding the girls
who turn and back-peddle
their feet keeping tempo
on the grassy meadow
as the night-outlasting

moon reddens and sets
over our heads.
Have we done this correctly,
have we done it well?   870

MESSENGER *(entering out of breath)*
    Alcmene, I have news of the sort
    that you love to hear and I to report.
    We beat them! Our men are stripping their dead
    for battle trophies. They have sent me ahead.

ALCMENE
    Thank the gods for this. This news frees you.
    But wait! I have something more to ask you—
    How did things go today for my grandsons?

MESSENGER
    They live and are praised by the men of Athens.

ALCMENE
    And Iolaus too—

MESSENGER
                                Another survivor,
    and his fortune improved by the Thunderer.   880

ALCMENE
    What happened? Did something—

MESSENGER
                                Miraculous.
    The gods have transformed him from an old man to a new.

ALCMENE
    Incredible! Magic? But the magic can wait.
    Tell me first of the fight, of my Hyllus' fate.

MESSENGER
       One anecdote encapsulates it.
       Once our ranks were in place
       and we stood, face to face,
       Hyllus pulls up in his fast chariot,
       hops from the still-bound-
       ing car to the ground,   890
       and midway between the Argives and us,
       as he coasts to a stop
       one foot down, one foot up,
       across the field yells,
       "Eurystheus, general,
       let's have a detente between Athens and you.
       Let Athens be. This
       is just between us.
       Here is my advice.
       One life pays the blood-price.   900
       Yours or mine, Eurystheus. Just you and I
       can settle this thing.
       A man-to-man meeting
       at midfield. You win
       and I give up my kin
       and myself. If you lose
       you restore to me those
       titles and benefits that are mine legally,
       the Heraclids' house
       and whatever else   910
       was his and is mine—my patrimony."
       You should have heard
       how his words stirred
       in the Argives a whirring of "yesses" and "thanks
       for thinking of us,
       you're a god, Hyllus!"
       But Eurystheus, wanting to seem nonchalant
       at his army's murmur
       and Hyllus' bold offer,

and thinking a cool non-response the intelligent　　　　920
way to settle it,
sat back in his chariot!
Showing all what scum he is! This coward
expects us to yield him the sons and the mother
of Heracles? Please.

So Hyllus withdrew from that no man's land
and rejoined his lines.
When the priests had divined
that no man-to-man combat would settle the score
they caucused, took votes　　　　930
and opened the throats,
the pale throats of the luckless victims of war.
From their generous veins
the lucky life drained.
Then we climbed into cars
and the foot-soldiers
fell in behind us and shouldered their spears,
and one young captain
yelled, "Gentlemen,
we have practiced for this, you all know the drill,　　　　940
back up your buddies,
kill plenty of Argives!"
The Argive, likewise, made rallying talk
but all so down-beat—
"don't yield, don't retreat"—
you'd think that Argive
is a language of negatives.
Then the trumpets blatted, and the battle began.
A mish-mash of notes
from the metal throats　　　　950
of the brazen trumpets and the beating and beaten
fighting back pain,
the slayers, the slain.
The Argives hit first, a flood tide of iron—

rolling in, rolling back,
retreat, then attack,
wave on successive
wave of Argives,
till toe-to-toe, it was line against line.
Bodies were flying,   960
fought dazed, fought dying,
and over it all you heard one of two cheers—
"Athens forever,"
or "Never surrender."
Better to die
than embarrass your city.
With a burst, finally,
at the limits of energy
we turned their front lines and applauded their flight!
But it gets even sweeter. At that very instant   970
old Iolaus
spots your Hyllus,
who's hot at his own work, and snatches the reins
and shouts in his ear,
"Son, lend me your car,"
for old Iolaus
was after Eurystheus
all by himself and—now, I didn't see this,
this sequel, in person.
So from this point on   980
I'm relying like you on another eyewitness.
There is a park here. It is consecrated
to the goddess Pallas,
and as Iolaus raced past
the Pallene (as it's called) someone heard him pray
to Hebe and Zeus,
as he closed on Eurystheus,
"May the gods rejuvenate me today,
to make things even and Eurystheus pay."
Then the miracle: we all saw two stars   990

from nowhere descend
on the car's front end
and cover in gloom and cloud the whole car.
The experts surmise
that materialized
in each star were Hebe and Heracles.
Then out from that surg-
ing darkness emerged
Iolaus, young, all biceps and brawn.
Now *Battling* Iolaus   1000
caught up to Eurystheus
in a fast four-horser beneath the Skironian
Hills, grabs the chariot
by the yoke and stops it,
and captures alive the Argive general,
the once-prosperous
King Eurystheus
hand-cuffed in back, like a stuffed animal!
His disgrace is a powerful
lesson for mortals.   1010
Envy no one who's happy until he is dead.
For luck changes quickly.
Need proof, look at me.

CHORUS

Zeus, turner of battle-fortunes,
thanks for your help. Our terror is gone.

ALCMENE *(to the sky)*

Thanks for me too. You took your time, Zeus,
in getting to me. Now I have one problem less.
I am also convinced, if I wasn't till now,
that my son is in heaven. There can be no doubt.
Now, children, now, we are totally free   1020
of that damned Eurystheus. We are problem-free.
You will see for yourself where we all came from,

repossess our estate, and thank God we are home
with hecatombs to the gods of your father.
We are back to ourselves. We will wander no farther.
(suddenly pensive)
But why did Iolaus not kill Eurystheus
there on the spot? He can fight, that Iolaus,
but you capture a bad man, and how smart can you be
not to finish him off immediately?

MESSENGER
He did this for you. With your own eyes to see   1030
Eurystheus here miserable
and in *your* control. Eurystheus fought
wildly not to and is really distraught
at the thought of submitting to *you*. He is caught—
and held by Hyllus—in a god-set snare.
So goodbye, old mother, and you will remember
that you promised me freedom when I announced
good news was coming. In things this immense
it only makes sense
that the high-born should keep their promises.   1040
(Exit messenger.)

CHORUS
The best is when
the dance begins,
and the music pressed
from the instruments
adds a drowsy note
to the feasts of blessed
Aphrodite!
Today our tally
of blessings mounts
since we have new friends   1050
whose bad luck ends
in good. Fate, you bring

never one thing
but double blessings,
one is requested,
one unexpected.
Fate, whose wife,
Time's daughter, is Life.

So stay the course
my steadfast city   1060
of righteousness.
Do not let go
of your anxious hold
on the gods. Fear God
and you can ignore
the boastful and wrathful
for we now see more
clear proof before us—
God reveals it to us—
in a young Iolaus   1070
and a broken Eurystheus.
God advertises
the dangers of pride:
the noble but arrogant
had better relent.

And he is in heaven,
Alcmene, your son,
be assured of his
apotheosis,
and rest assured   1080
that the idle rumor
that he wanders through Hell
like a common mortal
is gossip. Instead,
he is sharing a bed
with Hera's daughter,

your boy and Hebe
in a golden suite.
Two children of Zeus
honeymoon there—   1090
what a glorious honor!

And what a correspondence
rules these phenomena!
Heracles was assisted,
they say, by Athena,
then Heracles' children
receive their assistance
from Athena's city—
coincidence?
There's a goddess in this,   1100
Athena's her name!
She disables the reckless
and wrecks the vain
self-regarding losers
who make bad things worse,
turn blessings to curses,
choose discord over discourse.
She takes them to school!
God forbid that my spirit
get so out of control!   1110
Prudence forever above enmity!
God's will over man's eternally!

(The servant enters with Eurystheus in restraints—handcuffs perhaps—
and his clothing tattered but still somehow princely.
Eurystheus is a man about the age of Iolaus, not as
young as Demophon, well-spoken and impeccably
mannered.)

SERVANT

Though you'll see it yourself, Alcmene, give me
the pleasure of announcing it formally:

Eurystheus Bound. A glorious surprise
for you, for him you're no sight for sore eyes.
Here's a man never dreamed it could come out this way—
captured by Iolaus—when he left Mycenae
at the head of his army, all bloated with pride,
come to push around Athens. But luck loaded the dice.   1120
Hyllus and Iolaus were about to install
a statue to Zeus, the Turner of Battles,
were just getting started then stopped suddenly,
looked at each other, and grinning, told me
to bring him to you. Said you'd get a real kick
at seeing this blowhard so down on his luck.

ALCMENE *(approaching Eurystheus)*
So here you are, scum. Your luck has run out.
Turn your head, look at me—no, don't look down.
Look me in the eye. I will talk, you will listen.
Answer me this: are you the same one   1130
who made a career of bossing my son,
who, they say,
(to the chorus)
                    is in heaven? You can't be the one
who sent my boy off sweeping stables, bagging lions,
who sent him to Hell? I won't even go into the rest of your evil, I would never be done.
And once he was dead, it was asking too much
to let bygones be bygones. That wasn't enough,
you wanted his future. So you came after these
children and drove them from one end of Greece
to the other saddled with two refugees   1140
as their bodyguards. Did you bank on this—
a city courageous enough to accept us
and to love us? Now you'll pay for your crimes
but still be a winner. You can die just one time.
*(The chorus steps in between Eurystheus and Alcmene, reproducing the
                precise position it assumed when it blocked access to
                Iolaus by Copreus at the beginning of the play.)*

CHORUS *(moving in)*
    He must not be killed.

ALCMENE
                    Why not? He's a captive.
    Or was that just rehearsal?

CHORUS
                    You must listen: he must live.
    And he must be returned.

ALCMENE
                    What law would we break?

CHORUS
    Our leaders agree. It would be a mistake.

ALCMENE *(honestly confused)*
    I'm lost. Is it wrong to kill enemies?

CHORUS
    When they're taken in battle.   1150

ALCMENE *(increasingly impatient)*
    And did Hyllus agree
    or not with this thinking?

CHORUS
                    Hyllus concurs.
    He has no choice.

ALCMENE
                    But the man is a prisoner.
    He should shut his eyes on the sunlight.

CHORUS

                              Is it right
     not to ransom a prisoner?

ALCMENE

                         I don't know. Is it right
     that a criminal walks?

CHORUS

                    Talk to Hyllus. He
     controls this prisoner.

ALCMENE

                         Whom we will let free?
     Who won't pay for his crime? Because Hyllus blundered?

SERVANT

     There is one other problem: There are no volunteers
     to execute him.

ALCMENE

                    Me, I volunteer.

SERVANT

     Big trouble for you if you *do* volunteer.   1160

ALCMENE

     You know I love Athens. My loyalty is clear.
     But he, who has come to me out of the blue,
     to *me*—not Athens—is past mortal rescue.
     So call me an outrage. Say I've lost my mind,
     but this man dies. He will pay for his crime.

CHORUS

     Your rage, Alcmene, is savage, excessive.
     And dangerous. Yet it's also persuasive.

EURYSTHEUS *(slowly and deliberately; the actor should without overdue*
emphasis pause slightly at the line-endings)

    Woman, understand me: I will not
    resort to flattery
    because it's beneath me.   1170
    This lot fell to me. I did *not*
    want to outrage my own kinsmen—
    you, my cousin, and your son,
    Heracles. Like it or not,
    this was God's doing. Hera
    overwhelmed me with the mania
    to undertake this. And since I did not
    see an expedient to this feud
    with your son I saw it through,
    became a genius at making trouble,   1180
    spent my nights dreaming up ways to hassle
    Heracles. Because I could not
    imagine myself terrified
    night after night, because I could not
    hide from facts: here was no
    lightweight but a true hero
    whose shadow I would never
    evade, whom I had made my enemy—
    no counterfeit but a heavyweight. I can not
    dismiss his strength or his dignity   1190
    though he and I were enemies once, but no
    longer. With Heracles not
    here to haunt me any more
    there was nothing to stop me settling scores
    his children would settle with me. No man's
    hatreds escape his children.
    They would live to kill me if I did not
    kill them first. And, by the way,
    it doesn't matter what you say,
    you will do likewise should the roles reverse—   1200
    sheltering the lions' cubs in Argos?

I don't believe it. I really don't think so.
The point is this, though: you did not
execute me on the spot
when it was sanctioned. And now you *can* not.
If you should you violate statutes
all Greece honors. You pollute
your lives in taking my life from me—
you advocates of sanctuary!
Athens is acting prudently.   1210
"Prudence above enmity,
God's will over man's eternally."
You have asked, I answered. The gods not only
forbid my death but the gods agree
to honor whoever honors me.
And so it is. I live. I am not
afraid to die. But I would rather not.

CHORUS
  Alcmene, please, defer to me:
  Leave him to us. Obey the city.

ALCMENE *(approaching the Chorus)*
  I know how to kill him and still comply.   1220

CHORUS
  Tell us.

ALCMENE
      It is this: it is really simple—I kill him,
  then deliver the corpse to whoever comes to claim him.
  Athens violates no legal conventions.
  He dies and I get my satisfaction.

EURYSTHEUS
  Kill me. I will not beg you not to,
  but I leave this city

which so scrupulously
respected me and fought for my release
this benediction:
it's an old prediction   1230
of Loxias, and its coming true
will glorify Athens—
not now, but then.
You will bury my body, the forecast reads,
near Athena's shrine,
by Athena Virgin,
in Athenian soil, where I'll lie always,
a friend and a savior
to Athens, forever.
But to them, the bitterest enemy   1240
to the generations
of Heracles' children
who in time will shark up a hostile force
and attack your city,
and *exit* generosity
and Zeus Xenios.
And if you wonder
still why I came here
knowing all that I knew and so far in advance—
Hera's the answer.   1250
My fate was with her.
A goddess can cancel
the worst oracles
and predictions of mortals.
Hera would never betray me. You must not
allow them to come
anywhere near my tomb—
especially her,
from me, keep her far,
no blood, no libations.   1260
And in consideration
of this I will ruin their trip back home.

If you will do it my way, your gain will be double.
You'll get assistance and they'll get the trouble.

ALCMENE *(impatiently, gleefully)*
    So why are we stalling? Since even he says
    it's a foregone conclusion, why this delay?
    Let's get it over with. You heard what he said.
    This man is no friend. We'll do fine with him dead.
    Lead him off to the slaughtering lot
    and get rid of the body.   1270
(to Eurystheus, mocking his speech)
  I sure hope you are *not*
    expecting that you
    will somehow make it through
    this alive. You will not.
(Gathering around Eurystheus and Alcmene the chorus forms a circle.
                  Eurystheus disappears from view. Alcmene's arm
                  can be seen rising above the crowd as the lights
                  come down and the chorus speaks its final lines.)

CHORUS
    Uninvolved
    means absolved
    of all trace of guilt.
    Let him be killed.
    Let him be killed.   1280

The Madness of Heracles

Translated by
Katharine Washburn and
David Curzon

Translators' Preface

When David Slavitt, in the early days of his editorship of the Penn
Greek Drama Series, announced that Euripides' uncanonical masterpiece
Heracles remained among a number of plays still to be assigned, I renewed
an old and long disrupted attachment and chose it at once. I had been a
student in Helen Bacon's seminar on Euripides in the chaotic spring of 1968
at Columbia University, and when student strikes shut down the campus
and academic mayhem prevailed, the paper I hoped to write on *Heracles*
was abandoned. To have the opportunity to reread and translate the play
nearly thirty years later was something more than fortuitous. While my
notes from Professor Bacon's class lay intact in a folder, this particular play
continued to haunt me. What a stroke of fortune not only to engage once
more with its enigmas but also to locate a collaborator equal to the metrical
demands of its verse and able to set the words we translated to verbal music.
Godfrey Bond's edition and commentary had become available in 1981.[1] My
heavily penciled notes in Gilbert Murray's 1913 edition[2] were still intelli-
gible: I see that I carefully wrote in April 1968 that Heracles' bow "becomes
an instrument of rescue, then of madness," and that Heracles' epithet in
this play, *kallinkos*, is linked to "the re-founding of the Olympic games . . .
and their imagery." Those notes look quaint to me now; the play, however
deepened and grew in its significance.

When David Curzon joined me as cotranslator, we swiftly came to agree
with Michael Walton, the editor of another series of Greek drama in translation, that this problematic but dazzling play might in fact be the "most
underrated of all Greek tragedies."[3] In the course of our eighteen-month
collaboration (I with my gaze on with the Greek text and my own notions

---

[1] *Heracles*, intro. Godfrey F. Bond (Oxford: Clarendon Press, 1981).

[2] Oxford University Press, 1913.

[3] *Plays Five / Euripides*, trans. Kenneth McLeish, intro. Michael J. Walton (London: Methuen
Drama, 1997).

of diction and how to craft a lyrical line in English, David Curzon with his prosodic skill and taste in place as well), we arrived together at a new translation and at a reading of our own in which the seeming flaws of this play of Euripides are subsumed into its complexity, its mystery, and finally, its simplicity of intention.

Not readily datable by traditional methods (only its archaizing use of trochaic trimeter suggests that this Euripidean drama was performed as late as 415), not a canonically sanctioned work in the Euripidean corpus (its "broken-backed" structure led to its dismissal as the classical equivalent of the unruly "problem play"), and not at home in the hierarchy of the patriotic and humanitarian works of Greek theater to which it was assigned by generations of classical philologists and unfavorable critics, *The Madness of Heracles* is, nonetheless, a masterpiece, defying conventions yet still accountable to them.

But the play's richness, density, and resonance, its subversive theology, and its opulence of meaning and theme still resist easy classification. Is this simply a ragged and unruly "suppliant play," beginning as it does with the huddle of Heracles' doomed family around the altar of Zeus the Savior awaiting the arrival of a hero and protector too long missing in action and now presumed dead? Not quite. By line 290 Heracles is on the threshold, striding forth with bow and club to savage the swashbuckling usurper about to slaughter his old father, his loyal wife, and his three small children. And then, by line 655, the *deus ex machina* arrives in a savage parody of the familiar suppliant/rescue formulation. A corrupt messenger from Olympus swoops down, hand-in-hand with the nightmarish figure of Madness. Divine intervention will indeed take place, but not in the manner in which we (Euripides' audience then and now) would like it. The shattering blow from the realm of something more alien and dangerous than even the underworld from which Heracles made his return destroys the family he came back to save. Heracles, roused from a deep sleep in the aftermath of a bloodbath, will have to be saved in turn. Without the intervention of Theseus he will not survive the awakening from madness. Probably the audience was mindful of Ajax, the greatest warrior (after Achilles) at Troy, who succumbed to a fit of rage in which the innocent appeared as his mortal adversaries. Like Sophocles' hero, who destroyed a flock of sheep in a delusional state, Heracles has slaughtered his own small flock, but unlike Ajax, whose wild rampage closed with the decision to commit suicide, Heracles is persuaded to live on and to suffer with no real end to his wakening. He walks away from the city, bereft of family, of gods, and of the enfeebled chorus, old men leaning on their staffs. We can imagine him leaning on the arm of Theseus, a hero whose parentage—perhaps half-man, half-god—is as ambiguous as his own. Heracles may or may not be the son of Zeus; Euripides' audience knew that Theseus may or may not have been the son of Poseidon.

Heracles overturns many expectations. In the close reading our translation demanded, we had to look at a number of models to recreate it in English. Perhaps we were translating a play of *nostos*, or homecoming: a hero returns, like Odysseus, to his anarchic household, and his enemies, in a great scene of slaughter, are held accountable for the ruin of his patrimony. The *nostos* is a theme familiar from not only the *Odyssey* itself but as part of a lost epic cycle of the trials of heroes and returning veterans after the Trojan War. So attractive was this idea, with all its Euripidean irony, that in translating the title of our play we were tempted to manipulate the traditional title *The Madness of Heracles* into one that encompassed a mock-triumphal and paradoxical meaning. *The Homecoming of Heracles* began to sound increasingly plausible as a translator's title. But in the end we were thrown by the play's catastrophic turn from victory into disaster back to its familiar title *Herakles mainomenos*. In our play, the blameless Heracles, through divine malevolence, is indisputably driven mad: no sooner is Lycus dead than the bow and the club, the arms with which he civilized the panhellenic world and rescued his family, are turned on the household itself and all his pretty ones are dead by Heracles' own hand. (His use of the word for small birds, fledglings or chicks, an echo of Megara's words in lines 12ff., is grotesque and horrifying.)

So the reader is driven once more to consider the presence of this *deus ex machina*, a hideous mime of the divine intervention of Aeschylean theater that rights wrongs and sets straight the derangement of family, culture, and society. The message is heaven-sent, by Iris, the courier of Olympus. The instrument of its accomplishment is—like those unshapely creatures of which Heracles tried to sweep clean the earth—Lyssa, an unclean demon, a monstrous birth, the one such entity against which Heracles' strength and valor is utterly useless. Lyssa, whose name in Greek suggests a rabid dog, is the one beast Heracles' valor cannot master, and the great hero's manic rampage through his own household becomes still another ferocious parody, this time of those extraordinary feats of strength and skill that Lycus mocked and the chorus so poignantly, and prematurely, celebrated.

Another title, with an abrasive flavor of its own, proposed itself: *The Last Labor of Heracles*. Despite our reading that Heracles' final battle in the chronicle may be the one fought in this play with either the demon of madness (a defeat), the malevolence of the distant gods (a clear defeat), or the human impulse to suicidal despair (a great victory), we returned once more to the traditional title and must trust its editorial wisdom. The play best abides its conventional name and *The Madness of Heracles*, although seldom used by modern translators, still holds its own.

Although the tradition varies as to the nature of Heracles' labors, ancient arithmetic rounds them off at twelve. What precisely those labors were remains as problematic as his parentage, since this most popular and broadly worshiped of Greek heroes is generally agreed to be mortal, not divine. His theophoric name means "glorious gift of Hera"; his origins are as ambiguous, mortal, and murky as those of his friend Theseus. Their friendship, as I've suggested, may be sealed by the common issue of their disputed paternity. Ancestry is unreliable here, so are native cities, invisible fathers and undependable gods. Heracles, at the end of the play, seems to turn his back on the question altogether, weary of fathers, distrustful of the gods, and preferring a self-imposed exile from the city that has proved as unstable and unreliable as the Olympians. Theseus, like the Prince Theseus who enters at the end of *A Midsummer Night's Dream*, *is* Athens, restorer of law and order and refuge from the night with its fantastical and wild imaginings.

The mythological catalogue of labors, held constant at the number twelve, remains, however, artificial. It still generally includes the conquests of the Nemean Lion, the Hind of Ceryneia, and the Hydra of Lerna, as well as the capture of the wild boar that lurked in the thickets of Mount Erymanthus. (Euripides prefers to substitute here Heracles' killing of a homicidal innkeeper along the route, possibly because this deed parallels his friend Theseus' slaying of the equally murderous Procrustes.) Some registers of his labors include the slaying of the savage mares of Diomedes and a trek into the Stymphian Marsh to take on a notorious flock of brazen-winged man-eating birds, obscenities, voluraptors, which shed razor-sharp feathers and foul droppings on the surrounding marshlands. The accounts

of Apollodorus, Diodorus Siculus, Hesiod, and others are not easily recon-
ciled, although all of them seem to agree on the cyclical encounter of this
hero with a chaotic world. The labors of Heracles seem to take place on an
earth like that in the sixth chapter of Genesis, when giants, monsters, and
unnatural creatures still prowled an antediluvian wilderness.

To clear our own way through such thorny uncertainties, both ancient
and modern, we sometimes supplied an extra line or two where a contemporary reader might be at a loss. Thus, when Heracles killed Cyncus, the
fairy-tale ogre who preyed on pilgrims to Delphi and cut off their heads to
build a temple from their skulls, we wove that narrative into our translation.
Euripides uses the same word for him in Greek as Homer used for the archaic psychopath of the *Odyssey*, and we felt that the interpolation was jus-
tifiable. (In Euripides' *Iphigenia in Tauris* the epithet for Cyncus turns up
again, suggesting a mythical terrain where human sacrifice is still accept-
able.) In translating a passage hymning Heracles' quest to the Amazons on
the border of the known world, we added some words necessary to remind
the reader that it was Theseus who accompanied his friend on that journey.
Where we took liberties with the text, our intention was not to assume the
role of translator as *auteur* but to mimic the echoes and riddles that are
clamorous in the Greek text but elusive in English.

The most significant of the labors on that list, whether they count an
imbroglio with a wild boar, a voyage to the mist and darkness of the Black
Sea, or a cleansing of the Augean stables, involve variants on the theme of
the conquest of Death. The battle with Death reverberates through the narrative of treks to steal the cattle of the monster Geryon on an island in the
extreme West, the theft of the golden apples from the dragon-guarded tree
at the end of the world, and, of course, the actual descent to the House of
Hades to steal an infernal watchdog. In the simplest and most antique versions of Heracles' combat with Hades, Pindar's "Olympian 9" refers to the
"death-god's" succumbing to Heracles' staff. Earlier still the *Iliad* recalls
how "the strong son of Amphitryon . . . / struck . . . Hades the gigantic . . .
and gave him to agony."

Whatever the antique sources may choose to emphasize in their lists of
all of Heracles' combats with death and infernal creatures, a third of the way
through this play he has just returned from a journey to the netherworld.
Back from hell, something of hell now lives inside his own head. That's why

we read Megara's call to him, in line 277, summoning him to return as a phantom, a ghost, or an apparition, as a version of a fairy-tale with an old implicit warning. In the conventional wisdom of folklore and fairy-tale, it is bad luck to call on the dead, for what comes back may not be the human being you love and the object of your desire may turn out to be an instrument of your own doom. Because we heard her cry as a desperate (and dangerous) recourse to magic, our English version reinforced the incantatory language of her appeal with a rhymed couplet. Her attempt at communication with the dead, her sequence of imperatives, and what is almost a taunt to stimulate the return of the dead has the force of a spell.

The translators as close readers had to deal with an abundance of clinical explanations for Heracles' madness, ranging from a solemn nineteenth-century diagnosis of epilepsy to Wilamowitz's conviction that his insanity rose out of the depths of his own soul. The great nineteenth-century textual critic was confident that the storm of heroic frenzy engaged by the strenuousness of the labors must necessarily mirror itself in the pathological rage of the returning hero. But we know that Heracles has been to the underworld and back, and that the experience may have altered him in ways unknown to himself or to the family he savages in a fit of madness. Our fashionable contemporary notion of post-battle trauma syndrome has perhaps had its day; not every veteran of every battle takes the life of his loved ones on return. Ancient commentaries on the text supplied the not very helpful idea that the rock hurled at Heracles to prevent the crime of patricide might be a real meteorite: we decided to let the nightmare of Heracles' madness remain mysterious. Euripides himself found room in the narrative for the wrath of Hera and its barbarous vengeance.

The Madness of Heracles is packed with warnings, not the least of them those that suggest that the gods are not all we wish them to be. They are not only undependable but, sometimes, lethal. No wonder the play delivers two stunning messages, perhaps even a double climax, contributing to the endless debate as to whether this play, which Swinburne called "a grotesque abortion," truly satisfies the Aristotelian requirements for a "normative" tragedy. The hero, like Verdi's Otello, realizes that in his pursuit of making the chaotic world safe for humankind he has left his wife and children vulnerable to human predators: thereafter he says farewell to all his labors. He turns to the task at hand, in order to preserve the family from the murderous Lycus, the usurper whose name in Greek recalls a wolf. After Heracles slays the "Wolf," he confronts Lyssa, the personification of a mad dog. Waking to reason from her triumph over his sanity, Heracles, like Shakespeare's Othello, wants to die, although he has done the state some service and they know it.

He is persuaded by Theseus, whom he rescued from hell (in an act of pure generosity and friendship, not one of the formal set of labors and never included in its tables), to go on living. But Heracles will live now as mortal, not god or even demigod, and it is in the rhetorical and thematic design of our play that we finally came to terms with *Herakles mainomenos*.

The Madness of Heracles engages so closely with issues of hierarchy, mortals, demigods, gods, and heroes that it required in its Englishing a prosodic mirror for these distinctions. Even the famous chorus about youth and old age, which many commentators have found a redundant filler, seemed to us to suggest more about the diminished role of the gods (the old order) in human life and a Euripidean blasphemy. Heracles walks away from the traitorous gods: his departure is a metaphor for reality in a transitional period wherein what Nietzsche called "the indispensable dark spring" of action at last belongs to humans. The gods are weary, flippant, and corrupt; the world of city and state is at worst homicidal and at best prosaic. The real heroism of Heracles and Theseus gets its due in this translation with the assignment of the solemnity and gravitas of monodic blank verse. The Olympian pantheon is cracked wide open. Civil war has divided Euripides' Greece, and Heracles' exile answers better to his grief than staying at home in a town that no longer protects its heroes, its old men, its women, or its children.

The speech of the chorus on old age, for all its poignancy, seems to signal something about the diminished significance in this play of familiar ties and hierarchies, about the passing of an old order under an astringent Euripidean skepticism. What survives in the ruins of Thebes (whose long and horrific history is the deep background of the play) is not the power of gods, families, or the state, but the loyalty of Theseus, who, out of friendship, comes from another city to return a favor. In Greek legend, Heracles dies, eventually, after another quarrel, immolated in a tunic poisoned by the poison of a Hydra (from a smear on his arrows) and the blood of an old enemy, the Centaur Nessus. The image of his immolation has passed into the language as an idiom: to put on "the shirt of Nessus" means to take on a deadly labor; its reward will be fatal to the hero, his family, and even his tribe. Once again, the archaic audience most likely knew every fold of the story, just as we read Othello from Shakespeare through Verdi, and at last through Orson Welles.

This translation acknowledges several favors, with thanks both to David Slavitt, coeditor of the Penn Greek Drama Series, whose spirited encouragement made this labor available to us, and to the late William Arrowsmith in grateful remembrance. Professor Arrowsmith's translation of *Heracles* cast a long shadow over our own task many years later. His advice to the translator of Greek tragedy was, invariably, to look for the generic, at a "huge crystalline structure with organic lines," to look at an archaic play for the unity in its strange diversity of the translucent, the opaque, and those ritual elements of Euripidean drama that ultimately must disclose themselves with the living language.

—Katharine Washburn

*   *   *

Like all translators, we were concerned about accuracy, an issue that is never simple. Our aim was to produce an accuracy of effect, a performable translation that would convey something of the dramatic vision a Greek audience might have comprehended. Consequently, explanations that might have been relegated to a footnote were inserted into our text. One of the most extensive of these passages, and one most critical to an understanding of the play, occurs at the beginning of the chorus on the Labors of Heracles. Our interpolations are italicized.

> Linus, son of Apollo—
> *the one who taught Orpheus*
> *and, as Heracles' music tutor,*
> *attempted to correct his playing of the lute,*
> *provoking the fury of Heracles, who,*
> *raging like an Achilles on the kill,*
> *let loose in his madness*
> *and slew the great musician—*

used to add to his paeans of praise
as he swept the strings of his lute
with a plectrum of gold
    the howl of a dirge. (140–51)

Here the passing allusion to Linus reminds those who know the story that Heracles had in the past lost control and killed an innocent person. Since the most dramatic action of the play, and a major reference of its moral concerns, is Heracles' murder of his wife and children, this is not a point to be missed, even though Euripides merely alludes to it in an aside. We briefly considered putting such insertions in italics, following the precedent of the King James Bible, but dropped the idea as too pedantic. Our insertion also permitted us to refer to a notion of archaic madness that has no real counterpart in modern psychology, the frenzy of a warrior like Achilles who willfully releases civilized controls during a battle.

The play starts with confusion and rises to a great poetry of clarification at its end. Its subject is the response of mortals to the arbitrary fates that the cavalier deities of Euripides can inflict on them, and the potential of mortals to rise above the prose of confused existence to the nobility of spirit that the heroes represent. The human chorus comments, but cannot participate in the dramatic action in the same way as the other mortals, and its function is altogether different. A powerful sense of distinctions between one category of person and another was natural to the audience of Euripides' theater, and this sense of a speaker's status is of critical importance in *The Madness of Heracles*.

These considerations led us to translate the play into a mixture of prose and poetry in a number of different metrical forms. Such a mixture is not usual in translations from the Greek and doesn't attempt to correspond to Greek metrical forms. We have attempted instead to create an appropriate emotional undercurrent for the speeches of each caste of person by means of a corresponding metric. We wanted a modern audience to hear subtexts of difference between normal mortals, the chorus, the heroes, and the visitors from divine realms.

For the witty, garrulous, and casually cruel exchange between the messenger of the Gods, Iris, and the demon, Madness, we used rhymed pentameter couplets, with many lines stretched to hexameters. The heroes speak in iambic pentameter blank verse, the norm for high diction and elevated thoughts in English poetry. The mortals speak prose, often a little convoluted in the emotional turmoil at the beginning of the play. (Euripides' prologues are frequently indicted for their wooden archaizing. We let that be, and sometimes made his prosiness even more extensive.) But even the prose of the mortal characters is lifted close to blank verse at the end of the play in the dialogues between the mortal survivors and the heroes.

For the poetry of the choruses we chose a modern version of the Anglo-Saxon strong-stress metric. Descriptive or sententious questions and comments by the chorus in Greek plays can seem gratuitous or vacuous, and the inability of the chorus to take simple steps to find out what is happening is also a problem. This poses serious difficulties when a murder, accompanied perhaps by blood-curdling screams, is taking place just off stage. We tried to convey the weight that the contribution of the chorus should have by means of bunched stresses and alliteration or assonance:

> Don't falter! Don't drag your laboring legs
> as if under the tug and strain
> a young horse has who hauls uphill
> a huge wheeled wagon, its hooves
>   striking stone. (43–47)

Here, as in most other choruses, the ending of a succession of four-stress lines is usually indicated by a change of cadence to a final two-stress line.

In the choruses in the middle of the play, where the speech is not somber and weighty but quick and excited the norm chosen is a two-stress line:

> Overturning of wrong!
> Our great lord's life
> turns round again,
> returning from death. (517–20)

For the choruses or parts of choruses where a more dance-like rhythm is needed, the metric was closer to iambic. Here, for example, we have a succession of lines all ending in an unstressed syllable:

Add yours to our voices
which hymn the victor,
which sing at the crowning
of Heracles the hero. (615–18)

The justification of these metrical experiments is left to the ear of the reader
or audience. But the greatest betrayal of this great play would be to not
attempt to convey in English the extraordinary poetry of the original. And
since no one has ever had any sustained success in reproducing the Greek
meters in English, and many have tried, we made our own attempt to use
as fully as we could the linguistic resources natural to English, in both poetry and prose.

—David Curzon

Cast

AMPHITRYON, father of Heracles and an elderly man
MEGARA, wife of Heracles, daughter of Creon the former king
  of Thebes
CHORUS of old men of Thebes, citizens and veterans of
  former wars
LYCUS ("Wolf"), usurping monarch of Thebes
HERACLES, hero of disputed parentage, son of the god Zeus
  or the mortal Amphitryon, believed dead at the opening of
  the play
IRIS, messenger of the gods
MADNESS (Greek Lyssa, "the unbinding one"), goddess of
  madness or divine frenzy
MESSENGER, who circulates news among mortals only
THESEUS, King of Athens, whose temple was a sanctuary for
  runaway slaves and criminals
NONSPEAKING
  Sons of Heracles and Megara (traditionally named
    Therimachus, Creontidas, and Deicoon)
  Attendants of Lycus

*(Outside the palace of Heracles at Thebes, Amphitryon, Megara,
  and the three small sons of Megara and Heracles are crouched
  on the steps of the altar of Zeus the Savior. The altar, their refuge
  as suppliants, was once dedicated by Heracles himself, but the
  hero never returned from the underworld. Heracles went to
  Hades on the last of the labors to which he was bound by his
  enemy, Eurystheus; the spite of the goddess Hera sentenced him
  to this servitude. The danger is extreme, since Creon, Megara's
  own father, is dead, Heracles' family is in the power of Lycus,
  and they are locked outdoors, awaiting the fury of this usurper
  from Euboea who intends their death. Amphitryon, Heracles' old
  father, rises and speaks the prologue, using the archaizing and
  sometimes garrulous voice of a man of his many years and long
  memories.)*

AMPHITRYON

Everyone in Thebes knows who I am: Amphitryon. Those who
    trace pedigrees know the whole tale. My own
    father was the son of Perseus who killed a sea-
    monster and we are the children of their star-
    myth, the offspring of Perseus and Andromeda.
    When I was young, I came to a country where
    one wild harvest gave us the Sown Men—
    Spartans, to you. And those who were left after
    the battle—the sparings of war who settled the
    city—our city, city of Cadmus, I mean! I mean
    Thebes—although its name is unlucky, to say
    the least! Must I draw you a chart? Or lose you
    in the labyrinth of names and races and disputed
    descents while what matters here is the start of
    our story?
Zeus and I were bed-mates, as you are all well aware. We had
    Alcmene in turns, and either of us could be
    called, if you will, the godfather of Heracles. Now
    to return to the dragon's teeth dynasty, and the
    children Strewn Men. One of them was Creon, a
    stopgap name in the tradition, wherever a prince
    turns up in our legends, for His General
    Lordship, but our Creon, now slain, was the
    father of Megara, Heracles' bride. I remember
    the time we sang their wedding, to the wailing
    of flutes when Heracles, our great hero, one way
    or the other my son, brought her home to my
    house.
And then, forsaking Megara, the small ones, and the rest of the
    clan, he fled our country for Argos and the Lion
    Gate to take back the terrain that outlawed me
    once for killing some fellow or other whose
    name, if you seek it, the scribes still recite, sifting
    their notes and sorting out shadows.
His name was Electryon, and there's some version of the legend

in which he's said to be Alcmene's father, but put
that aside and bear with me now when I tell you
how Heracles, driven by some destiny of his own
or stung by the spite of his namesake, Hera,
the wife of great Zeus, swore to plough the
wilderness and clear the world of monsters:
his fee my return to the land where I was born.
And when he had spent himself with all the other labors, one
last task remained. He went down to Hellmouth,
taking the dark road south to Hades to haul the
three-headed beast—whose name is never
spoken—back up to the sunlit world. He has
not returned from that journey.
Once—so the local legend has it—there was a king here in
Thebes, a Lord Lycus who married one of our
queens, seized power in the high-gated city,
before the twin riders ruled the land. The Wolf
had a cub, heir to his name although no son of
this place. Lycus the Younger saw a palace shaken
by Oedipus' great fall, murdered Creon, and took
the throne. And now my kinship to the dead
regent puts us at great risk. While my son hunts
with the lost in the dark caverns of the earth, that
Wolf, Lycus, who rules our land hunts us to the
kill: Heracles' wife, his sons, and my useless self,
too old to count in the scoring of blood
staunching blood. All to one purpose: that these
boys become men might settle accounts, and
avenge the murder of Creon.
I was left here to nursemaid the children, to be keeper of the
flame, while my son took the night-road to the
underworld places. Now, to keep the young safe
from the slaughter, their mother and I sink to
our knees at the altar of Zeus the Savior, and
for this our salvation, we give great thanks. Its
stone table was raised by my son whose glory is

everlasting, a token of his triumph over a distant
tribe, a remote people who come trailing legends
of their own.
(Their name can mean little to you. We know them, however,
as Minyans. Their harbor was a port of call for
Jason and his sailors in another story.) In our
own, we sit here on the open ground, wanting
food, drink, and cover for our skins, locked out
of the house and despairing of rescue. When
I look to our friends, I see some untrue, the
rest without means to come to our help. Foul
weather tests friendship when we're far at sea:
Watch out for the friend who watches your disaster,
Ill fortune is our only master.   10

MEGARA

Old man, old campaigner, in your great days you led the army
of Thebes and took that far-off northern village,
while Zeus, as you yourself admit, seduced your
Alcmene before you made your way home. Who
can justify the ways of the gods to men? Surely
fortune smiled on my birth, since my father was
Creon—"rich as Creon," they still say around
here—and when he was king men ate their
hearts out, and the long spears leaped with
longing for the fat land he ruled. His women
ripened with children too, and in time he gave
one of his daughters—he gave *me*—to your son.
Now the shadow of death wings over us all—house, hero,
ourselves, and these children. The small ones
slip under the shadow of my death. I look after
them, weeping, whimpering to me: "O mother,
where is my father, where did he fly, to what part
of the world, what does he do there and when
will he return?" Like small bird cries, their voices
call one after another for their father. And I, I tell

them the old legends, I hush them and say all
the right words: always, always, the father returns.

(lowering her voice)

They startle in hope at the swing of a door gate, the fall of a foot
on the threshold, thinking to settle on the knees
of a father sweeping them up in his returning
embrace. Hopeless, I keep looking to your great
age for counsel—while you know and I know
how closely the borders of this country are
guarded, and where the watchmen patrol the
seven gates. We have no friends in high places,
none who can save us:

I await your wisdom, old man, while we both know that the only
knock on the door, the tap of greeting will be
the sound of Death, coming closer. Now tell me
plainly. Do you have a real plan, or are we simply
to lie down and die?

AMPHITRYON

Daughter, none of this comes easily to me. My thoughts too are
labored. Time worries the weak who must wait
these things out.

MEGARA

How you still love daylight, old sentinel of the dark.

AMPHITRYON

So, I still live in the moment, and look to the break of day: I
remain in love with hope.

MEGARA

You and I both, old man. But hope demands the possible. No
rescue will arrive, only a short respite here.

AMPHITRYON

Something like a respite may come with this wait. But perhaps
it's only a prelude to something worse.

MEGARA

    It's the sting of that respite, in which I find no repose.   20

AMPHITRYON

    Daughter, once more I call you daughter, let me remind you
                that a fair breeze may yet come after the storm
                gathering on you and on me, and it's possible my
                Heracles and yours may make his way home. For
                now, be the calm wind that wipes away all the
                tears from their eyes, and dries up these living
                fountains. Comfort them with legends where
                heroes return and graves give back their dead,
                feed them old fairy-tale endings. Let fables
                defraud them with those lies which sweeten
                the sad day.
  Misfortune must come to an end: the gale wears out its breath,
                the luck of men fails too, the gods tire, and
                we do well to remember: *Change alone is*
                unchanging. The same road goes both up and
                down. The brave hope against hope. Let cowards
                eat despair; we'll leave it for them.
(Chorus of elders of the city of Thebes enter, limping along, leaning on
                their staffs.)

CHORUS

      Strophe

    Aching with age,
    stumbling with my staff,
    I've managed to come
    to the old man's couch,
    to stand under his ample roof,
    wanting to assist a friend,
    though my body is so frail
    it no more than transports my voice.   30
    I am like the voice of sorrows

inhabiting a dream.
Like some decrepit cock I crow
    sad songs.

Greetings, children—
all are orphaned of father!—
and greetings to you, old man,
and you, unhappy mother,
mourning your husband
your absent lord,   40
away in the unseen kingdom,
    the halls of Hades.

    Antistrophe

Don't falter! Don't drag your laboring legs
as if under the tug and strain
a young horse has who hauls uphill
a huge wheeled wagon, its hooves
    striking stone.

Old man! Help another old man clamber
up this steep slope,
help him to grasp a hand, a garment,   50
hold him, your aged friend,
just as he held his friend
in the press of battle when
spears struck
and he upheld
    his country's glory.

    Epode

Look at the eyes of the children,
their fire is their father's fire!
But his misery, too, is with them,
and his straight-backed pride.   60
Greece! What allies you'll lose
    if you lose these.

Look. Lycus approaches. Why would the tyrant come
loping here? The sight of this wolf strikes me dumb.
(Lycus enters with his attendants.)

LYCUS

You, father of Heracles, and you his wife, I would like, if I may,
            to ask a question or two. Not that you have a
            choice: I am master of the house and can ask
            whatever questions I please. How long do you
            expect to cling to life? What can you possibly
            hope for except certain death? Do you count on
            the father of these boys, your hero-under-the-
            ground, to come halloaing back from Hell?
Your grief is out of bounds. You know you're bound to die, you
            who set Hellas ringing with your hollow claims:
            you, a husband, cuckold of the Great Father
            himself, getting a child with the Sky, and happy,
            happy Megara over there, radiant bride of the
            best of men.
Now for the high deeds of this husband of yours. He killed
            a water-snake, I beg your pardon, a *hydra*, in
            some swamp, and slew the Rogue Lion of the
            woodland with snares—not with the bare
            stranglehold his stories claim.
You try to build a case on these exploits? For the sake of these
            marvels, the sons of Heracles should live?
            Children of a born coward, a man who boasts
            like a savage of battles with beasts, a man whose
            left hand never bore a shield, who kept a safe
            distance from the spear, and carried a bow, the
            cheap weapon of small men, although handy as
            hell when fleeing the field.
(Lycus turns from the suppliants and addresses the audience.)
To be armed with a bow is no proof of courage. It takes a real
            soldier to wait and hold his ground, to look
            without flinching as spears fall like scythes,
            slashing through the ranks of the brave.

Old man, you think me ruthless in what I do; I'm simply far-
        sighted, a man of strong purpose. I don't forget I
        killed Creon and took his throne. Nor will these
        children—I cannot leave them to come of age
        and take revenge for what I've done.   70

AMPHITRYON

    Let Zeus take care of his own. Leave wonderworks to the Father
        of gods and men.

(looking away)

    O Heracles, I have only words to combat this mountebank: I
        cannot abide the filth of his sophistry.

    First, the slander, the unspeakable lie, when he names you,
        Heracles, a coward. Gods! Be my witness in the
        high court: I call on thunderbolt and storm, on
        the chariot of Zeus that carried you, when there
        was war in heaven against the hell-brood, when
        there were giants in the earth. Then you shot
        your arrows, winged spears sent straight to the
        mark, and you sang the triumph in the great
        processional of the gods.

(turns to Lycus)

    Go north to the backwoods of Thessaly, and ask His Royal
        Obscenity, king of the four-legged folk, who
        among men is most fearless? Even a centaur,
        snorting and pawing, will answer: my son—
        the man you call coward. Or go—go straight to
        the mountain and ask Lord Nobody from the
        country that bore you: there no one will sing
        songs of praise for you. No place, nowhere, is
        there a soul to bear witness to the fine deeds of
        Lycus.

    You sneer at the bow, O great dialectician, at gear fashioned by
        men far wiser than you. Hear me and learn what
        wisdom is. The foot-soldier with spear is the
        slave of his weapon. When his comrades fall,
        then he falls too, and their lucklessness is his

doom. If his spear shatters he has no hope; death
is on him when his sole defense is gone.
But the archer whose hand is attuned to his bow can unloose
a thousand arrows. He has it best from start to
finish, driving death away and standing fast,
aiming at blind ranks who see just the blood
track of his shafts and see no more. There's
battle-lore for you, there's wisdom: to wound the
foe and stay alive yourself. The man with spear
and shield is fortune's toy. The archer saves his
skin. And wins.
I rest my case. Every word I've said flies in the face of your barbs,
your ready opinions, your stale rhetoric.
Why do you want to kill these innocents? What can you hope
to achieve? Yes, in one way you're wise enough:
lowlife does well to fear the sons of virtue. Yet it's
a heavy thing for us, dying to score a point, when
it's you who best deserve death at the hands of
your betters. But Zeus has turned away his face,
and there will be no just retaliation here.

(He falters.)

Look now, if you seek the scepter and the throne, let us go and
take refuge far from this place. Restrain your
violence, lest violence visit you. The wind
changes at the gods' will.

(Amphitryon kneels, beats his breast, and keens.)

Country of Cadmus, where victory spells ruin! I turn back to you
with more words of chastisement. Is this how
you watch over Heracles' boys? When the
Minyan tyrant took tribute from us and the
bronze tower watched our land, Heracles alone
fought and set us free.   80
And I have harsher words for Hellas—unspeakable contempt—
for the army which could have come with flame
and sword to save these fledglings: so the shining
Hellenes reward the man who made clear the

paths of the sea and safe the roads of the
mainland.

Dear children, Thebes and Hellas have repaid you well. You look
to me, mouthing words, all strength gone, shaky
of gait—what is left is a slender reed and
memories of my onetime power. God! God,
to be young once more: I'd lift my spear—

(He lifts his staff and holds it like a weapon.)

and—with that—your sandy plumage, my fair-haired fellow,
caked with blood, my spear prodding at your
coward's back, you'd run—ah, run, and faster
run—past Land's End and the gates of Ocean
where sailors never dare. I see you running still.

CHORUS

Words still come to good men, although
the pace is halting and tongue is slow.

LYCUS

Talk on, talk on, this soaring tower of words is staggering.
Simply . . . staggering. Enough: I'll return the
favor and match your vicious words with some
action.

(He turns to his companions.)

Get going. Take the mountain trails—sacred, I believe, to the
Muses—and you, over there, go to sun-burnt
Helicon—and you, you climb Parnassus and tell
the woodmen there to mow the hillsides, cut
down the oak, and haul the brushwood to the
city. Heap up the kindling around this altar, and
set it alight. Burn them alive. The dead king has
had his day. Lycus alone is King, Lord of Things
As They Are. What is, is.

Now, reverend sirs, old geezers, you'll pay for your gabble and
grieve, not only for the children of Heracles but
for the fate of this house. Disaster will follow

disaster until you understand you are slaves and
here I have absolute power.

CHORUS
Feeble men of Thebes, who were once teeth
ripped from the dragon's savage grimace   90
and sown by Ares, by the God War,
into this earth which brought you forth,
brandish the canes your hands clutch,
and crack and bloody the unholy head
of that foreigner, that stranger, the catastrophe that came
        to rule our youths.
(to Lycus)
You can't rule me without cost.
I didn't accumulate riches for you.
I curse you! Crawl back to your place,
continue your insolent whinnies there.   100
While I'm alive you'll never kill
        Heracles' children.
He's underground, hidden deep in Hades,
has outpaced his sons,
and you, the ruin of this land, rule
        and not its savior.

Does it make me meddlesome if I attempt—
is it agitation—to help the dead?
Don't the helpless need help?

How you need to hold a spear, my hand!   110
But a known weakness undercuts impulse,
or I'd stop the mouth naming me a slave
and live in honor where you now luxuriate.
Thebes is a city so sick with schemes
it has disease in mind, not right in mind,
        or you'd never rule us.

MEGARA

    Amen. Amen. Thanks once again, to your committee of good
            old men.

    True friends speak up for each other in the heat of a just anger.
            But don't slide to ruin yourselves for the sake of
            our own calamity. Amphitryon, hear me out if
            whatever I say makes sense to you.

    I love my children. How could I fail to love the children of my
            travails? Their death is horrible to imagine, but
            to grapple with necessity—how grubby, horrible,
            and hopeless for us about to die. And to die in
            your fire, burned alive in the double flame of
            heat and hostile laughter! It would be better just
            to die. A good house can always lay claim to a
            good death.

(turning briefly to Lycus)

    You owe us that, wearing the wolf-lord's sleek muzzle on your
            helm, the fearless victor who has no dread of a
            coward's death.   120

(back to Amphitryon, her hands stretched out)

    My long-gone, my husband, needs no friends at court: Heracles'
            children would rather die than live through the
            largesse of lesser men. The high-born do not
            abide the disgrace of their kind, and I am wife of
            Heracles still. I'll follow his lead in this and beg
            you to think from whence comes your hope.

    Do you think Heracles will come back from his chase through
            the paths underground? Who ever returned from
            the House of the Dark? Who has ever slipped
            away from the grasp of the Unseen, the King of
            Shadows, and how, how, do you think to soften
            his heart with your prayers? This is the common
            enemy; avoid him, avoid him and yield when you
            must to the wise. Fall on your knees only to
            adversaries on a level ground who give and take
            and deal like noble men.

I was tempted to think that our prayers might buy a lighter
             sentence. But to banish these children is to keep
             them safe in beggary, little paupers at the feast
             where men stare at their guests until sunset, and
             then, as we know, send the exiles creeping away.
             Share in our death since you're bound for it too.
Old man, greatheart, I call on you to come, come along with us.
             The brave man who sets course against the winds
             of fate takes passage on a ship of fools.
Don't war with what exists. Necessity
determines all that is, all that will be.

CHORUS

If my old arms retained their strength and skill,
no one would insult you. I would stop his mouth.
But I'm now nothing. I've become a nothing.
Amphitryon, it falls to you to find   130
             the path from disaster.

AMPHITRYON

I am no coward. I don't long for life. I don't fear death. I want
             to save these boys, and all I want, it seems, is the
             impossible—victory over what will be.
(He turns around to Lycus.)
Just as you like. Here's a throat to slit, a body for stabbing, and
             a throttled corpse to toss over a cliff. But now,
             your lordship, grant a favor to both of us: Kill
             me, kill this poor woman before you slaughter
             the children and save us the sight that stinks to
             high heaven of these boys choking and crying at
             the end for mother and father—I mean, their
             father's father. And then, your will be done.
             Finish. We have no defense but death. Finish it.

MEGARA

In your graciousness, gracious lord, grant one grace more. Do
             one thing and be blessed, and then bless you,

bless you. Let me dress these children for death.
Open the gates locked against us; admit us to the
house and let them at least take a grave-offering,
scraps of cloth, to spirit away as their share of
their father's estate.

LYCUS

By all means. Go inside, go right in. Get dressed. You there,
(addressing his attendants)
fling open the doors. Deck yourselves out for dying—there's no
shortage of clothing, robes, what have you—but
when you have wrapped yourselves in fancy
dress, suitable for the occasion of your demise,
I'll send you on your way and dispatch you
straight to darkness.
(Lycus exits.)

MEGARA

Come, children. Hurry. Walk with your sad mother into your
father's halls. Other men own his house; we still
carry his name.
*(Megara and her sons enter the palace. Amphitryon and the chorus are
alone on the stage.)*

AMPHITRYON

Zeus, Zeus! What a joke, our bed swap with my wife! What a
joke, your godfathering of my son! You were not
the great friend you seemed. I'm no more than a
man, but better that than a god like you—you
are not the measure of all things. I did not turn
away from the sons of Heracles. You were clever
enough to come like a thief to my bed, taking
what was never yours.
And where's that divine cunning now—can you come to the
rescue of those you love? What kind of god are
you, O Laziness—clumsy lout or common
criminal?

CHORUS

Strophe 1

Linus, son of Apollo—   140
the one who taught Orpheus
and, as Heracles' music tutor,
attempted to correct his playing of the lute,
provoking the fury of Heracles, who,
raging like an Achilles on the kill,
let loose in his madness
and slew the great musician—
used to add to his paeans of praise
as he swept the strings of his lute
with a plectrum of gold   150
    the howl of a dirge.

And I, now that Heracles, the son of Zeus—
or is he just Amphitryon's child—
has descended to dark Hades,
dedicate to Heracles,
a wreath of triumphal formal song
    praising his labors.

First,
he saved the grove sacred to Zeus
by killing the lion in its cave,   160
and made its gaping jaws a hood
which swallowed up his golden hair,
and its hide became his cape
    trailing behind him.

Antistrophe 1

Next,
he destroyed with poisoned arrows
that untamed mountain race,
the Centaurs, the horse-men,
giants whose spears were entire pine-trees,

whose hooves trampled on harvests,   170
while the owners of homes hid,
while whole towns trembled
in the wide plains surrounding
Peneus, the gliding river,
    witness to terror.

And then
he slew the spotted hind
whose antlers were made of metal,
a gold that spread desolation,
and gave its carcass to gild   180
    the altar of Artemis.

    Strophe 2

And then
he slew with bridle and bit
the jaws of Diomedes' hideous horses,
that champed with foul euphoria
    the flesh of men,
              and then
he crossed the eddies of Hebros
spangled with silver
to continue the tasks of the tyrant
    who ruled Mycenae.   190

And then,
at the strand of the streams of Anauros,
on the path taken by pilgrims to Delphi,
he came to the inn kept by Cycnus
and his arrows killed the ogre who savaged
    every guest.

    Antistrophe 2

And then
he came to the singing women
in the gardens of the sunset

where the golden apples grew   200
which he plucked among their leaves
after killing their coiling guard,
    the amber dragon.

And then
he went down to the depths of the sea
and purged its caverns of monsters,
made straight its paths,
so men who sail in ships
could plough their oars
through calm waters,   210
    a silent sea.

And then
he came, at the gates of ocean,
to Atlas, and held the hall of heaven,
he bore up the Immortals' palace
    splendid with stars.

    Strophe 3

And then
he assembled for expedition
the host of the Hellene—
Theseus was among these comrades—   220
and, braving the dangers of the Black Sea,
he crossed its waters to wage war,
attacking the Amazons on the shore of Maeotis,
a watersmeet, to seize from the Warrior Queen
the ceinture that circled
her gold-threaded garments,
her warrant of sovereignty,
and carry back to Hellas
as prize for Mycenae
    this spoil.   230

And then
he burned the monster dog of Lerna
and smeared the venom of its many heads
on the arrows he used to kill
the cattle of the herdsman
who was king of Geryon,
who lives in the country
where the sun sinks
    red in the west.

> *Antistrophe 3*

And then,   240
after many other struggles,
victorious in all,
he went in the last of his labors to Hades,
he came to the place of weeping, of grief,
and will never again be seen by us.
Charon will ferry the children to death,
a trip that is no homecoming,
killed against all law and justice.
Your house searches out its champion,
    its lord gone.   250

Were I as strong as I once was,
when the companions of my youth and I
brandished our sharp spears,
I'd be the champion your children need.
But alas the glory of youth is gone
    which once was mine.

> *Epode*

But now I see the children of that Heracles
we'd named the great
coming our way clothed for the grave,
his dear wife dragging step by step   260
children stiff with the terror of death,

and the feeble father of Heracles with them.
And I, wretched as I am,
can't prevent tears welling
    in these old eyes.

MEGARA

What now? Who is the high priest, the holy cut-throat who
                comes to put us out of our misery? Still living,
                we are creatures shambling to the dark. Children!
                How obscene this final drive to the death: the
                old, the young, the mother, under one dingy
                yoke. This is a squalid fate for me and my sons.
                I look at them for the last time; for the last time
                my eyes meet theirs.
I gave birth to you and reared you well. Well done, good work:
                to breed live fodder for the scornful, the spiteful,
                and the predator's knife.
My hopes for you were all absurd
and perished with the promise of Heracles' word.
(She addresses the children in turn.)
Firstborn, we named you Hothead. Your father would have
                left you all Argos. You would have lived in the
                great hall, king of broad pasture and summer
                farmland. He wrapped you in the lion-skin
                he wore: you would have been Lord of the
                Lion Gate.   270
And you, my father's namesake, for you there was a throne in
                Thebes, city of coursers where streets are like
                racetracks, the mother-land I passed on to you.
                You coaxed it from your father. He made it your
                share. When he played a game with you of hide-
                and-seek, you won first prize, the club in your
                hand, the emblem of Thebes, the playful present
                of a treacherous toy.
And you, my baby, what did you get? A minor province with
                a forgettable name. He took it once from the

archer-king; his bow and the place were meant
for your hands.

Three of you, three kingdoms, three gifts, there's a lion-skin
for you, and a club for you, and a bow for the
smallest: he meant well by his sons, all three of
you, there was space in his heart and pride of
possession.

I looked out for brides, picking the prize goods. I had Athens in
mind, and Thebes, and Sparta as well, shoring up
the house with marriage on marriage, laying
anchors in every safe harbor, so that you might
secure calm voyage through rough waters. That's
all over. The wind has shifted. You'll get brides
with faces like ruin; they'll have dowries in the
dark world, ghost-girls from Hades.

What wedding is this, where the waters of ceremony run in a
wash of tears? My dreams turned to destruction;
the marriage to funeral. Your father's father is
crying: We have arrived at this feast spread by
Father-in-Law Death, and you will wed his
daughters.

Heaven! I don't know where to place the first kiss or the last,
or which of you to hold in my arms or press
to my mouth. Better to cut this short, to shed a
single tear for the many, swallow sorrow like
nectar in one short flight skimming from face
to face.

My darling, my long-gone, if you can hear me among the dead,
I am calling to you. Heracles, I am calling your
name, come forth. Heracles, come forth. Your
father is dying. Your children are dying. Megara,
once called blessed among women, is dying.
Come, come, come as demon or ghost or dead
hero: come back in a dream.

Man or god or demon, come.

Come in a dream. Save us. Come.

AMPHITRYON
>   Dear woman, pray on, and send your prayers to the dark address.
>   I look up, I name Zeus, I call on high heaven.
>   Zeus! Patron of the helpless, if you will save these
>   children, do it now. Later is too late. I keep
>   calling and calling. My labors count for nothing!
>   I see death coming closer and no way out.   280
>   Life is short, old men. Eat the honey of the world and cram
>   the sunlit hour with lotus: grief is the great
>   distraction from the daylight. Time has no time
>   for our small hopes and desires. It makes its
>   rounds and skims away.
>   Look at me: I was the great compass of the world, all eyes
>   watching me, the hero of the hour, but fortune
>   lifted everything from me like the light wind
>   pocketing a feather for the sky.
> *(He turns directly to the chorus, walking away from Megara and the*
> *children.)*
>   Great wealth, good name, all in a day,
>   blasted, dried up and blown away.
>   Farewell. I was your cohort and your friend.
>   Look now on fellowship's end.

MEGARA
>   Sir, dear heart, old man: I see someone coming!

AMPHITRYON
>   Daughter. I see—I don't know what I see. The words are gone—

MEGARA
>   It's him. The man we knew who went underground, dead and
>   gone with the rest of them. My eyes ache with
>   dreaming and I don't trust my sight. Old man,
>   look at your son! Children run, run fast, take
>   hold of his cloak, clutch it tight and don't let go.

Our savior is here, and the High God comes at
last at his side.
(Heracles strides in, carrying bow and arrows and holding his club. He
doesn't see his family, but stands before the walls of
his house.)

HERACLES

Hello, my house, my hearth my halls! I have   290
returned to daylight and I greet you all with joy!
(He sees his family.)
What's this? My family's beyond the shelter of the house!
And small heads crowned with leaves, dressed for a burial!
And my wife standing in the stench of a crowd,
my father crying for some nameless loss.
Why is he crying? I'll get close enough
to ask my questions, come to understand.
My wife! My woman! What is going on?

MEGARA

My darling! Greatest of men!

AMPHITRYON

Daybreak returns! Sunlight shines on a father!   300

MEGARA

You've come back. You're alive. You came in our dark hour, our
savior.

HERACLES

What are you saying? Father, what's occurred?
Tell me what has happened in this house.

MEGARA

We were dead. They were about to kill us. Forgive me, old man,
if I misspeak. Women weep more easily than
men. They were about to kill the children and
myself with them.

HERACLES

Apollo, give me light! What a start to your welcome speech!

MEGARA

My own father is dead. My brothers are dead.

HERACLES

Enlighten me. Who killed them, by whose spear?
What happened, in the name of every god?

MEGARA

There was a usurper. His name was Lycus. He killed them all.

HERACLES

A plague, a revolution, war?   310

MEGARA

A war. His side won and took the city and its seven gates.

HERACLES

Why was that so dreadful for you and the old man?

MEGARA

Listen to me. He was about to kill your father, your children, and
           your wife.

HERACLES

Were orphans such a threat to him? They are
too small for harm, and have no friends.

MEGARA

Friendless children grow up. They might have gone after him to
           avenge Creon's death.

HERACLES

These robes, these graveclothes. Why dress the boys like this?

MEGARA

Listen to me. We dressed to attend our own funeral: we prepared
to die.

HERACLES

I'm reeling! Someone wants to kill my children! Mine?

MEGARA

There was no one here for us at all. We heard you were dead.   320

HERACLES

And what made you despair of me, and why?

MEGARA

Messengers came from the king himself. You are officially dead.

HERACLES

On the force of that, you walked out of this house?

MEGARA

He used force. He flung your father from his bed.

HERACLES

There's such a thing as shame! Who treats old men like that?

MEGARA

Lycus has gods of his own. Shame is not one of them.

HERACLES

When I was gone, were there no friends around?

MEGARA

Friends never fail to favor the fortunate.

HERACLES

No one recalls the war I fought up north?
Do all my friends piss on my great campaigns?   330

MEGARA
> Listen to me. I said a man without fortune walks without friends.

HERACLES
> Strip off those hellish wreaths; this journey won't take place.
> Open your eyes to your salvation. Lift
> your faces to the day and banish darkness and death.
> True labor comes at last, and I must strike
> the tyrant's house and raze it, and cut off
> his filthy head, and feed the mash to dogs.
> There'll be a reckoning from the victor's bow
> and hails of arrows for those men of Thebes
> who gave me evil for the good I gave.   340
> I'll ram the river with their corpses, I
> will set the current swirling with their blood.
> All that is worth defending is
> your children and your father and your wife.
> I say good-by to all my labors. I
> disown my glory. The great hunt is done.
> *(He gestures toward his family.)*
> I chased folly while death was chasing you,
> hunted monsters when what mattered most
> were humans doomed to die because I was their father.
> What honor is there in taking orders from   350
> King Craven's circus—wrestling snakes in swamps,
> swordfights with freakish foes—when my last labor was
> the death of these? Where now is my good name,
> the Victor, the Triumphant Hero of the World?

CHORUS
> Speak on, you have right on your side.
> What is there better for a man than to defend
> his boys, his father, and his wife.

AMPHITRYON
> How like you, this love of friends and bitter anger against
>   enemies. Don't ever forgive. But slow down,

slow down, do nothing quickly—let's not have
another civil war.

HERACLES

Tell me, your son, my father, what's too swift, too soon?

AMPHITRYON

This Wolf has his sheep, a flock without pasture but with broad
claims of its own: the unemployed, the old
moneyed class, the idle rich, their patrimony
spent, are up in arms. The scorpion has turned
its twisted tail to sting the body politic. The
sowers have sown sedition's crop.   360
These pirates on dry land saw you entering the city. They've now
had time, having spotted you, to reconnoiter, so
keep watch or you'll stumble without knowing it
into their calculations.

HERACLES

I do not care if all the city saw me.
We can invent a story packed with birds
and omens and a whiff of augury:
Let's say I saw a crow: its perch was sinister.
I knew my house was in trouble. Like Odysseus,
I got a warning and made a secret landfall.

AMPHITRYON

Splendid! Go in now, and greet the goddess who watches the
household fire. Look at the house of your father,
let it survey you in turn. Someone is coming
soon to haul us all away and kill us—wife,
children, and father: his lordship himself is
on the way.
Stay here then, and we'll be secure and all will be well, my child,
if you don't worry about the rest of the city until
you've finished what has to be done here and
done now.

HERACLES

> I'll do it. I will walk inside at once   370
> and greet the household gods who called me up
> from the caverns where the Dark King and his Goddess rule
> deep under earth. How could I fail to kneel
> and greet the household gods, under my roof at last?

AMPHITRYON

> And did you really go to that dark place, my child?

HERACLES

> I did. And dragged Hell's Watchdog up, three heads and all.

AMPHITRYON

> By force, or was he a gift of the Goddess?

HERACLES

> By force. With club and collar. Father, I
> saw the Mysteries, the rites, the blessings, the hymns
> by torchlight, forbidden to all except the citizens   380
> of Athens. It was my good fortune, lucky outlander!
> I was a student down there in the dark.

AMPHITRYON

> Is the beast in the kennel of Eurystheus?

HERACLES

> No. I stowed him in Demeter's grove,
> a neutral place, behind the Mother's temple.

AMPHITRYON

> Does Taskmaster Eurystheus know you've returned to the sunlit
>   world?

HERACLES

> No. I came here first.

AMPHITRYON
> Why were you gone below the earth for such a long time?

HERACLES
> Father, to harrow hell and set free Theseus took time.

AMPHITRYON
> Where is Theseus now? Has he returned to Attica, to his own
> > land?   390

HERACLES
> Released from the underworld, he made for home.
> *(turning to his children)*
> > But children, lift your hearts up, go
> > inside the house, follow your father, since
> > your going in will be better than your coming out.
> > So dry your tears, don't be afraid. And you,
> > my woman, shaking like a quail, you too
> > should pull yourself together. All of you!
> > Please stop this clutching at my hem, please stop.
> > Do you see feathers on me? Am I a bird,
> > a birdman about to fly away from the nest?   400
> > What's this, no letting go? Still clinging to
> > my robes with all your might? What did you think—
> > you came so close to death that death was after you?
> *(Heracles lays down his bow and club and takes his children by their*
> > *hands.)*
> > Then hold my hands. I'll tow you in like some
> > great sail that tugs along small boats in its wake.
> > I'm not too proud to be a nursemaid in
> > this service. We're all equal here, both haves
> > and have-nots love their children. Money is
> > important to them too, perhaps, and yet
> > I know that children count for everything.   410
> > That is what makes us men and women, not beasts.
> *(Heracles exits with the children, followed by Megara and Amphitryon.)*

CHORUS

Strophe 1

I yearn for youth.
Age weighs on me as Aetna weighed
when mounted on the monster Typhaeus.
Heavy age presses my head
lowering eye-lids into dark
    shrouding sight.

If I were offered the wealth of Asia,
houses stocked with coin, with spoil,
in trade for youth,   420
which lavishes its loveliness
on the impoverished as on the rich,
I would refuse this counterfeit
    for the riches of youth.

I despise old age.
If only that predator would slip
under the wave,
never to haunt houses and towns
where mortal men live out their lives,
if only wings would lift old age   430
    away into air.

Antistrophe 1

If wisdom and wit,
which now are only all too human,
were given to gods,
that godlike wit and wisdom would allow
the devout to be distinguished
by letting those, the twice-born, live
    a second youth.

Then the enlightened
would be redoubled back to sunlight   440

to allow their lives another lap,
while those who were not noble
would race through life in a single lane,
head straight for the string, break it,
    and collapse at the finish.

And from this signal
the wicked as well as the noble would know,
like sailors who, when clouds part,
see in a constellation the star
    by which to steer.   450

But now no bound
is set by the gods to separate
wicked from noble,
and the gods allow men to acquire,
as their lone time on earth
whirls on, wealth alone,
    only wealth.

    Strophe 2

Although I now am old
I will not cease to sing,
to link and mingle still   460
my musings with sweet grace.
No life without the Muses,
no life without the Graces.
Let me be garlanded,
with those whose brows are crowned,
let me live on in memory,
memory is origin of song,
old singers celebrate
memories that spur to song.
And I will sing forever   470
of the Heracles that victory has crowned
and the feast of Dionysus
and the lyre of seven strings

and the wail of the desert lute.
Although I am now old
I will not cease to sing,
or cease to praise the Muses who
    set all things dancing.

Antistrophe 2

Outside the temple of Apollo,
the god of music and of song,   480
the women of Delos,
whirling in all the figures of dance
lift their voices to sing praise,
    to hymn the paean.

Within your halls,
like an ancient swan
who sings from a silver throat,
I celebrate in my old age
all that is good,
    all that is.   490

And sing of Heracles,
who is the son of Zeus,
famous beyond his godlike birth.
He labored to grant us tranquil life,
he labored, a man against the shapes
of lions' jaws, the hooves of centaurs,
antlers of metal, dragons of amber,
he labored for us even in
    the halls of Hades.
(Lycus enters with his attendants. Amphitryon comes out of the palace.)

LYCUS

Right on time, Amphitryon, and here you are. You did however
        take your time scenting the corpse, getting
        dressed up for the grave. Now, hurry. Tell

Heracles' wife and boys to move right along now,
and show their faces outside the walls. I believe
we had a mutual understanding: that you'd have
time to get dressed just in time for your death.   500

AMPHITRYON

Your lordship. You dance up and down on a poor helpless man.
Outrage reaches out for more, outruns us on the
way to death. If you are lord here, if you are so
powerful, then mend your pace. Yours is the
force that sends us to die; yours the force to
which we yield: your will be done.

LYCUS

Where is that woman Megara and where are the children?

AMPHITRYON

It looks to me as though from where I stand out here, it would
seem . . .

LYCUS

How, indeed, does it seem to you? Or do you have anything that
can be called evidence?

AMPHITRYON

She . . . crouches in the ashes, breathing on them to call Hestia of
the Hearth . . .

LYCUS

If she calls on heaven to save her life, her prayers are prattle.

AMPHITRYON

And she calls and calls for her husband, calls in vain for a
dead man.

LYCUS

Your own *idée fixe*. He's dead and gone and never coming back.

AMPHITRYON

> Never. Unless the grave, with the help of a god, open and give
> back its dead.

LYCUS

> Get in there. And quickmarch her outside the house.   510

AMPHITRYON

> Then her death is on my head.

LYCUS

> Very well. Since that's the way you take it, this death-on-your-
> own-head scrupulousness, I, who've said good-
> bye to all that, will go and fetch the lady and her
> sons. Come along, guards, and let's clean this up:
> I want a *finis* to this labor at last.

(Lycus sweeps into the palace with a train of guards.)

AMPHITRYON

> Get on, walk right in to what must happen. Someone else, I
> think, will keep an eye on your path.

(to himself)

> Things won't turn out the way you plan.
> Revenge tracks every evil man.

(He turns at last to the chorus.)

> Look, old friends, at the Great Coward walking into the web
> where a sword lies waiting, his murderous mind
> savoring our death: What sweetness, this sword-
> snare, how delicious to see him die, justice
> waiting for him at the end: I want to watch
> him trussed up, his throat slit, I want to see
> my enemy dead, the debt discharged.

(Exits into the palace.)

CHORUS

Strophe 1

Overturning of wrong!
Our great lord's life
turns round again,
returning from death.   520

A howl! A howl!
The river justice
flows back to us
drowning the wolf:

Your time has come.
In death pay
its penalty.
Go where they go,

those with hubris
who act with hubris   530
against their betters.
Go there, go.

He's overthrown!
In my delight,
my eyes flood
with tears of joy.

I had despaired
but now is the hour
this lord of the land
never foresaw.   540

If only we,
an old chorus,

could go inside
or look inside,

to exult at the sight,
to see our foe
suffer as we
wished he would.

LYCUS *(from within)*
    Help me! Help me!

CHORUS

> *Antistrophe 1*
> A sweet song sounds   550
> inside the house:
> a cry, a shriek,
> a prelude to death.
>
> What a great groan!
> It seems the lord
> fears slaughter,
> expects death.

LYCUS
    Country of Cadmus! A dead man—a deceit—destroys me!

CHORUS
    As you'd have destroyed.
    Face death,   560
    pay the penalty
    of justice done.

    Who was the man
    who flouted law,

mindlessly mocked
the very gods,

overturned all
orders of heaven,
said the gods
lacked strength?   570

Old men!
the impious man
is no more.
His halls are silent.

Turn to the dance!
Fortune returns
as I had hoped
to those I love.

Strophe 2

The dancing and the dances,
the feasting and the feasts,   580
take hold on the lovely city
and wipe away its tears,
taking its misfortune,
giving birth to song!

The wolf is gone now
who ruled before!
The true king rules now,
returned from the black shore.
We hadn't dared hope for
him who came now   590

Antistrophe 2

The gods! the gods!
The gods concern themselves with us!
The gods consider right and wrong!

But the gold of good fortune
turns heads that are mortal.
It is mortals who follow
the power of injustice.
No man wants to think of
reversals, the race-course,
that by flouting the law he   600
whips on the lawless,
and though (black with tarnish)
his chariot now prospers,
turns can careen him
into wreckage.

Strophe 3

Wreathe your garlands
by the river Ismenus!
Start dancing
in the seven-gated city!
Dirce's the source of   610
our bright waters,
and with her are many
daughters belonging
to our sister river.
Add yours to our voices
which hymn the victor,
which sing at the crowning
of Heracles the hero.

Rock of Apollo,
graced by forests!   620
Helicon's our dance-floor,
the home of the Muses.
Come into our city,
where joy is shouting,
where the Sown Men sprouted
an army of soldiers

bearing brass shields
who leave their earth to
their children's children,
a line that is sacred,   630
the light of Thebes.

Antistrophe 3

We'll celebrate now
the bed of marriage
where a bride was shared by
two bridegrooms.
One was a mortal,
and Zeus was the other
who claimed a woman
who was Perseus' daughter.
Zeus! we had doubted   640
this marriage had happened
but now we believe it
since time has revealed
Heracles' strength.
He returned to the living
from the inner chambers
of the House of Hades
deep under earth.
Zeus! you are better
than the low-born monarch,   650
since, when the struggle
comes down to swordplay,
you show us the high gods
still delight in justice.

(Iris and Madness descend, with a crash of thunder, on the roof. Madness
is gorgon-faced and carries a goad, riding in a
black chariot. Iris faces her on the other side of
the roof.)

What horror is this we see above!
We cower, we panic, we're merely old men.

What specter is this over the house?
Run away! Run away!
Our legs falter, but lead us on.
Holy Apollo! Healer and Lord!   660
Turn away terror! Turn away evil!
Turn terror away!

IRIS *(to the chorus)*
Be brave; it's Madness there, the child of Night.
I'm Iris, servant of the gods. No need for fright.
We haven't come to destroy your lovely city.
We war on one; on him we have no pity.
I refer to the son of Zeus, to Heracles,
who was immune until his labors ended. He's
been under the shield of Zeus who wouldn't let
our Hera get the revenge she longed to get.   670
But now his labors are completed and Hera's free
to prod him into killing off his progeny
and labor him with murder, a fine prospect to me.
(to Madness)
Let's go, unmarried Madness, harden your heart,
and madden him, use your nocturnal art
to make his feet insanely dance until
death engulfs his sons in Hera's will.
Let out the sails of murder, speed him on
his passage over river Acheron
which he, with his innocent sons, must navigate,   680
and learn from this the strength of Hera's hate,
and mine, against his kind. The gods will fail
and mortals win if this one can prevail.

MADNESS
I'm noble from my birth; I am no acolyte:
my father is Uranus, my mother is the Night.
And yet my work has made me loathed by all the gods
since I visit only those with whom I am at odds.
But let me give you some advice, and Hera, too.

If you don't want mistakes, I warn you, hear me through.
The man against whose house you'd have me act   690
is famous in heaven and earth: you'll have to face that fact.
He tamed the pathless land and raging sea
and the honor of the gods was saved by none but he
when they had shriveled up confronting evil men.
You're urging something wicked. Think again.

IRIS

Hera and I don't need advice from the likes of you.

MADNESS

I have a better plan than what you'd have me do.

IRIS

Don't try to show us all how sane you are.

MADNESS

Heaven be my witness! I'm pushed to an act I tried to bar.
But since I have to act as you and Hera ask   700
I'll do it like my huntsman's hounds, I'll run to the task,
I'll break in Heracles like the ocean's breaking waves,
he'll feel me like a quake, I'll rave like lightning raves!
I'll smash his roof and then I'll drop into the hole
and make him kill, and while I'm in control
he'll kill not knowing whom he kills, or why.
Look! His head is writhing and his eye
is bulging, and his pupils roll, and now you see
how he heaves like a bull about to charge, how he
bellows, howls up each one of his hell-mates,   710
and groans and shouts to the crazed pipe of the Fates.
So fly to Mount Olympus, Iris, be at ease,
while I sink down into the house of Heracles.
(Iris and Madness vanish, to the music of the flute, playing softly, then
loudly, then with dissonance and a break in
rhythm and pitch. Then the stage is silent.)

CHORUS

> Cry! Cry! Now is time for lament.
> Heracles, true son of Zeus,
> cut down, a disaster for Hellas,
> by frenzied dance, music of Madness
> whose flutes he hears.
>
> Madness ascends in her heavy chariot!   720
> her horses driven with harsh goads;
> a Gorgon, Daughter of Night, her glittering eyes
> and a hundred hissing serpent heads
> unloose lunacy.
>
> Soon, a god comes closer.
> Soon, great change of fortune,
> soon the children die, their lives
> snuffed out by a
> doomed father.
>
> Horror, horror, I look on nothing but horror!
>
> Zeus! this unloosed revenge   730
> ends a line, a termination
> with no mercy, unjust,
> unforgiving, a blood fee
> too severe.
>
> The horror! the house! the horror!
>
> Now, to no sound of cymbals
> a different dance begins.
> But Bacchus has departed.
> No ivy-covered staff
> weaves here.   740
>
> Horror is in the house!

A new vintage spills,
its color blood-red.
No Dionysian wine, no
god-pressed grape, makes
    a flow like this.

Run away! Children—run from this place!

The flutes pipe death,
murder's music. He hunts
his children. The bitch is mad.   750
Her bark leads the pack.
None get away, none,
    when she hunts.

Horror, evil, hell itself, let loose.

Weep for
the old one,
and the mother who
bore these children
    into nothing.

And now witness: 760
a whirlwind shakes
all the house, the roof
shudders, tears off,
    and falls.

AMPHITRYON *(from inside the palace)*
    Ai. Ai. Daughter of Zeus, what are you doing to this house? You
                have turned hellfire loose on this ground, you,
                hurler of stones when giants rebelled, the She-
                Who-Stuns-With-Her-Shield is here: Athena.
(A messenger arrives, stepping outside the palace.)

MESSENGER
    Excellencies, elder statesmen!

CHORUS
    We know who you are. Don't shout at us. We can hear.

MESSENGER
    What's happened inside is the scourge of high heaven.

CHORUS
    We know it all without the gift of prophecy.
    We need no second guessing from a courier.   770

MESSENGER
    The children are dead.

CHORUS
    Ai. Ai.

MESSENGER
    Go on crying. This is hard to say.

CHORUS
    Slaughter.
    Cruel slaughter.
    Slaughter at
        a parent's hand.

MESSENGER
    There are no words for what we've just seen.

CHORUS
    Try. Speak. Tell us how this atrocity occurred,
    this thing we weep for, this atrocious ruin,   780
    father-murdered sons, how did it happen,
    this ruin rushing on this house from heaven:
    How did the children die?
    They were so small.

MESSENGER

All was in holiness: the victims stood in place before the altar of
Zeus. The house had no trace of the death of the
king; Heracles cast his corpse out of doors, and
stood in the sweet circle of children and mother
and grandfather to begin the ritual of cleansing
before the hearth.

Holy, holy, holy, and the basket stuffed with barley, and the knife
swerved—like a nest sounding with small bird-
cries swung around the altar—just so—the
domestic rite before the dinner.

Then Heracles held out his hand to take the torch and dip it in
the water. He stood stock-still. He stood there
rigid. The children stared at this statue until it
thrashed—and came to life again. But the man
was gone now. His eyes were rolling in his head.
The seizure took him. Rivulets of blood sprouted
in the wild eyes—spittle spilled down the
bearded chin—and when speech came he
laughed like a lunatic.

Like Ajax slaughtering the flock of sleep in a manic dream—he
was doubled over with laughter—

"O father," he cried,
"Why should I clean the house with holy fire?   790
There are twin objects of desire:
I'll kill two birds with a single stone—
foolish to take one head alone.
Eurystheus' head is standing still,
empty basket; water spill,
wash our hands at final kill—"

Laughing, hooting, he went on and said, "Give me my bow and
fetch my club, I'm on my way to the Lion Gate,"
and running around the pillars, he went on
to say:

"Fetch me a chisel, a crowbar and pick,
and I'll take down the walls the horse filth built
when they laid them out stone on stone—   800
I'll grind them back to bone on bone."

And then he thought he saw a team just behind the pillar and
               vaulted over its rails riding round the hall,
               flicking the goad over the horses, the coursers
               of his double chariot of dreams. "Just ride," he
               said, "and ride," while our hearts were divided
               between laughter and fear.
One looked at another and said "The lord of the house is playing
               a game again for the children—or has he gone
               mad?"
But he kept running and riding through the great hall of the
               house, driving the wild horses and saying he'd
               come to the port-town where once a man,
               turned to sea-eagle, chased a treacherous child.
               And he thought he was there. He was at home in
               his mind.
Inside, once again he lay on the floor, his hands scrabbling for an
               invisible feast. He took his time there, and then
               he said he had reached the valley where they hold
               the great games: city of the plains, where he
               stripped off his mantle and threw off the buckles
               and wrestled with no one, calling for silence and
               proclaiming Heracles King of the Celery Crown,
               although the contest took place inside
               Heracles' head.
Raging, he returned to Eurystheus and his private war against
               Mycenae and Tiryns. Then his father grasped
               him by the hand, took that powerful hand
               and said:
"O my son. What are you doing and where are you going?
Are you drinking the blood of your prey like wine? You
are drunk with the blood of the victim and maddened by
               drink."

But Heracles saw someone else. Not his father, but Eurystheus,
    Taskmaster, suppliant, cringing and crawling to
    touch his manslaying hand, and he pushed him
    away. He was hunting his own children and he
    thought they were the Whipmaster's, the Wide
    Lord of Life. Unstrung, he unleashed arrows
    against them.   810
They were terrified. They were trembling. They ran here and
    there, the three of them. One slipped himself
    under the skirts of his mother. One slithered
    behind the shadow of a column. The smallest
    skittered away like a sparrow shivering beneath
    the altar, waiting for a great cat to set his paw.
Their mother cried out: "Stop it! You are their father! What are
    you doing? Would you kill your own sons?" The
    old father shouted and all the servants shouted
    out together.
We thought his games of hide-and-seek had gone too far. He
    chased the child round and round the column
    up to the kill. Circling him until he came face to
    face with the boy, who thought the pillar would
    protect him until he moved too quickly. And
    then Heracles caught him, pierced him to the
    heart, and said, "Got you!" The child fell
    backward, and his blood splattered over stone,
    and he died.
Then Heracles exulted and cried out for joy. "Alala alala!"
    he said.
"Alala alala!
Eurystheus hated me,
I hated him more.
Now all his pretty ones
lie dead on the floor.
Alalala."   820
Then he found a second target and picked up his bow. Before he
    could aim, the boy crouched at the foot of the
    altar, small bird in the covey, flew up and sank

to the knees of his father and touched his chin,
plucked at his beard, and cried: "Father! My
father, don't kill me! I am yours, your own child,
and not that man's son, no—!"
But he looked at him with that ferocious gaze; the child, frozen,
turned to stone. Frustrated, but not for long, he
saw he stood too close to stretch the bow, the
weapon that averted evil, once the toy in their
game. So he battered him hard, swung the club
down on the small skull, and smashed the downy
head like a smith striking the hot forge. And so
his second son was gone.
One more victim remained; the ritual almost done. He rushed
around to take him in turn. The mother was
quick, saw him coming, swooped up the child,
and ran with him and slammed the doors and
locked them. But he thought he was crashing the
great walls of Mycenae, and pried them open,
broke down the doors, ripped them from the
hinges, flung them down, and shot the arrow
that took both wife and son.
We thought he'd kill the old father too, in the wild ride. But
She came.
Like a vision: Pallas Athena, crested helmet, and like her statue,
the spear in her hand. She moved and hurled
a rock right at his breast. It stunned him into
sleep and cut short the rage as he slipped to the
floor and fell down next to the fallen column,
shattered in two when the earthquake turned
the roof into ruin.
We were freed from our terror and turned in flight. The old man
helped us leash him fast to the column with
ropes. We were afraid of his wakening and what
might happen then. Now he sleeps, swaddled
tight, on a sea of troubles. A troubled sleep for
this wretched man who killed his wife and slew

his sons. I've never seen anything like the
suffering of this man.

(The messenger withdraws.)

CHORUS
What is there left except to tell old tales?
The murder watched by the rocks of the Argos hills
was proverbial for horror. But the son of Zeus
has just outdone that ancient massacre,   830
that time when the heads of fifty murdered men
were left to lie by the winding road up there,
sons of Aegyptus, killed on their wedding night,
on the orders of the father, by their brides,
    by the daughters of Danaus.
And there was Procne and her only son.
She killed him and then served him as dinner to
her husband, the man who raped her sister. She
was turned into a nightingale, so think of it
as a sacrifice to the Muses, who made it song.   840
But Heracles! You had three sons and in
your frenzy killed them all, profligate parent.

I can't keep reciting the past like this.
What lament, what dirge, what funereal dance
    can I offer up?

Look at the sight we see, and grieve with us!
The double doors that lead from the great hall
    have opened up.

Look! Look! the children lie
near the wretched sleeping man   850
    who is their father,

who sleeps his miserable sleep
asleep after the terror of his waking
    murder of his own.

Cords with many knots bind
Heracles' body; lashed round,
he cannot move but sleeps cradled
in the sling between stone pillars
　　of his own house.

Like a bird mourning nestlings   860
that were too frail to fly,
the old man falters
'toward us, deep in his
　　bitter thought.
(The doors are now wide open and Heracles lies sleeping in a sling of
　　　　ropes hitched between two shattered columns.
　　　　Amphitryon walks out, and he and the chorus
　　　　speak to each other.)

AMPHITRYON
　　Softly, old men, old citizens. Soft. Let him lie deep in sleep. Let
　　　　him slip away from sorrow for a while.

CHORUS
　　I cry, old friend, for you,
　　the children, the royal head,
　　the wreath in the dust.

AMPHITRYON
　　Back away. Back away. Don't make a sound. Don't cry out, don't
　　　　keep him from sleep. Don't disturb his short
　　　　peace.

CHORUS
　　What is this bloodbath? What horror happened here!   870

AMPHITRYON
　　Don't speak, don't make matters worse.

CHORUS
The blood he shed will rise and drown him.

AMPHITRYON
Sing your lament softly, old men, softly. Or Heracles will rise
from his sleep and, stirring awake, will rend his
ropes and destroy this city, kill his father, pull
down his own house.

CHORUS
I'm helpless; I can't stop; I cannot help it.

AMPHITRYON
I'm going to count his breath softly, my ear to his chest.

CHORUS
Does he sleep?

AMPHITRYON
Yes, he's dead asleep. He sleeps like the dead: this man who slew
his wife and children with the deadly hum of his
arrows.

CHORUS
Grieve. We now must grieve.

AMPHITRYON
I grieve.

CHORUS
For the death of children. 880

AMPHITRYON
And I, I—

CHORUS
>   For children, for your own child.

AMPHITRYON
>   I, I—

CHORUS
>   Old comrade—

AMPHITRYON
>   Soft now. Soft. He stirs, he's waking up. Where can I find a dark
>   corner in this house and hide myself?

CHORUS
>   Take heart. Darkness still seals his eyes

AMPHITRYON
>   Look out! Look out! But who am I to be afraid of death after all
>   that has happened?
>   I'm an old scarecrow, ready for the dark, but if he kills me, his
>   father, then he commits the crime of crimes in
>   the sight of the Furies. They hound the trail of
>   a parent's blood and they'll come for him.

CHORUS
>   Better than life now would be
>   to have died when you went,   890
>   after the sack of that northern port
>   to revenge relatives,
>   your wife's dead.

AMPHITRYON
>   Run away. Run away, old men. Run for your lives, leave the
>   palace before he wakes in rage. If not he'll soon
>   double his slaughter, and kill old men too, raving
>   and roaming through the streets of our city:
>   Heracles unleashed.

CHORUS

> Zeus, you hated him, hated him so much,
> set him adrift, your own son, on his
> > sea of sorrow.

HERACLES

> I . . . I . . . I . . . breathe . . . see, see
> heaven, earth, shaft, light, sun. I
> am, eyes now, nothing else.   900
> Vision a swim of surf, the sea I'm in
> surrounds, all here heaves, strange swell,
> heart pounds, chest pumps. I spit the water, air.
> I am. And here. And what is this, this tight
> body, forge and bellows, lashed, like
> a wrecked ship, cables coiled to it,
> columns anchor it to ruin's stones,
> a shattered stonework. This is no ship
> in wreck, though many sailors drowned.
> Corpses surround me, the deck is littered with   910
> debris, arrows, a bow floats on the floor
> of this, a desert of drowned. These were my arms,
> my guards and friends. I took good care of them.
> Where am I now? Where do I live? I think
> I'm back in the underworld, in hell. Did I return
> from the race-course Eurystheus set me on?
> But how could I still be in the house of Hades?
> I don't see Sisyphus, sly thief, sliding his stone
> up slope and it slipping down again. I can't
> see Hades' dark lord rich in corpses or   920
> the scepter of his consort, daughter of
> Demeter, dark queen.
> > > > I'm brushed aside? Lost here?
> Help me. Someone, some friend close by, or friend
> who's far from me, help me, cure me in my
> confusion. Whatever I understood has been
> swept away, and everything here is strange.

AMPHITRYON

> Old ones, should I walk straight into this hellish scene?

CHORUS

> Do so. I'll stay beside you,
> share suffering, share with you
> the hugeness of it.   930

HERACLES

> Father! You're crying. Your face is covered up
> and you stand far from me, your son. I know
> I'm still your son and that you love me still.

AMPHITRYON

> You still are, whatever you have done.

HERACLES

> What have I done to make you weep great tears? What crime?

AMPHITRYON

> Even a god, if he knew of this, would cry great tears—

HERACLES

> Great sorrow then, but what is its great secret?

AMPHITRYON

> See it for yourself; use your eyes if you can see what reason sees.

HERACLES

> Speak. Just speak. If you have something you wish
> to say about this strange turn of events.   930

AMPHITRYON

> I'll talk to you if you can swear you are no longer out of your
>   mind, a stranger spat back from hell—

HERACLES

What? What? What's that disgusting thing you said?

AMPHITRYON

I don't know if you have come to your senses yet. Or if you still
are out of your mind.

HERACLES

Out of my mind? When was I ever out of my mind?

AMPHITRYON

Old friends, what do I do now? Should I loose the ropes binding
my son? What else can I do?

HERACLES

Loose me! Who bound and shamed me in this way?

AMPHITRYON

Know what you must of your trouble and let the rest go.

HERACLES

So I'll be quiet, won't speak. Will that buy answers?

AMPHITRYON

Zeus! Do you see now what Hera has done from Her high throne
and Her long hate?

HERACLES

Is Her long war on me the source of our sorrow?   950

AMPHITRYON

Let it go, the feud with that Goddess, let it go. All this suffering
sits on your own shoulders, all of it.

HERACLES
I'm lost. Tell me the depth of this disaster. Speak.
*(Amphitryon slowly removes the shrouds from the corpses of the
children.)*

AMPHITRYON
Look at this. Look at the bodies of your children. They're dead.

HERACLES
How hideous! What are you showing me?
*(Still rubbing his arms after the removal of the ropes, he staggers back
and falls on his knees. Amphitryon has removed
the shrouds from the corpses of his children.)*

AMPHITRYON
You, my son, made war on your own sons. Nature forbids this.

HERACLES
What war are you talking of? Who killed my boys?

AMPHITRYON
It was you, and some god, and the bow you carry.

HERACLES
What did you say that I have done?
Horror, my father, are you horror's herald?

AMPHITRYON
You were mad. The answers to your questions could only be
horrible.   960

HERACLES
My wife, did I kill her? Did I? Her, too?

AMPHITRYON
Everything here is the work of your own hand. This is your
house.

HERACLES

    How terrible. This sight. How terrible.

    What storm, black cloud, what grief surrounds me,

    I am surrounded, stranded, by a distant sea.

AMPHITRYON

    Look at this. Look at me. I'm crying. Over your fate and what it

        brought on us.

HERACLES

    When I went mad, did I run wild through the house?

AMPHITRYON

    I know one thing only; this is the demise of your house, and you.

HERACLES

    Whose sting drove me mad and where did I succumb?

AMPHITRYON

    You were standing at the altar and cleansing yourself with fire.   970

HERACLES

    Why? Why? Why can't I die when I took life

    from my own children?

                     There are three roads from this place.

    I could be their avenger and leap off

    a cliff. Or plunge a sword into my side.

    Or set myself on fire since fire will burn

    madness away, the madness sticking to my skin

    like a flaming shirt, to the self which was sick and mad.

(Heracles looks away and sees Theseus coming.)

    Theseus comes, he comes as cousin and friend

    to stop me on the road I'll take to death.

    He must not see me. He's my dearest friend.   980

    And I am what I am, unclean, a murderer

of my own sons, a godforsaken man.
What can I do? Where can I hide
from all my crimes? If I had wings I'd fly
down, to the far recesses of the earth.
I'll cover up my head in darkness in
deep shame for every horror I brought on.
I'll spare him from the harm that the sight of me,
taboo, would inflict on innocence.
I'll hide. To look on me is to breathe contagion.   990
(Theseus enters. His men trail behind at a distance.)

THESEUS *(addressing Amphitryon)*
    I've come, old man, and brought my warriors,
    I've raised an army to assist your son.
    Athens is here, quick to its ally's cause.
    My men wait at your city's frontier,
    camping on the river's muddy banks.
    In the city of Athena and the Earth-born
    we heard a rumor, that the wolf lord seized your throne,
    made war on you and yours. And so I came
    for Heracles, because of what he did for me,
    bringing me back from the lower world.   1000
    I'm here, old father, I and my men,
    to help you in whatever way I can.
(He sees the bodies of the children.)
    What are these? This, this, and this. All heaped
    together on the ground. A violent crime
    preceded me. Have I arrived too late? Who killed
    these children? Children don't go to war.
    I can't make out that woman's face, who's she? What's here
    is something hideous, which waits to be revealed.

AMPHITRYON
    Lord of the citadel, where the holy olive grows—

THESEUS
    What is this hymn of grief that you're reciting?   1010

AMPHITRYON

> We speak from the grief which the gods sent us to endure—

THESEUS

> Who are these children? Why do you cry for them?

AMPHITRYON *(stammering)*

> My son, may the gods preserve us, my son begat them, and then
>> he ungot them, he killed them, his own sons,
>> ungot them.

THESEUS

> Speak, but speak more clearly, not like this.

AMPHITRYON

> I'll try. It's impossible.

THESEUS

> You speak of horrors, you speak horror.

AMPHITRYON

> We've lost, we are lost, everything has gone, is smoke and ruin.

THESEUS

> Tell me what happened, how, what did he do?

AMPHITRYON

> He ran amok, raving, he rained his arrows on them, the darts
>> dipped in the blood of the trophy, the beast with
>> a hundred heads, his Hydra.

THESEUS

> This was Hera's war against him and his own.   1020
> What a contest! But, dear heart, who is
> that living man who lies among the dead?

AMPHITRYON

> That is my son, mine, that man over there broken by hard fate.
> > There was a time when his spear slew Titans in
> > the great war where the gods battled with giants,
> > in the field where volcanos left their trace of fire,
> > lava and hot ash.

THESEUS

> Was ever a man, ever, in such misery?

AMPHITRYON

> You couldn't find one, however far you sought him, who was
> > smothered by greater suffering. My son was more
> > hard driven than Odysseus himself.

THESEUS

> Why does he cover his up his face with robes, poor soul?

AMPHITRYON

> He's afraid to meet your eye. Murderer of his kin, killer of his
> > own children, he's afraid of your kind good-will,
> > your kindred spirit.

THESEUS

> I came to share his suffering. Uncover him.

AMPHITRYON *(crouching on the ground next to Heracles)*

> My son, cast off the mantle which covers your eyes, and throw it
> > down before you, and show your face to the sun.
> > On my knees, let me wrestle you to the other side
> > of sorrow, supplicating, crying, begging, hanging
> > on you, on your neck, your knees, your hands,
> > tugging at your face. Sorrows are lessened when
> > the match is on a level ground.
> > Child, you have the spirit of a lion when you're in a rage. Tame it;
> > don't roar like a beast. Subdue it, it enslaves you

to the taste of savage death, to suffering grief on
grief, my son.   1030

THESEUS

I call on you, hooded in misery,
pull off that hood, lift up your head, take off
your veil and show your face to friends. No cloud,
however black, is dark enough to hide
such sorrow. Nothing can hide you. Don't wave me away.
Your hands signal their stain of murder's blood.
Why are you doing this? Are you afraid
that you'll defile me if I talk to you?
I'll share in your misfortune. Nothing wrong with that.
There was a time when knowing you was everything.   1040
Should I forget how you went down to darkness
for my sake, and hauled me safe to daylight?
What is more hateful than a friend grown stale
in gratitude, a friend whose friendship thrives
only in our prosperity but won't
set sail with us on a voyage that is lost
knowing we're fortune's outcast, when our luck
forsakes? Get up, my friend, unveil your face
and in your sorrow look at me, your friend.
The high-born must endure what heaven sends   1050
and never turn away. They face their fate.
(*Theseus raises Heracles to his feet and removes the covering from
his head.*)

HERACLES

Theseus, did you see my glorious contest with my children?

THESEUS

I heard and see the evidence of horrors.

HERACLES

Then why expose my head to the light of the sun?

THESEUS
What's this? No mortal can sully what the gods have given.

HERACLES
Dear fool, flee from the taint I carry with me.

THESEUS
Your tainted spirit can't defile a friend.

HERACLES
I thank you. I am glad I labored for your sake.

THESEUS
And now I pity you, who saved me then.

HERACLES
A man who kills his children is pitiful.   1060

THESEUS
I'm grateful to you still, and weep at your affliction.

HERACLES
Is there a man as afflicted as I am?

THESEUS
Your sorrow storms heaven in its wretchedness.

HERACLES
Let heaven know I'm set on death. I refuse to live.

THESEUS
Is this revenge? Does heaven care what you do?

HERACLES
Heaven is heartless, and I'm its true-born son.

THESEUS

    Stop. These wild words will bring more pain.

HERACLES

    The hold is crammed with cargo, and it's full;
    there isn't room to store more suffering.

THESEUS

    What now? Where does your wildness drive you now?   1070

HERACLES

    To die, and go back where I came. Under the earth.

THESEUS

    Such talk is commonplace, not fit for a hero.

HERACLES

    You talk like a man who's never known suffering.

THESEUS

    Am I talking to the Heracles who endured so much?

HERACLES

    So much, not this. I am beyond enduring.

THESEUS

    You were a good man, and the good man's friend,
                      you did so much that's good.

HERACLES

    What good are men to me? It's Hera's world.

THESEUS

    A banality for a man like you. A cheap despair.
    Greece won't permit this death. Find another platitude.

HERACLES

My friend, I can play this game as well as you,   1080
but let me answer your excellent advice
and hear me out. Hear a few stories from
the great scroll of my life. It never was
worth living, not then, not now. Look at my father there.
He killed my mother's father. What kind of man
would marry his victim's daughter, who
gave birth to me. A good beginning for the house.
With so much blood smeared on the cornerstone
who wouldn't think, "that house will inherit grief."

And Zeus, great Zeus,   1090
whatever you were and are and shall become,
thank you, thank you for begetting me
and thanks for granting Hera reason for
hating Heracles. How elegant these immortals be.
Don't be offended, Amphitryon, for I
consider you, not Zeus, to be my father.

What next? When I was still in swaddling clothes,
sucking milk from my mother's breast, the sweet thought came
to Hera to set serpents on me, and their eyes
glanced fire like gorgon's eyes as they   1100
crawled through the cradle of her bedmate's child
to murder him. I was that infant. I
strangled them, and grew. I grew up strong.
A muscular young man, the savior of
the civilized, and their prizefighter, too.

Do you need to hear the list of my labors? No?
I took the monsters on, I fought my wars.
Remember Typhon? He's not in the list
of my legendary labors, too exotic for
us Greeks, with his hundred heads and the foulness of   1110
three bodies. He was the spawn of an old fight

between the Gods and the giants, and I killed him.
Some say he was grandfather of the lion I killed.
I killed the lion and Typhon, killed them all,
and hordes of filthy horse-men, and I killed
the Hydra, the houndlike thing whose snakes
coiled and sprang back as soon as I cut them off.
And when I was done with these and with the swarm
of other labors, sweeping the earth of unclean things,
I went down to the sewers of the dead to fetch   1120
up to the light, on orders of Eurystheus,
the triple-headed dog who guards the gates of hell.

And now I'm finished. The worst labor was the last,
the murder of my sons. I've built my house,
my slaughterhouse, and as my final act
I set the coping stone on my great work.

I can't remain with those who are dear to me.
If I stay on in Thebes, what temple's ground
will welcome me, what gathering of friends
will take me in? The writing on my face   1130
spells ruin, repelling those who come too close.
To Argos? To a place I'm banished from?
Some other city, then. I see it now,
how I'll take flight to somewhere, and they will keep
a scornful eye on me, and everyone
will know me for what I am, flay me with words
and ask with a sneer, "Is this the son of Zeus,
the man who killed his wife and children?
He belongs in hell, not here. Godspeed him home."

I've come to the end of what I can endure.   1140
The earth itself will break its sacred silence
and from its depths will cry against my trespass on
the ground. Rivers and oceans will roar against
my crossing and forbid my passage. I,

like Ixion, another killer of kinsmen, will
turn and turn in chains forever on
the wheel of sorrow. Best for me to go,
to go away from shining Hellas where
I was rich and shone with greatness too.

Why should I go on living? What's the gain   1150
for an unclean and useless man like me?
On with the dance, Madame Zeus, go tap
your golden sandals on the floor of heaven!
She's had her heart's desire, she has cast down
a hero as true as Hellas ever had
and plunged him into the abyss. Who can
say prayers to gods like Her? Great Zeus preferred
a human woman to Her Majesty
and this was reason to destroy
the greatest friend Greece ever had, though he   1160
was blameless in all eyes but Hers.

CHORUS
    Yes. You comprehend. Her hate did this.
    No other god's at work in this disaster.

THESEUS
    I have only the dust of ancient answers.
    You must live on and suffer. None alive
    escape misfortune. No, not even gods
    unless our poets lie when they pick up the lyre.
    The gods commit incest, adultery,
    and get away with murder. They overthrow
    their cannibal fathers and gobble them in turn.   1170
    Their crimes are legend, but they breathe
    the rarified air of Mount Olympus
    and have some talent for living things down.
    What can a mortal say if he
    wishes to protest his fate to them?
    The gods on high have no cause for complaint.

Abide the law. Leave Thebes and follow me
to be an exile in Athena's city.
There, when I have scoured your hands of homicide,
I'll give you shelter and share what I have.   1180
All my abundance will be yours. I have
the gifts of citizens whose boys and girls
I saved from sacrifice to the Cretan Minotaur.
All over Attica are consecrated lands
held in reserve for me, and now they're yours.
Whatever belongs to Theseus belongs
to Heracles. And when you die at last
and vanish underground, then Athens will
establish monuments, and sacrifice,
to honor you. And this will be the crown   1190
of the noble story of great Heracles.
You saved me once, and now you need a friend.

CHORUS

Only those on whom gods dote don't need friends;
when gods help we cope without help of friends.

HERACLES

What's your theology to a wretch like me?
I don't believe the gods are adulterers.
I don't believe in gods in chains
fettered for the sake of petty rivalries.
That always seemed incredible to me.
I don't believe one god can dominate another.   1200
If the gods exist they must be godlike, perfect:
your versions are some poet's foul confection.

But still, I wonder, wretched as I am,
if the step into the dark is a coward's step.
When face to face in battle the man who can't
bear suffering cannot be valiant.
I'll soldier on. I will go on with life.
I'll go to Athens, and be thankful for your gifts.
(Heracles weeps.)

My labors were uncountable. And I
never turned away from one. I've never wept.   1210
Who could have thought I would dissolve like this.
I never thought that I'd be shedding tears,
but now my master is necessity. And I know Her name.

So be it. Father, I am going away
as you can see, and in me you can see
the butcher of my children. Bury them,
and when you do, be generous with the tears
I'm not allowed to shed. Lay them on their
mother's breast, and wrap them in her arms.
Make it the way it was, a sad reunion.   1220
The way they were before I—it was me!—
blundered to the kill, and killed them all.
And, when the earth has covered their small remains,
live on! However bitter life is, stay alive!
Stay here and share the pain of my misfortune.

Children, children, your father gave you life
and took it back again. You never mined
a fleck of gold from all my laboring,
the legacy of fame I labored for
which was for you. And you, poor wife,   1230
I killed you in return for your fidelity,
for your safekeeping of my house and bed.

Wretched wife, wretched children and the wretch
himself, named Heracles! I leave you now
in misery. I cannot bear the pain
of kisses, or the tug of this last embrace.
(He picks up his bow and arrows.)
You weapons, bitter partners, you whom I
have coupled with and carried all my life,
I don't know what to do, should I keep you
or cast you off? You'll clatter at my side   1240

and always say: "You wore us when you killed
your children and your wife, so put us on
and wear their deaths forever." Can I bear
these things? But if I'm stripped of them
how can I answer with no company of arms?
All through my days in Hellas I'd be helpless,
the shameful prey of foes. A former hero.
I'll carry them, though they're as heavy as my pain.

Give me your hand, Theseus, in one thing more.
I must lug a dog to Argos, though it seems   1250
the creature is much heavier now.
If I travel without a burden and alone
the weight of my lost sons will pull me down to death.

Country of Cadmus! people of Thebes! begin
the mourning and the shearing off of hair,
and grieve with me and walk in the long train
to my children's tomb. One funeral song will do
for all of us. The dead who are here, and me.
We died together when Hera ruled our fate.

THESEUS

    Get up, unhappy man. These tears are flooding us.   1260

HERACLES

    I can't get up. I'm rooted in this place.

THESEUS

    The strong are overthrown by fortune's overturn!

HERACLES

    I'd like to be a stone in this stony place
    indifferent to everything. Inanimate.

THESEUS

Stop; dry your eyes, give your hand to the friend who's
   helping you.

HERACLES

Be careful. I don't want to stain your robes with blood.

THESEUS

Be careless. Bloody them; it doesn't worry me.

HERACLES

My sons are dead; you are my son, and all I have.

THESEUS

Lean on my shoulder and I'll carry you on.

HERACLES

Love yokes us two, but one of us is a man   1270
who has had grief inscribed all over him.
(turning to Amphitryon)
Father, when you choose friends, choose one like this.

AMPHITRYON

The land is blessed that breeds such noble men and native sons.

HERACLES

Theseus, turn round once more. I want to see my sons.

THESEUS

Do not look back. What for? Do you want a drug
to drive your grief away? There's no relief.

HERACLES

I have to wrap my father in my arms once more.

AMPHITRYON

I'm here. And all that matters is what you want.

THESEUS

You are in tears. Don't you recall your long
calendar of labors in which no tear was shed?   1280

HERACLES

Those were no labor in comparison with this.

THESEUS

You won't crown them by acting the woman now.

HERACLES

I'm alive. I go on living. There was once a time
you never thought you'd see me sunk this low.

THESEUS

Is there some room in all of this despair
for Heracles the Great, the Savior of the Earth?

HERACLES

And you, my Theseus, I suppose you were
some kind of hero in the underworld.

THESEUS

Oh, I was the king of cowards when I was there.
A hero afraid at all times of the dark.   1290

HERACLES

Then why tell me that I'm diminished by my grief.

THESEUS

Go forward. Let's move on. I'm telling you to move.

HERACLES

Old man, old father, now it is good-bye.

AMPHITRYON

Good-bye, my son.

HERACLES
>Bury my children as I begged you to.

AMPHITRYON
>And who, my son, will come to bury me?

HERACLES
>I will.

AMPHITRYON
>When will you come?

HERACLES
>When your turn comes, my father, I'll bury you.

AMPHITRYON
>How? You're now a citizen of another town.   1300

HERACLES
>I'll send. You'll come from Thebes to Athens.
>For now, take my children out, and send them down
>with all the weight of grief they carry into the earth.
>And I, who brought my whole house to its ruin,
>towed in his wake like some small battered barge,
>will follow Theseus. Some men say money is
>the best, and some say power, but the soul is sick
>if it does not prefer the love of friends.

CHORUS
>We go, and go in grief.
>Thebes, downcast, is at an end.   1310
>*(Theseus and Heracles leave the stage by the left. The chorus goes to the*
>   *right. Amphitryon follows the procession with the*
>   *bodies of Megara and the children.)*

Iphigenia in Tauris

Translated by
Carolyn Kizer

The reputation of Euripides has had more ups and downs than that of the other two members of the Big Three, Sophocles and Aeschylus. The accusation that, unlike them, his plays were "impure" because they deviated from the classical standard continued to dog him even as late as the late eighteenth century. More than 2000 years after the death of Euripides, A. W. Schlegel said that Euripides hardly existed as a major figure except in comparison with Racine!

Euripides realized that times were changing; the diction in his plays approached the language of ordinary people. That upset the purists, but Euripides knew audiences were beginning to lack the training in prosody that had enabled them to enjoy the standards of ideal tragedy. It seems likely that his use of a more vernacular speech is something that appealed to his admirer Dante.

Above all, Euripides was concerned with close analysis of character: people as flawed humans rather than ideal types. These types or archetypes had served an important purpose: to individualize characters lessened their traditional value to Greeks, who considered themselves descended from gods and heroes.

Both Iphigenia and her brother Orestes are flawed because of their terrible pasts. They brood on their wrongs with obsessive passion. They are spoiled, having been raised as Princess and Prince without undergoing the seasoning of common life, as have the women of the chorus. This is reflected in Iphigenia's peremptoriness in her treatment of the Herdsman ("What were cowherds doing down by the sea?") and her paying scant heed to the laments of her handmaidens until, near the end of the play, she realizes that her safety and that of her brother depend on their loyal silence. This creates a wonderful moment of drama when, after her indifference, she throws herself on their mercy.

It would take a very great actress indeed—someone like Vanessa Redgrave (who would also be superb doubling in the role of the goddess

Athena, ablaze in golden light)—to make us feel that Iphigenia, who is very real, is a sympathetic character, unlike the idealized heroines of the past. As for Orestes, he is preoccupied with the wrongs done him, but shows singularly little remorse for having murdered his mother. Self-pity leaves little room for self-blame. In regarding these characters it is perhaps best to think of them as partly crazy. Pylades and King Thoas are the only rational people in the play. Pylades, Orestes' closest friend and companion in his wanderings, is difficult to portray without having him seem like a straight man. There is also the problem of long stretches of the play in which Pylades is silent. Rather than have him just stand there like Al Gore, I would suggest that he go over to the Chorus, Iphigenia's handmaidens, and be inaudibly sympathetic, leaving center stage to the sister and brother. I longed to make the Herdsman a comic character as in Shakespeare, but I found this impossible to do without spoiling the language of Orestes he quotes. A great comedian, however, might be able to bring this off.

As is probably plain by now, I have been thinking, throughout this version, of how to stage it. Nearly all the translations of this play treat it as an academic exercise rather than as living drama. Any liberties I have taken are to serve the latter end. For example, I have shortened Iphigenia's prologue, and limited her long account of her genealogy to figures with whom the audience has at least some familiarity. (I confess I am haunted by the account of the original libretto of *Idomeneo*, by Abbe Varesco, containing endless arias that would have succeeded in making Mozart boring for the only time in his life had he not cut them.) There are also a few speeches of Pylades (in italics) that I have plucked from the mouth of Orestes; these seem more natural coming from Pylades, and give him more interaction with the other two.

Euripides is a supreme ironist. The long scene in which Iphigenia interrogates Orestes before she realizes that he is her brother is heavy with the ironic responses of Orestes. In response to her query about Pylades, he says, "Does that make you happy?" When she begs him to tell her one more thing, Orestes, who expects to die shortly, says, "Why not? I have the time." Later, when he tells her that Clytemnestra was killed by her son, Iphigenia exclaims that this was horrible, but just. Orestes, thinking of his pursuit by the Furies, replies, "The gods have failed to recognize his justice." There are examples of ironic action in this play, such as the conventional drawn-out recognition scene when Orestes inquires whether Iphigenia has come back from the dead, and she tells him not to interrupt! And there is Euripides' portrayal of Thoas, "the barbarian," who seems more civilized than the protagonists.

My belief is that, in bringing on Athena as the *dea ex machina*, Euripides is saying, "There is really no reason for this miraculous intervention of the goddess. Poseidon has already calmed the waters, and Orestes and Iphigenia can sail out of the harbor and go home. But I know you people expect it, and so (sigh) here it is." There are periods in history when neither realism nor irony is appreciated. Revolutionaries and romantics alike reject them — or, perhaps I should say, would-be Romantics and Revolutionaries. The real revolutionary romantics, like Dante and Goethe, understood Euripides, and loved him.

Cast

IPHIGENIA, daughter of Agamemnon and Clytemnestra
ORESTES, Iphigenia's brother
PYLADES, Orestes' friend
CHORUS of Iphigenia's women
THOAS, king of the Taurians
MESSENGER
ATHENA, goddess of wisdom, crafts, and war, patroness
    of Athens
VOICE OF EURIPIDES
NONSPEAKING
    Temple guards
    Attendants to Thoas

*(The temple of Artemis in the land of the Taurians. There is a
blood-stained altar in front of the temple. By convention, stage
right leads to the country and the sea; stage left leads to and from
the town. These are the only entrances and exits, except for the
single temple door, approached by a wide flight of steps. Before
the door, Iphigenia enters to speak the prologue.)*

IPHIGENIA
    I am Iphigenia, daughter of Agamemnon.
    Clytemnestra is my mother.
    Yes, I am that same Iphigenia
    my father sacrificed to Artemis
    to comfort his brother, Menelaus,
    whose wife, Helen, was stolen by the Trojans.
    But Agamemnon's enormous fleet—1000 ships—
    was trapped in port by a series of terrible storms,
    and both sea and wind opposed Agamemnon.
    My father consulted Calchas, a seer devoted   10
    to blood sacrifice, who told him the only way

to free his ships to war on Troy
was to honor a vow made to Artemis long ago:
he must sacrifice the most beautiful child
born in that year. I was the child.
And I must die so the great fleet might sail.

The wily Odysseus invented the lie
that I must come to Aulis to be Achilles' bride.
Achilles!—the most eligible man alive.
And so I came, decked in my bridal finery,   20
radiant with expectation.
At that moment they seized me
and held me above the altar.
But just as the dagger struck
Artemis saved me!
and left a plump doe in my place.

Then Artemis carried me through the bright air
to this barbarous country
ruled by Thoas, its barbarous king,
so swift of foot he could run like a wild horse.   30
I was made priest of the temple of Artemis.
I preside here, over unspeakable rites:
Any Greek unlucky enough
to set foot on this shore is sacrificed.
My task is to consecrate the victim,
but I am spared his slaughter,
which is performed by those inside the shrine.

Last night I had such terrible dreams!
It may give me some relief
if I speak them to the sky: 40
I dreamed I was at home in Argos
in my childhood room
when a violent earthquake heaved me from my bed.
As the cornice of the house collapsed

I fled outside.
Only a single pillar was left standing.
Its capital sprouted long blond hair; it spoke
with a human voice!
I sprinkled it with tears and sacred waters
as is my duty to the dead.   50
It pains me to more tears as I am forced
to interpret the dream like this:
The lonely pillar represents Orestes,
my brother, last of our line.
Male children are the pillars of the house.
The dead are those on whom I sprinkle water.
I must give my brother what last rites I can,
being so far from home.
My handmaids will assist me.
Where can they have gone?   60
I will wait for them inside the temple.
(Iphigenia exits. Enter Orestes and Pylades.)

ORESTES

Watch out! There may be someone coming.

PYLADES

I've been looking everywhere.

ORESTES

Pylades, do you think this can be the temple
of Artemis?—the one we were sent to look for when
we sailed from Argos?

PYLADES

It looks like it, Orestes.

ORESTES

Horrors! See the altar
dripping with Greek blood.

PYLADES

Those have to be bloodstains.   70

ORESTES

And do you see the spoils—armor and shields
and skulls—hung from the beams?

PYLADES

Yes, the trophies of strangers who have died.

ORESTES

Phoebus, have you led me into a trap?
Must I see blood again? I've seen enough of blood!
I did as the God commanded: murdered my mother
to avenge my father. Furies with bloody eyes
drove me from my country, relentlessly pursued me.
I came to you and begged you, Phoebus, to relieve me
from these bouts of insanity and pain, to spare me   80
my endless hopeless wanderings. You sent me here
to discover the altar of Artemis, told me to seize
the image of the goddess which fell from the sky,
and take it to Athens. It was you who persuaded me
to risk everything, to come to this perilous place,
that someday I might find peace. So here I stand.
Pylades, advise me. What should we do? Look how high
the walls are! How could we climb them? We're sure
to be seen. If we had tools to pry open the bolts
and force our entrance! But we'd be caught and killed.   90
We know nothing about these people. Let's go back
to our ship.

PYLADES

No, no, we can't run away! We can't disgrace
ourselves before the oracle. Let's leave the temple
and hide among the caves on the shore.
We'll wait till nightfall, then come back
and steal the statue.

Look up! There's a space between the beams
where we might creep in. Cowardice will get us nowhere.
The harder the quest the greater the glory!   100
We haven't come this far only to turn around
and row back home.

ORESTES

I hear you, Pylades, I should have said those words.
Let's go and find a cavern we can hide in.
The God will take care of us. He won't want to see
the task he set us end in futility.
(They exit. Enter the Chorus and Iphigenia.)

CHORUS

Silence, we should keep silence, we
who live past the Clashing Rocks
beside the Unfriendly Sea.
We come to your garden, Artemis,   110
to the golden walls of your temple.
We, like Iphigenia,
exiled far from Greece,
lost to her walls and towers,
her forest-lands and fields.
We are far from Sparta's river,
far from its cool waters
where our horses cropped the grasses
outside the city wall;
the benches where our fathers   120
enjoyed the meadow flowers.

CHORUS LEADER

Iphigenia, tragic daughter
of the lord who led the fleet:
its thousand ships, ten thousand men
in armor, to the towers of Troy—
why have you sent for us?

IPHIGENIA

    Oh pity me, my women!
    Hear what I learned in a dream:
    I have lost my only brother.
    Alas, alas for the sorrows of Argos!   130
    The house of my fathers is no more.
    Our race is banished forever
    and my brother sent to hell.

    I must sprinkle the death-libations
    here on the stony earth:
    milk of the mountain cattle,
    the shining wine of Bacchus,
    the taste of tawny honey.
    Give me the golden bowl.
    I offer this to Death.   140

    Orestes, beloved brother
    now numbered with the dead,
    accept these holy gifts.
    I'm unable to leave a lock
    of my golden hair on your tomb;
    I can't weep on your grave
    which lies so far from here.
    There they believe me murdered,
    there they believe I'm buried.
    But I'm exiled far from home.   150

CHORUS

    We will sing you a lament
    echoing to the sky
    to answer your song, O Queen.
    We wail in an Asian mode,
    a wild, barbaric cry,
    a litany of grief
    to mourn the perished ones—

our dead, as well as yours
caught in the breath of Hell,
no triumph in their hymns.   160

The house of Atreus
once gloried in its kings.
Now all the kings are fallen,
their gleaming scepters too.
Murder is heaped on murder,
and woe gives birth to woe.

The Sun, flung from his chariot,
turns his face away, and then
he who once rose in the west
has reversed his shining course   170
and rises now in the east.
The famous golden lamb,
that symbol of mighty kings,
was a curse on fathers and sons,
the line of your brilliant house.
Now only vengeance echoes
between the empty walls.
Since no heirs remain,
the ugly zeal of the Fates
is visited on your head,   180
Iphigenia.

IPHIGENIA
Misfortune has been my fortune
since the time I was conceived
on my mother's bridal night,
she who was Leda's daughter,
the wretched Clytemnestra.
I was schooled by a hard fate.
Then later I was sent
by chariot to Aulis

to marry the mighty Achilles.   190
But it was all a hoax!
So now I am here, unfriended
beside the Unfriendly Sea,
without husband, child or city.
So I can't dance for Hera,
surrounded by lovely songs,
or work the designs on my loom
of Titans or Pallas Athena.
I must face this blood-soaked altar,
I must listen to dreadful music: 200
the moans of terrified strangers,
their unheeded lamentations,
the silence of their tears
as they prepare to die.
But now the tears are shed
for Greece, and my fallen brother.
O Orestes, I saw you last
when you were a little child
clasped to my mother's breast,
the royal prince of Greece!   210

CHORUS
   We see a herdsman, Iphigenia,
   who is approaching us with news.
(Herdsman enters.)

HERDSMAN
   Daughter of Agamemnon,
   I have something strange to report.

IPHIGENIA
   Why are you so excited?

HERDSMAN
   A foreign ship has landed.
   It sailed through the Clashing Rocks

Two young men were on board.
They'll make a splendid sacrifice!
Artemis will be happy.   220
So get the barley ready
and bring out the holy water!

IPHIGENIA
Do you know where they come from?

HERDSMAN
They're Greeks. That's all I know.

IPHIGENIA
Did you hear either of their names?

HERDSMAN
One called the other one Pylades.

IPHIGENIA
So tell me how you found them,
and then how you captured them.

HERDSMAN
We had gone right down to the seashore . . .

IPHIGENIA
What were cowherds doing down by the sea?   230

HERDSMAN
Why, to wash our cows in salt water.

IPHIGENIA
Now tell us the whole story,
all the details, if you please.
This altar has waited a long time
to be drenched in Hellene blood.

HERDSMAN

We were driving our cattle down
from the forest to the shore
near a cave that was hollowed out
by the pounding surf of the sea.
One of our herdsmen saw   240
a pair of godlike men,
and came tip-toeing back to us:
"There are couple of gods in the cave!"
One of us—he was religious—
peeked in on them and prayed,
"Lord of the sea, our savior,
be gracious unto us."
But another, an unbeliever,
laughed at his prayers and said,
"They're only shipwrecked sailors   250
who hide in the cavern because
they've heard of our nasty custom
of sacrificing strangers."
We thought he was right. We decided
to capture them for the gods.

Just then, one of the strangers
came screaming out of the cave.
He trembled from head to foot
in a fit of craziness.
He cried, "Pylades, do you see her?   260
That viper from Hell come to kill me?
There's another one, wrapped in flame,
flapping her wings of slaughter.
She carries my murdered mother,
my mother, turned to stone,
to hurl at me and kill me!
Where shall I run? I can't see!"
There was nothing to be seen,
just the sounds of our dogs and cows.

He thought they were sent by the fiends!   270
We cowered in silence—but then
he rushed among our animals
brandishing his sword
and began to stab our cattle!
He believed he beat back the Furies,
and the sea bloomed with bright blood.
When we saw him killing our livelihood
we blew on our horns to call
our neighbors to come help us.
We knew we were too puny   280
to beat those tall strong men.
A lot of folks came running,
but the young man's fit was over.
He collapsed onto the ground;
foam ran down his chin.
So we began to stone him.
His comrade wiped his face
and held up his heavy cloak
to ward off our hail of stones.

The first man, now recovered,   290
saw the circle of enemies
drawing ever closer.
Then we heard his battle-cry:
"Pylades, we shall die!
So let us die like heroes!"
We saw them brandish their swords,
and most of us ran away,
but others kept attacking;
and the first who had run came back
to throw more stones. But here   300
was a miracle! None of the stones
we had flung at them struck home!
They were unblemished victims
to sacrifice to the goddess.

At last they grew so tired
they sank to their knees, and then
we knocked the swords from their hands
and carried them to the king,
who will send them for purification,
and then for sacrifice.   310
So, Iphigenia
you'll have your revenge on Aulis,
Aulis, that tried to kill you.

CHORUS

What a wild tale! Who is this madman who comes
from Hellas to our Unfriendly Sea?

IPHIGENIA

That's enough. Go bring the strangers here,
while I prepare for the sacrifice.
Oh once, poor heart, I was compassionate.
Once I wept for strangers who fell into my hands.
But now my dreams have made me brutal;   320
they tell me plainly
I have lost my brother. Orestes
will not see another day. Now my heart is stone.
Whoever comes will find a cruel woman,
a woman without a tear.
(She speaks to the chorus.)
Friends, I find that old saying true:
those who are unfortunate will show no mercy
to those who are more unfortunate.

No breeze arrived from Zeus, no ship came through
the Clashing Rocks to bring me Helen or Menelaus   330
who ruined me—so that I might pay them back.
Menelaus, Agamemnon, those brothers who would kill me—
my own father playing priest!
When he lifted me to the altar how I clung to him!
How I clutched his knees and cried,

"Father! Shame! I came here to marry, not to die.
You lured me here in your chariot to this bloody bridal.
Treachery! Right now, Mother and her maidens chant
marriage hymns that echo through our house
as you prepare to kill me.   340
Flutes play, as I am dying at your hands.
My groom is not the son of Peleus, but Hell.
I am the bride of Death."

When I was sent for, in my bridal clothes,
I wore a veil like gossamer, and hid my blushing face.
So I did not embrace my brother,
who, I believe, is dead now. I did not kiss my sister.
I prepared to meet my groom, Achilles.
I would see them all again one day soon
So I saved up all my kisses for my return.   350
Orestes, if you are dead, what a heritage is lost!
The power and pride of kingly generations.

As for Artemis, subtle hypocrite! She condemns any mortal
whose hands are stained with blood, any woman
who just gave birth, and every corpse. They are unclean!
She bans them from her altars.
Yet she seems to enjoy sacrificial murder. I don't believe
that her mother, Leto, the wife of Zeus,
could give birth to a creature so depraved.
And I don't believe in that tale of Tantalus   360
who served the gods a feast of his own flesh and blood—
his son! No, I am sure that the people of this country,
murderers all, blame their own crimes on the gods.
I don't believe that any god is evil.
(Iphigenia exits.)

CHORUS
Dark, dark cliffs, where two seas meet,
gateway from Europe to the land of Asia;
who are these travelers who survived the sea?

Do they come from Sparta's gleaming river,
green with rushes,
or from the holy stream of Thebes?   370
What are they doing in this sullen land?
There is no safety here
where the altar of Artemis, daughter of Zeus
is stained with the blood of strangers.

With pinewood oars
that flung the surf to either side,
a breeze that sang through the tackle,
their ship raced before the wind.
Did these men really hope
to fill their boats with treasure?   380
Winsome hope leads men to ruin.
No matter how much they possess
they still lust for more.
They wander on dangerous seas
and pass through alien cities,
vainly pursuing wealth
while others have riches thrust at them.

How do they manage to steer
between the Clashing Rocks
beyond, the capes of Phineas,   390
then coasting near the beach
to where the fifty daughters
of Nereus circle and sing?
They rush before the winds
that blow from South and West;
the sails strain, the rudder creaks
as they pass by that bird-haunted beach
to the long white shore, the track
where Achilles trained to race.
Still his ghost-feet skim the sand   400
beside the hostile sea.

If only the prayers of Iphigenia
could bring Helen here from Troy
to have her throat cut,
Leda's darling daughter!
If Iphigenia could kill her,
those blond curls soaked in blood,
that would settle the score.

But how full of joy we'd be
if a ship brought news from Greece   410
that would free us from our slavery;
not only from this place
but free of the deadly cycle
of killing and revenge.
Now all we can do is dream
of the city of our fathers,
that someday we might return
to sing in unison
with the women who stayed at home,
healed of our bitterness,   420
to embrace a world at peace.

CHORUS LEADER
     Look! Here they come,
     those two men, roped together,
     new victims for the goddess.
     Silence, my friends! The herdsman spoke the truth.
     These men, the pride of Greece,
     approach the temple. O Goddess,
     if the rites of these barbarians give you pleasure,
     accept this sacrifice.
     Though it would revolt the Greeks,   430
     it is the custom of this place.
(Enter Orestes, Pylades, guards, and Iphigenia from the temple.)

IPHIGENIA

First, I must think how to please the goddess.
Untie the strangers. Now they are sacred victims,
and must not be chained. Attendants, go into the temple
and prepare what is needed and customary.

(Guards leave.)

Young men, you were once little children.
Who was the mother who gave birth to you?
Who was your father? Who your sister?
Did you have a sister? It would be tragic for her
to lose such a fine pair of brothers.   440
Gods move in mysterious ways!
No one can predict the evil that lies ahead.

Tell me, where do you come from, unhappy men?
You have traveled so far to reach this land.
Now you can never go home.
The gods are dark, and you go into the dark
For all eternity.

ORESTES

Woman, why do you weep?
You only add to the agony we must face,
bravely, I trust. How can we sympathize with our killer?   450
Are you trying to comfort us on the brink of death
with no hope of rescue?
Please don't pity us. Fate will take its course.
We don't need your tears. We understand
the customs of this place.

IPHIGENIA

Which of you is called Pylades?
First, tell me that.

ORESTES

He is. Does that make you happy?

IPHIGENIA
    And he is a citizen of which Greek city?

ORESTES
    What good would it do you if we tell you?   460

IPHIGENIA
    And you two are brothers?

ORESTES
    Brothers in friendship, not by birth.

IPHIGENIA
    What name did your father give you?

ORESTES
    Call me Unlucky. That's all you need to know.

IPHIGENIA
    That's not what I asked. That is your Fate.

ORESTES
    If I die nameless, no one can insult me.

IPHIGENIA
    Why do you begrudge me this?
    Are you so proud?

ORESTES
    You may have my body but not my name.

IPHIGENIA
    Please, tell me the city you come from.   470
    At least, do me this favor.

ORESTES
    Argos is my native land.

IPHIGENIA

In the gods' name, is that the truth?
Is that where you were born?

ORESTES

I'm from Mycenae, once so proud and prosperous.

IPHIGENIA

Are you in exile then? Tell me what happened.

ORESTES

Exiled by chance, not by choice.

IPHIGENIA

Please tell me just one more thing.

ORESTES

Why not? I have the time.

IPHIGENIA

Oh, I am so glad that you have come!   480

ORESTES

Enjoy yourself. But I can't share your pleasure.

IPHIGENIA

I expect that you have heard of Troy.
Everyone knows of it by now.

ORESTES

Gods! I wish I'd never even dreamed of it!

IPHIGENIA

They say it is fallen; the town is gone.

ORESTES

That's true. Whoever told you that is right.

IPHIGENIA
> And Helen? Is she back in the house of Menelaus?

ORESTES
> She is—and she brought a curse to one I know.

IPHIGENIA
> She brought an earlier curse to me.
> Every Greek hates her; I am not alone.   490

ORESTES
> I too have been a victim of her marriage.

IPHIGENIA
> Has the Achaean army returned, as rumor says?

ORESTES
> Rumor is right. But you demand the whole story
> in a word.

IPHIGENIA
> I want us to share the story before you die.

ORESTES
> Ask me then, and I will try to answer.

IPHIGENIA
> Did Calchas, the priest, come back from Troy?

ORESTES
> He is dead, or so they were saying in Mycenae.

IPHIGENIA
> Thank you, Artemis! And what has happened
> to Odysseus?   500

ORESTES
>He is not home yet—but they say he is still alive.

IPHIGENIA
>Curse him! I hope he dies, and never gets home.

ORESTES
>Don't say that. His life is already cursed.

IPHIGENIA
>And is Achilles, Thetis' son, still living?

ORESTES
>No, he's not; his wedding at Aulis
>did not save him.

IPHIGENIA
>A treacherous wedding, as some of us
>know too well . . .

ORESTES
>Who are you, anyway, who seem to know so much
>of Greek affairs?   510

IPHIGENIA
>Hellas was my home.
>I was lost while still a child.

ORESTES
>So it's natural that you long for news.

IPHIGENIA
>And what's become of the great general,
>called "The Fortunate"?

ORESTES

    The general I knew was far from fortunate.
    Whom do you mean?

IPHIGENIA

    I mean Agamemnon, son of Atreus.

ORESTES

    I don't know. Please drop the subject!

IPHIGENIA

    I beg you, don't refuse me. I'd be so happy   520
    to have news of him.

ORESTES

    He's dead. And his death destroyed another life.

IPHIGENIA

    Dead! What happened to him? I am in despair!

ORESTES

    Why are you crying? What was he to you?

IPHIGENIA

    It's the memory of his greatness
    that makes me weep.

ORESTES

    His end was terrible—murdered by his wife.

IPHIGENIA

    Oh, Gods! I weep for both of them.

ORESTES

    No more questions! I've said all that I can say.

IPHIGENIA
  Just tell me this; is his wife still alive?   530

ORESTES
  She is not. Her own son killed her.

IPHIGENIA
  Oh ruined House of Atreus! Why did he do it?

ORESTES
  He avenged his father, whom she had stabbed to death.

IPHIGENIA
  How horrible! How evil!—but it was just.

ORESTES
  The gods have failed to recognize his justice.

IPHIGENIA
  Do any of their children live at home?

ORESTES
  Only Electra, who is still a girl.

IPHIGENIA
  What about the daughter who was sacrificed?
  Does anyone mention her name?

ORESTES
  Only to say that she is dead.   540

IPHIGENIA
  She is to be pitied; so is the father who killed her.

ORESTES
  She was destroyed for the sake of that evil woman.

IPHIGENIA

And what has become of Orestes,
the dead king's son? Is he alive?

ORESTES

The wretched man lives nowhere and everywhere.

IPHIGENIA

He's alive! So much for my worthless dreams!

ORESTES

Yes, even the gods whom we call wise
are as deceitful as our fragile dreams.
In the gods' world, as in our own, all is chaos.
Wise men weep when ruined, not by their folly,   550
but because of their faith in heavenly oracles.

CHORUS

And what about us? Who cares for us
who were born humble? We loved our parents
but no one bothers to tell us of their fate . . .

IPHIGENIA

Listen! I have a plan: If I save you, stranger,
can you take word to Argos?
I have had no one to be my messenger.
It seems, by your manner, that you are nobly born.
You know Mycenae, and the people there I loved.
Just carry this little letter, and you are saved!   560
But your friend here must still be sacrificed.
The state demands it.

ORESTES

Strange lady, I agree to all you say,
except that my friend must die.
That would be more than I could bear!
I steered him to this fatal enterprise.

He came with me out of pity for my troubles.
No, give him the letter and let me perish.

IPHIGENIA

O noble heart! You must be of royal blood.
I hope that my brother, the sole surviving male   570
of our illustrious family, may resemble you.
Yes, I have a brother, though he is a stranger,
but still my brother. You shall have your way.
He goes, and you must die.
How odd of you to be so in love with death!

ORESTES

Who is the cruel priest who will end my life? '

IPHIGENIA

I am. This is my function, set by Artemis.

ORESTES

A terrible task for a woman!

IPHIGENIA

I have to do it; I must obey the law.

ORESTES

Can a woman take up the sword and kill a man?   580

IPHIGENIA

No, I only sprinkle water on your head,
for purification.

ORESTES

And who, may I ask, performs the slaughter?

IPHIGENIA

There are people inside the temple
who take care of this.

ORESTES

    What sort of tomb will I have when I am dead?

IPHIGENIA

    In the temple there is a sacred fire,
    and then a huge cleft in the rock.

ORESTES

    Oh how I wish my lost sister could dress my body!

IPHIGENIA

    That is a futile wish, poor fellow,   590
    whoever you are! She lives far from this barbaric land.
    But since we are from Argos, I shall give you all the honors
    that I can. I'll pile rich gifts on your grave;
    I'll drench your body in yellow olive oil;
    then I'll pour flower-scented honey on your pyre.
    But now I'll go and get my letter from the temple.
(as she enters the temple)
    For what I have to do,
    don't think I am your enemy.
(The guards come back.)
    Men, guard them well, but do not chain them.
(to herself)
    Now perhaps word can be sent   600
    to him I love the best,
    to say that one he took for dead
    is alive, will speak to him, and bring him joy.
(She exits.)

CHORUS

    We grieve for you, that drops of holy water
    doom you to the shedding of your blood.

ORESTES

    I don't need pity, but I thank you.
    And now farewell, good women.

CHORUS
>
> Pylades, we are happy for your happy fate.
> Your feet will once again touch native soil.

PYLADES
>
> There is no happy future when   610
> my dearest friend must die.

CHORUS *(to Pylades)*
>
> You will go on a voyage of tears.

(to Orestes)
>
> And you will go to a pitiful death.
> Which is more bitter, your life or your death?
> Our hearts hesitate to make a choice
> between grief and grief.

ORESTES
>
> God, Pylades, are your thoughts the same as mine?

PYLADES
>
> Friend, I don't know. What do you think?

ORESTES
>
> Who is this woman who knows about the wars
> of Troy, the kings' return, the wizard Calchas,   620
> and the dauntless Achilles?
> She must have been born an Argive.
> She pities poor Agamemnon and asks about his family.
> She acts as if her welfare
> depends on in the city's fate.

PYLADES
>
> You are ahead of me, friend, but I agree.
> Except that all places which are visited by ships
> have heard of the fall of mighty kings.
> But let that be. I think of other things.

ORESTES

    Friend, share your thoughts with me.   630

PYLADES

    How can I live if you are killed?
    I would be disgraced. I have shared your troubles
    and your voyages. I must share your death.
    If I sail home to Argos and to Phocis,
    I shall be branded knave and coward.
    People who are knaves themselves
    will say I have betrayed you.
    Or even that I killed you,
    so that I as your sister's husband
    might gain your throne.   640
    I must breathe my last with you,
    and, as I love you,
    give my body to the knife and fire.

ORESTES

    Don't talk like that! One pain is enough;
    I can't bear two.
    It's no great sacrifice to lose my life
    when the Gods pursue me. You are a happy man.
    Your heritage is clean, not stained like mine.

    When you escape, you and Electra will bear sons.
    Through you my name shall live, my father's line   650
    not be blotted out. Live, Pylades!
    Live in my father's halls.

    Only do this for me:
    build me a memorial,
    and let my sister come and weep,
    and dedicate her lock of hair.
    Tell how I ended here,
    doomed by an Argive woman—

that I was purified
before I died.   660

And, dearest friend, never leave my sister,
though you see our house destroyed and desolate.
As boys we hunted together on the hills of Greece;
we grew up together, Pylades, our lives entwined.
You've shouldered many burdens of my awful fate.
But I, I am Apollo's dupe. I did his bidding
and killed my mother. Now I too must die.

PYLADES

I'll build your tomb, and I'll not betray
your sister. But though you are close to death,
there is still a chance that your ill luck is over.   670

ORESTES

Don't say any more. Phoebus will be
no help to me. But here's that woman
coming from the temple.
(Iphigenia enters.)

IPHIGENIA

Go in now, guards,
and prepare for the sacrifice.
(Guards exit.)
Here is the letter. But still, I have a qualm.
A man in fear of death will promise anything.
But once he's safe, and that fear fades
He may not trouble to carry out my mission.

ORESTES

What reassurance can we give you?   680

IPHIGENIA

Let Pylades swear that he will take my letter
to Argos, and deliver it to my friends.

ORESTES
    And will you too swear an oath to Pylades?

IPHIGENIA
    What should I swear to, then?

ORESTES
    Swear you will send him from the country
    alive and safe.

IPHIGENIA
    But of course! How else could he take
    my message?

ORESTES
    But will the king permit you to do this?

IPHIGENIA
    I can persuade him. And I'll escort Pylades   690
    to the ship myself, and see him safe on board.

ORESTES
    Swear, Pylades. Make it a sacred oath.

PYLADES
    I swear to take this letter to your friends.

IPHIGENIA
    And I will send you through the Clashing Rocks.

PYLADES
    What god bears witness to the oath you swear?

IPHIGENIA
    Artemis, who made me priestess of this temple.

PYLADES
    I swear this oath by Zeus, the king of heaven.

IPHIGENIA

> And if you fail me . . . ?

PYLADES

> May I never see my home again. And if you fail?

IPHIGENIA

> I'll never get to Argos while I live.   700

PYLADES

> But wait!—there's one thing we've forgotten.
> What if my ship is wrecked, and all my goods are lost,
> including your letter, and I escape with just my skin?
> Then the oath should not be binding.

IPHIGENIA

> I've thought of this. I'll tell you now
> the contents of my letter. You can repeat them
> to my friends. Thus my message will be saved
> if you are saved.

PYLADES

> Good. That serves us both. To whom, then,
> shall I take this letter, or take the message
> which I'll memorize?   710

IPHIGENIA

> Say this to Orestes, Agamemnon's son:
> "This message comes from your sister, Iphigenia.
> She who was sacrificed at Aulis and is dead
> to all her friends, is still alive . . ."

ORESTES

> Alive? Where is she? Did she come back
> from the dead?

IPHIGENIA

> I'm she. Don't interrupt. "Bring me to Argos,
> brother, before I die. Free me from this barbaric country,
> and free me from this bloody priesthood,
> where my chief function   720
> is to slaughter strangers . . ."

ORESTES

> Pylades, where are we? Is this all a dream?

IPHIGENIA

> ". . . or I shall haunt your house, Orestes,
> with this curse." I'll repeat his name, Orestes,
> so you'll not forget it.

PYLADES

> Ye gods!

IPHIGENIA

> Why call on the gods? I'm speaking of my brother.

PYLADES

> Excuse me. For a moment my mind wandered . . .
> (This is incredible. No point in questioning her now.)   730

IPHIGENIA

> Tell him that Artemis saved me from my father.
> As he believed he plunged his sharp blade into me,
> a fawn took my place; then Artemis brought me here.
> This is the message that is in my letter.

PYLADES

> This is the easiest oath I ever swore!
> I hasten to pass along your letter. Here, Orestes!
> I give you this message from your sister.

ORESTES

>   But with this joy, why do I need written messages?
>   My beloved sister, I am thunderstruck,
>   but let me hasten to embrace you! Happiness, at last!   740

CHORUS

>   Stop! Don't touch the priestess!
>   You'll defile her sacred garments.

ORESTES

>   Sister, don't turn away! We're both the children
>   of Agamemnon, Iphigenia, whom I never hoped to see.

IPHIGENIA

>   How can you claim to be my brother?
>   Don't talk like this. Orestes lives in Argos,
>   or else he is in Nauplia.

ORESTES

>   My poor sister, your brother is not in Argos now.

IPHIGENIA

>   You claim the Spartan Clytemnestra is your mother?

ORESTES

>   Yes, and I am Pelops' grandson.   750

IPHIGENIA

>   But have you proof of this?

ORESTES

>   Of course I have. Just ask me questions
>   about our father's house.

IPHIGENIA

>   You tell me of your proof and I will listen.

ORESTES

> All right, here's something that Electra told me:
> You've heard of the quarrel between Thyestes and Atreus?

IPHIGENIA

> Yes, they fell out over a golden lamb.

ORESTES

> And you wove that story on your loom.
> And your design showed the sun changing its course.

IPHIGENIA

> Yes, I wove that picture.   760

ORESTES

> And your mother sent holy water to Aulis . . .

IPHIGENIA

> Yes, because I was going to marry a prince.

ORESTES

> And you sent your mother a lock of your own hair.

IPHIGENIA

> Yes, as a memorial for my grave.

ORESTES

> Now I'll tell something that I saw myself.
> The ancient spear which hung in our father's palace,
> the one which Pelops used to kill Oenomaus at Pisa,
> was hidden in your room when you were a girl . . .

IPHIGENIA

> Orestes, my darling little brother!
> Let's embrace each other, both so far from home!   770

ORESTES

    I hold you in my arms who was thought dead
    by everyone. So let us weep together—
    tears of grief and joy.

IPHIGENIA

    This is the child I last saw in his nurse's arms.
    A little baby, light as a bird. Unspeakable happiness!
    It's more than marvelous, the bliss of our reunion.

ORESTES

    Let's hope we have a happy life together.

IPHIGENIA

    Friends, I'm afraid this joy will slip from my hands,
    that it will grow wings and float into the sky.
    Thank you, Mycenae, thank you for giving us life,   780
    thank you for nurturing my brother!
    Holy hearth and altar the Cyclops built,
    thank you for this child to light our house.

ORESTES

    We come from a noble house and race,
    But I believe our destiny is cursed.

IPHIGENIA

    I know too well. I remember
    when my dreadful father
    put the knife blade to my throat.

ORESTES

    Though I didn't see it,
    I see it in my mind's eye.   790

IPHIGENIA

    There were no wedding hymns for me,
    only tears and lamentations

as I was promised to cold sleep.
That was my sacred purification!

ORESTES

I shudder too at my father's awful act.

IPHIGENIA

How can I call him father
who was capable of such a crime?
That began our chain of suffering,
as if the gods had willed it.

ORESTES

But think, my sister, how near you were   800
to killing me!

IPHIGENIA

Terrible, terrible,
how near we came to horror.
I have done dreadful deeds
here at this place of death.
But how may the chain be broken,
how can I find a way
to send you safe to Argos?
I'm unable to send you by land
among the barbarous tribes   810
on roads that are no roads,
where Death will wait in ambush.
But the long escape by sea
is equally perilous.
The Clashing Rocks may crush you.
Is there no god to save us?
Who will aid the lone survivors
of the house of Atreus
and end this agony?

CHORUS

We here can testify to these events,   820
not legends, but what our eyes have shown us.

PYLADES

> Orestes, you and Iphigenia must not linger,
> embracing and weeping, although it's natural. But now
> we must concentrate on finding freedom!
> Let's make a plan
> to escape from this terrible place.
> Now, if we make haste, more joy may lie ahead.

ORESTES

> Yes, you are right. If we want God's help
> we must help ourselves.

IPHIGENIA

> But first I must have one word of Electra.   830
> How is my sister?

ORESTES

> She is married to Pylades; she is well and happy.

IPHIGENIA

> Who is your father, Pylades, and what is your
> native land?

PYLADES

> *My father is Strophius the Phocian.*

IPHIGENIA

> Why then we are cousins! You are Atreus'
> grandchild.

ORESTES

> A cousin, and my closest truest friend.

IPHIGENIA

> But he wasn't even born when my father killed me.

PYLADES

> *I was a late child of my father.*   840

IPHIGENIA

    Give me your hand, Pylades, friend of my brother,
    husband to my sister.

ORESTES

    And don't forget. He saved my life!

IPHIGENIA

    But tell me, Orestes,
    how could you kill our mother?

ORESTES

    I thought I must avenge my father's death.
    But I beg you, let that story be.

IPHIGENIA

    Do you know why she killed our father?

ORESTES

    Enough. There are things which are not fit
    for you to hear.   850

IPHIGENIA

    All right, I'll be silent . . .
    Are you now the lord of Argos and its hope?

ORESTES

    My uncle, Menelaus, reigns.

IPHIGENIA

    Did he take advantage of our misfortune
    to betray you?

ORESTES

    No. The avenging Furies drove me from our home.

IPHIGENIA

> I suppose that explains the fit you had
> on the shore. I was told of it . . .

ORESTES

> That's not the first time that strangers
> have seen me suffer.   860

IPHIGENIA

> The Furies haunt you for our mother's sake.

ORESTES

> Yes, my mouth drips blood under their cruel bridle.

IPHIGENIA

> Why in the world did you travel to this friendless
> coast?

ORESTES

> Apollo's oracle commanded me.

IPHIGENIA

> Can you tell me about it, or must it be kept
> a secret?

ORESTES

> I'll tell you. This was the beginning of my
> sufferings. When my hands were first bloodied by my
> mother's . . . with—but I'll not speak of it!—the Furies   870
> didn't cease to hound me. Finally Apollo directed me
> to Athens, to go on trial in the court of Zeus.
> God's hate preceded me, so no man would give me shelter.
> Finally, some people took pity on me,
> and gave me a table in their house,
> though I was forced to sit alone under their roof.
> And no one spoke to me so that I would not pollute
> their food and wine. But they gave me a cup to drink from

separately. Silently I mourned my mother,
and that I was her murderer.   880
I hear they have turned my pain into a religious rite
which is still practiced once a year:
the Festival of the Cups.

I took my place at the Areopagus, and the oldest Fury
stood opposite, to charge me with my mother's murder.
The votes were a tie when Athena raised her hand
for my acquittal. But the Furies did not relent.
They hounded me from place to place
till I approached Apollo's holy ground.
I flung myself before his shrine, prostrate and starving.   890
"God Phoebus, here I am, and here I die,
if you refuse to aid me!"
Then from his golden tripod the god spoke to me.
He told me to come to this country and rescue the image
of Artemis, which had fallen here from Heaven
and set it up in Athens.
So if we seize the image, I can escape my madness.
Sister, don't shrink! You can save me
and save our father's house as well.
Then we can board my ship with many oarsmen   900
and head for home!

CHORUS

The wrath of God has fallen like hot rain
upon this cursed house, and drives its children on
to further tribulations.

IPHIGENIA

Brother, your will is mine. But I am terrified.
How dare we deceive the goddess and try to escape the king?
When he sees that empty pedestal I am bound to die!
If we could accomplish this in a single action—
steal the statue and get on the ship—
then it's worth the risk.   910

But how could we do this? No, I must remain behind
and die, and you and the image escape.
But I don't shrink from dying. And I will have saved you.
No house can afford to lose its heir. Women's lives
are not as worth preserving.

ORESTES

I won't be the killer of both my mother and my sister!
I've shed too much blood already. Either in life or death,
we'll share and share alike. If we can get out of here
I'll take you home. Otherwise we die together.
But listen to my thoughts: would Apollo have ordered me   920
to come here and retrieve the image if he believed
that Artemis would take offense?
Perhaps his plan was to send me here to reunite us!
Taking all this into account,
I believe we're meant to see Argos again, you and I.

IPHIGENIA

How can we steal the image without dying?
God knows I have the will but I don't have hope.
Even so, let's try to work out a plan.

ORESTES

Could we manage to kill the king?

IPHIGENIA

More blood! But no, when I was a stranger   930
he took me in.

ORESTES

But if it's the only way of saving us?

IPHIGENIA

You're very brave, but I cannot agree.
Besides, it would break the sacred laws of hospitality.

ORESTES

Is it possible for you to hide me in the temple?

IPHIGENIA

Then we could wait for darkness, and escape!

ORESTES

Yes, night is the time for thieves, daylight
for the honest.

IPHIGENIA

But the temple guards are there, and they
would see us.   940

ORESTES

If there is no other way then we are ruined.

IPHIGENIA

Wait . . . another plan has occurred to me.

ORESTES

What is it? Speak!

IPHIGENIA

I think I can put your misfortunes to good use,
and manage to deceive the king.

ORESTES

Oh the cleverness of women may save us yet!

IPHIGENIA

I'll tell him you're impure—that you have
your mother's blood on your hands.

ORESTES

If we can put my torments to good use,
so much the better.   950

IPHIGENIA
I'll say it would be a sin to offer one
so polluted to the goddess.

ORESTES
How would that help us to retrieve the statue?

IPHIGENIA
I'll say I need to wash your body in the sea.

ORESTES
But what about the statue?

IPHIGENIA
I'll say you touched it,
so it must be purified as well.

ORESTES
Where will you perform the cleansing?
On the foam-drenched rocks of the headland?

IPHIGENIA
Yes, near where your ship lies moored.   960

ORESTES
Who carries the idol?

IPHIGENIA
I must. Only I am permitted to touch it.

PYLADES
And what part must I play in all of this?

IPHIGENIA
I'll say you too are tainted with the crime.

ORESTES

I suppose the king must know . . .

IPHIGENIA

I'll tell him. I'm sure I can persuade him.

ORESTES

Our ship's crew is poised and waiting for us.

IPHIGENIA

This part of the plan I leave to you two men.

ORESTES

Can you persuade your women to keep our secret?
I'm sure you can arouse their pity. The rest is up to us.   970
May fortune bless us.

IPHIGENIA *(to the chorus)*

Dear friends, I must count on you once more. My future
rests with you. I will find peace or I'll be nothing.
I'll never see home again, or see my brother and sister.
We are all women. Women have solidarity with one another.
We keep each other's secrets; we help each other when we
are periled. Now help us escape! Tell no one of our plans.
And I swear to you that if I live, I will come back,
and bring you all to Greece, to share in my good fortune.
I plead with you, each of you, one by one. I touch your   980
cheeks; I kneel before you. Think of your own relatives
at home! Think of all those you love—mother, father,
children—some of you have children?—will you help us?
Otherwise we are doomed.

CHORUS LEADER

We swear by Zeus we will keep your secrets.

IPHIGENIA

May the gods bless you and make you happy.
Orestes, Pylades, go into the temple. The king will be here
before long, to see if the sacrifice has taken place
and carried out correctly.
Artemis! You who once saved me from my father's sword,   990
now save us all. Consent to leave this savage place,
to prove to everyone that Apollo keeps his word.
This miserable land is no fit place to make your home.
Come with us to Athens, that fair city,
where happiness awaits us.

CHORUS LEADER

Halcyon, sweet bird of peace,
your song a piercing cry
over the stony cliffs,
touching our stricken hearts,
you never cease to lament   1000
your spouse, now lost forever.
You match your grief to ours,
we who are birds but wingless.
There is only a single song
for those who mourn like us.

I miss the old Greek markets
where people used to gather.
I long for the happy Artemis
who soothed the pangs of birth,
who lived by the Cynthian hill   1010
among the slender palms.
the branches of sweet laurel.
The sacred groves of olives
sheltered Leto's labor-pains,
by the round pool of Delos.
There the melodious swan
sang devotion to the Muses.

CHORUS

    Tears of fear and pain
    streamed down our burning cheeks,
    our ears deafened by noise   1020
    when our cities' towers fell.
    Then they dragged us to the ship
    manned by furious enemies.
    We had been traded for gold,
    the prey of vicious men.
    We were sent to this barbarous land
    to serve Agamemnon's daughter.
    This altar is crimson with blood,
    not the blood of lambs, but of strangers.
    Now we envy the unhappy   1030
    who have never known anything else.
    They are accustomed to tyranny,
    while we, who once knew bliss
    are crushed by our misfortune.

CHORUS LEADER

    And you, Iphigenia,
    will sail home on an Argive ship.
    The sound of the pipes of Pan
    will urge the oarsmen onward.
    Or will prophetic Apollo
    with his dulcet seven-stringed lyre   1040
    sing you safely to your home?
    Athens, which gleams in the sun,
    will welcome you with joy,
    while we are forsaken here.

CHORUS

    Oh, that we could follow
    the brilliant path of the sun
    in his gleaming chariot

over the homes of our childhood!
Then we might see, below us,
the dancers at a wedding,   1050
as we danced when we were girls
running from our mothers
to join our happy friends.
There we were rivals in beauty,
comparing our glorious hair,
our rarest jewels and gowns,
our shimmering veils to shade us—
Oh lost, lovely days that were!
(Enter King Thoas and attendants.)

THOAS

    Where is Iphigenia, the temple guardian?
    Have the rites begun? Are they over?   1060
    Are those bodies blazing in the shrine?

CHORUS

    Here she comes, O King!
(Enter Iphigenia, with the statue in her arms.)

THOAS

    Tell me, priestess, why are you carrying the statue?
    How dare you move it from its sacred pedestal!

IPHIGENIA

    King, stay where you are! Don't take one step forward!

THOAS

    Iphigenia, has something happened to profane the temple?

IPHIGENIA

    Let that evil word be unsaid! I spit it out
    and give it to the gods.

THOAS
Tell me plainly what has happened.

IPHIGENIA
These men you captured are unclean.   1070

THOAS
Is this a guess, or your discovery?

IPHIGENIA
The goddess turned her back.

THOAS
Did Artemis do this by herself, or did an
earthquake move her?

IPHIGENIA
She did it by herself,
shuddered, and closed her eyes.

THOAS
What caused this? Was it the guilty strangers?

IPHIGENIA
Yes, that and nothing else. Their crimes
are dreadful. They killed their nearest kin.

THOAS
Whom did they kill? You've aroused my curiosity.   1080

IPHIGENIA
They murdered their own mother: two men with
a single sword.

THOAS
Good god! Even a barbarian would balk at that.

IPHIGENIA
>They have been hounded from every city in Greece.

THOAS
>Now I see why you removed the image.

IPHIGENIA
>It's here, under the light of heaven,
>to be cleansed of blood.

THOAS
>How did you learn these men were tainted?

IPHIGENIA
>I questioned them when I saw the goddess tremble.

THOAS
>Your Greek intuition served you well.   1090

IPHIGENIA
>They too were clever. They tried to win my heart
>with word of Greece. They told me my brother Orestes
>was flourishing.

THOAS
>They thought this news might make you merciful.

IPHIGENIA
>They told me my father was alive and well.

THOAS
>But you were intent on carrying out your duties.

IPHIGENIA
>I loathe all Hellas, for Hellas ruined me.

THOAS
So what do we do with these two miscreants?

IPHIGENIA
First I must bathe and purify their bodies.

THOAS
In fresh spring water or the salty sea?   1100

IPHIGENIA
The sea can wash away all human sins.

THOAS
Then Artemis can accept their sacrifice.

IPHIGENIA
(And my own plans be achieved.)

THOAS
Doesn't the surf break right beside the shrine?

IPHIGENIA
I require privacy. Other, more secret rites
must be performed.

THOAS
It's not for me to inquire of sacred matters.
Do as you think best.

IPHIGENIA
The statue also must be purified.

THOAS
If it is tainted by the mother's blood . . .   1110

IPHIGENIA
> If not, I never would have moved it
> from the temple.

THOAS
> You are a prudent, pious woman.
> What can I do now to assist you?

IPHIGENIA
> Put these men in chains.

THOAS
> Why? How could they escape?

IPHIGENIA
> Never trust a Greek.

THOAS
> Guards, bring the chains.

IPHIGENIA
> Have them bring the strangers here,
> but with their heads covered by their robes . . .   1120

THOAS
> So that the sun won't see their pollution.

IPHIGENIA
> Send some of your soldiers with me,
> and one of them shall give instructions to the city.

THOAS
> And what must he tell the people?

IPHIGENIA
> That no one is permitted out-of-doors.

THOAS
　For fear that these men might contaminate them?

IPHIGENIA
　Yes, their pollution is infectious.

THOAS *(to one of the guards)*
　Go, issue this order.
　Iphigenia, you really care about my countrymen.
　No wonder our city pays you honor!   1130

IPHIGENIA
　And I look after my friends as well.

THOAS
　I believe that you include me too.

IPHIGENIA
　But of course!

THOAS
　What more can I do to help?

IPHIGENIA
　Stay here at the temple and wait, my King.
　Remain, and cleanse the shrine with fire.

THOAS
　So you'll find it pure when you return.

IPHIGENIA
　When the men emerge from the temple,
　cover your eyes with your cloak.

THOAS
　So that I may avoid pollution.   1140

IPHIGENIA
If I am away for awhile . . .

THOAS
When should I expect you to return?

IPHIGENIA
Please don't concern yourself.
I can't really estimate how long it will take.

THOAS
Go serve the goddess. Take your time
carefully to perform the needed rites.

IPHIGENIA
May the gods grant us success in this enterprise.

THOAS
I join my prayers to yours.
(The temple doors open and Orestes and Pylades enter, their heads
covered and their arms bound. Thoas enters the
temple.)

IPHIGENIA
Now the strangers enter from the temple!
Attendants carry the sacred robes, and the two young lambs   1150
whose pure blood will cleanse the stain of murder
among the gleaming torches.
All of you, stand back!
(She holds up the statue.)
Take flight, run away! Especially those who are about
to marry, those who are near to giving birth, flee
lest defilement stain you!
Artemis, child of Zeus and Leto, have pity on us!
If I can cleanse these sinners of their crime,
you shall have a perfect sanctuary, and we shall be happy.

For the rest, I am wordless, but the gods who know   1160
everything, will know what I mean. And Artemis,
you will understand my prayer.
(Iphigenia, bearing the image, leads the procession, followed by Orestes,
Pylades, and the remaining guards, heads covered.)

CHORUS
    Long ago in Delos
    in a valley of fruit trees,
    two beautiful children were born:
    Apollo, with golden hair
    so skillful with the lyre,
    and Artemis, gifted with the bow.
    Leto carried them to Parnassus
    where the revels of Dionysus   1170
    rang out on the slopes of the mountain.
    There a bronze-scaled serpent
    coiled in the shade of the laurel,
    guarded the ancient oracle,
    the voice of Earth itself.
    You, Apollo, were still a child
    who broke from your mother's arms
    and killed the dragon.
    You succeeded the sacred oracle.
    You are throned on the golden tripod   1180
    replying to mortal queries.
    Your prophecies are infallible,
    sprung from the center of Earth.

    When Apollo drove Earth's daughter
    from her sacred place as the oracle,
    Earth struck back, with apparitions.
    Strange dreams flew to the cities of men
    as they tossed in their sleep,
    telling the past, foretelling the future.
    So Earth, to avenge her daughter, Thetis,   1190

stole the privileges of Apollo.
Then Apollo rushed to Zeus, on Olympus.
His little hands, still childlike, gripped the throne.
Zeus laughed to see the boy, intent on profit
from those who appealed to the oracle!
He nodded, put an end to the nighttime voices.
So the dark, prophetic dreams were lost.
Apollo had his privilege restored,
and the mortals who thronged his throne
trusted his word alone.   1200

(Enter messenger.)

MESSENGER
    Temple guards, you who tend the altar,
    where is Thoas, lord of the land?
    Wrench open these temple doors and bid King Thoas
    to come out at once!

CHORUS
    Dare we ask what has occurred?

MESSENGER
    The two Greeks have fled the country.
    It is all a plot of Iphigenia!
    They've taken the sacred image, which now lies
    in the hold of their ship!

CHORUS
    Incredible! But the king just left   1210
    the temple, in a hurry.

MESSENGER
    Where did he go? He must be told
    of what has happened.

CHORUS

We have no idea. You'd better look for him.
Run to the palace as fast as you can!

MESSENGER

Never trust a woman! You're all liars.
I'm sure that you're mixed up in this.

CHORUS

You're mad! How could we be involved? Run!

MESSENGER

Not till I know for certain that the king's
not in the temple. Ho! You inside, unbolt the doors!   1220
Tell the king I have bad news for him.
(Messenger hammers on the doors till Thoas emerges.)

THOAS

Who's that battering at the doors of the temple?
How dare you disturb the peace of this holy shrine?

MESSENGER

These lying women tried to make me go away.
And you were in the building the whole time!

THOAS

But why would they do such a thing?

MESSENGER

That will keep, and this is urgent.
First I must inform you that Iphigenia and her friends
have fled. And she has stolen the sacred image of Artemis.
That whole story she spun of the cleansing was a lie.   1230

THOAS
What do you mean? Why would she do a thing like that?
What wild hope . . .

MESSENGER
She did it to save Orestes.

THOAS
You mean her brother?

MESSENGER
Yes, the man who was to be sacrificed.

THOAS
It must have been a kind of miracle. What else
could you call it?

MESSENGER
Never mind that now, just listen to me.
When you understand the facts, we must plan our strategy.

THOAS
Tell me everything. They have a long hard journey   1240
ahead of them before they can escape my power.

MESSENGER
When we reached the sea shore where the rites
were to be performed, we whom you sent to guard the Greeks,
were waved away by Iphigenia. She said she was busy with
mysteries of fire and sacrifice. She herself now led them
by their chains and marched ahead; all this made us uncertain.
Then she began to scream incomprehensible stuff, as if to
make us think she was washing away the stains of murder.
Time passed, and we grew more and more uneasy. Could the
prisoners have killed her and run away? But still we waited,   1250

afraid of seeing what was forbidden. But finally
we agreed that we must search for them.
Then we see the hull of a Greek ship, her oars in two rows,
raised like pairs of wings, and fifty oarsmen at the ready.
The two strangers, free of their chains,
are standing near the stern. Some of the sailors
steady the prow with poles; others hasten
to pull up the cables with their hands. Still others
are letting down ladders into the water
so that the Greeks might come aboard.   1260

When we took in this treachery, we grabbed Iphigenia,
and seized the cables. We tried to unship the steering oars
as we shouted at the men, "Who are you that are trying
to steal our image and our priestess?"
And one replied, "I am Orestes, come to take my sister,
Iphigenia, back to her home in Greece."
We tried to hang on to her, and force her
to return to you. But as you see,
it was a fierce struggle, though none of us had weapons.
We fought hand-to-hand, and the Greeks used their feet,   1270
so we have these bruises and broken heads and bleeding eyes.
We ran to the cliffs where we could make a stand,
and began pelting them with stones.
But there were archers on the stern who held us off.
Then a huge wave swung the ship towards the beach.
But Iphigenia was afraid to step into the surf.
Orestes swept up his sister on his shoulder
and with one giant leap reached the ladder.
She was set down safely on the ship,
along with the image of Artemis.   1280

Then from the middle of the ship a voice rang out:
"Men of Greece! Seize your oars and churn the waves
till they turn white! We have everything we came for
when we passed through the Clashing Rocks."

The crew let out a roar of triumph, and set to with the oars.
All went well within the quiet harbor,
but outside the bay the sea was rough. A hard wind fell
on the vessel and was driving it back to land.
Then Iphigenia stood and prayed:
"Artemis, save your priestess! Return me to Greece   1290
with my brother, and forgive my theft of your image.
You also have a brother whom you love.
It's natural for us to care for them."
The sailors responded with a hearty song,
but no matter how they struggled they were forced closer,
closer to the rocks.
Then we could wade into the sea
with ropes and grappling hook.
I was sent to tell you all of this. There is no way
they can escape. We must rush there   1300
with chains and halters. Poseidon, lord of the sea,
still grieves for Troy and hates her enemy.
He will hand over Agamemnon's son and his daughter
who betrayed Artemis, her savior.

CHORUS

Ah, poor Iphigenia, you are back in the
power of Thoas, and you must die.

THOAS

I call on every man in this city
to bridle his horse and run to the shore.
Sailors, drag all your fast boats down to the sea
so we can trap them by water and by land.   1310
Then we'll fling them down the cliffs,
these godless ones, or impale them alive on spikes!
You women, I know you were in the plot.
When I have time, I'll take care of you!
*(In a flash of light and a thunderbolt, Athena enters, on the roof of
the temple.)*

ATHENA

> Hold on, King Thoas, stop right there!
> Call back your soldiers and listen to Athena.
> Orestes was following Apollo's orders when he came here,
> fleeing the Furies, to find his sister and take her home,
> and bring the sacred image to my country.
> Then he will be freed of his pain and spells of madness.   1320
> Listen to me, Thoas! You mean to kill Orestes
> when you catch him. But Poseidon, at my behest,
> has calmed the waters so that his ship can sail.
>
> Now you listen to me, Orestes! You can hear me
> although you are far away. Do as I tell you,
> take your sister and the statue to glorious Athens.
> In Attica there is a sacred place called Halai.
> There you must build a shrine and install the image
> who shall be called the Taurian Goddess,
> in memory of this place and what you have suffered.   1330
> Establish there this custom: at festival time,
> let the priest hold a sword to a man's throat,
> and draw one drop of blood as ransom
> for the blood that is not shed here.
> In reverence to Artemis
> Men will gather and sing hymns to her forever.
>
> Iphigenia, you shall hold the keys to the sanctuary of
> Artemis. When you die, you will be buried there.
> And your grave will be adorned with fine-spun cloth—left
> behind by women who have died in childbirth.   1340
>
> Now Thoas, you must release these women and send them
> home to Hellas . . . Orestes, I've already saved you once.
> At the Areopagus, when the vote was even, I decreed
> mercy. Now let that stand as law: when votes are even,
> the accused is spared. Orestes, take your sister home.
> And Thoas, contain your anger.

THOAS

Goddess Athena, those who refuse to obey the gods
must be out of their minds. I renounce my anger at Orestes
though he has taken the image. I forgive Iphigenia for
deceiving me. Let them take the statue and give it a   1350
home. Good luck to them! And I'll send these women back
to Greece, as you request. Now I'll call off my army
and my ships.

ATHENA

Good. Even the gods must yield to necessity.
Blow, winds, and send the children of Agamemnon back
to Athens. I will accompany you, to protect the holy
image of my sister, Artemis.
(Athena disappears.)

CHORUS

Go with good fortune,
numbered among the blest.
And you, O great Athena,   1360
whom we all hold in awe,
mortals, immortals too,
your edicts we obey;
obedience brings joy!
We who were dead to hope
Now hope to live in bliss.

VOICE OF EURIPIDES

Beautiful victory,
wreathe me in garlands.
Stay with me always.
Crown me eternally.   ·   1370

Orestes

Translated by
Greg Delanty

Translator's Preface

At the beginning of *Orestes* Electra asks, "Why should I rehearse my family's nightmare once more?" By the time *Orestes* was performed, in 408 B.C., the nightmare of the house of Atreus had been recycled on the stage for fifty years. The great age of Greek tragedy that begins with the *Oresteia* of Aeschylus approaches its end with this work, which was, scholars report, the most popular of all tragedies.

Orestes is a play that deals with a murder in which Orestes and his sister Electra (and their friend Pylades) are complicit. The victim is their mother, Clytemnestra, and their motive is revenge for her murder of their father, Agamemnon. Angry, the citizens of Argos want to execute Orestes and Electra for their hideous crime. The Furies have tormented Orestes into delirious sleep. Electra's concern for her brother is perhaps the only positive family tie in this drama—as Pylades' friendship is the only human bond outside of family. These connections are what still link the half-crazed Orestes to a sane and stable world. But with the arrival of Helen, Orestes' aunt, and Menelaus, his uncle, it appears the disorder will continue, for they only add to Orestes' and Electra's terror and confusion. Desperate, condemned to death by all of Argos, and lacking support from their uncle and aunt, Agamemnon's son and daughter plan to murder Helen and protect themselves by kidnaping their cousin Hermione, daughter of Helen and Menelaus.

I have translated the play mostly into prose, in part because in the Greek the individual characters speak in dialogue that doesn't achieve a high level of lyricism. I have, however, written the chorus' lines in verse, including the chorus Electra leads herself, beginning "O Pelasgia, let me lead the keening chorus." I have also translated the final scene into verse. The chorus and the Apollo scene are significantly separate and heightened from those of the main characters and warrant the elevated treatment of verse. But I have translated the speech of the main, dread-full cast of characters in ordinary speech to suggest something of the melodrama of their dire plight.

Toward the end is a baffling scene in which the Phrygian slave, a crazed and somewhat ridiculous character, interrupts the play's grave progress. It is as if one of Shakespeare's comic characters—"Bottom" from *A Midsummer Night's Dream*—were to get his cues mixed up at some drama festival and run onstage in the midst of *The Tragedy of Titus Andronicus*. In *Orestes* a Phrygian slave, originally from the boondocks of Asia Minor, runs out of the kidnaping scene spouting an alien dialect. This slave, a captive, was brought to Argos from Troy, where he was already an outsider. For a Greek audience, he was a legitimate target for abuse and ridicule. Both N. Wedd and William Arrowsmith explain that the slave embodies Athenian feelings toward Persia, whose help they needed in the war against Sparta but who sided with the Spartans instead. Euripides, then, was insulting Persia and the Persians, yet the topicality of the scene is lost on today's audience and seems bizarrely out of place.

In my version, to suggest that the slave is an outsider or foreigner, I have made him Irish and the kind of person who, because he is from the country, would be called a "culchee," a "mucker," or what Americans call a "hick." Where other translators, such as Arrowsmith, have made the slave's speech semiliterate or pidgin, I have pitched his language in the demotic speech of my own city, Cork. I thought his mix of hysteria, confusion, and incongruity might be appropriately rendered by that dialect. As I worked on translating this play, my feelings were such that I often felt somewhat like that slave, who, in the dialect of Cork, does his best to explain the action.

The hysteria of the slave is almost matched by that of the main characters. Electra is about to set fire to the palace. Orestes holds a knife to Hermione's throat—reminding us of the sacrifice of Iphigenia, which first set this household on its homicidal course. It's not enough that Troy went up in flames, Argos will now burn, too. Finally, and out of the blue—or, one might say, the black—of the play, Apollo, about whom Orestes has complained for his tardiness, at last arrives for the dénouement. His intervention turns the moral order upside down once more. Marriages are arranged on the spot between Pylades and the bitter virgin Electra, and between the corrupt Orestes and the blameless and abused Hermione (whom he was just about to murder). And in the most astonishing and paradoxical reversal of all, the tainted Helen will be hoisted heavenward. In this play she is the unrepentant woman who, despite her own betrayal of her house, is spared her sister's fate and raised to the stature of a goddess.

These oddities—of the slave's characterization and of Apollo's intervention—have been the cause of much conjecture down through the years. For the most part scholars and translators, while acknowledging the peculiarity of the play, have argued on its behalf in one way or another. As Arrowsmith declares, this unpopular and neglected play doesn't fit into "the pat handbook theories of the well-constructed Greek play, and its very 'queerness' and bravura of bitterness have seemed to violate both the idea of tragedy and tragic dignity itself."[1] Wedd, at the end of the nineteenth century, argues:

> Originally the tragic trilogy was followed by a satiric play of a humorous character, the object of which was to relieve the strain of the preceding serious plays: but in time presumably because it was felt that a consistently humorous play was not appropriate after every tragic trilogy, the satiric drama could, if the poet wished, be replaced by a fourth play which would be in a form a tragedy, but would differ from the three preceding tragedies in being of a less serious tone.[2]

Wedd believes that Orestes is a play in this particular category of tragedy. He suggests, as does Arrowsmith, that this play, if measured against the Aristotelian rules of drama, is a failed tragedy, but he goes on to argue that it is "appropriate to and indeed the distinctive marks of those tragedies of the secondary order which aimed at producing something different from the tragedies proper and [closer] to the modern drama" (p. xvii).

The evidence Wedd cites, however, for such tragedy "of the secondary order" is less than convincing because there are not enough extant plays

---

[1] Arrowsmith, Introduction to *Orestes*, in *The Complete Greek Tragedies*, ed. David Grene and Richmond Lattimore, vol. 4, *Euripides* (Chicago: University of Chicago Press, 1960), p. 186.

[2] *The Orestes of Euripides*, ed. and intro. N. Wedd, Pitt Press Series (Cambridge: Cambridge University Press, 1895, rep. 1942), p. vii.

to support his taxonomic supposition. With due respect to Wedd, Arrowsmith, and other scholars and translators, their arguments seem aimed more at legitimizing the literary importance of *Orestes*. After all, it is a work by one of the greatest playwrights that has survived for thousands of years—therefore, it must be above reproach. These interpreters and translators argue that the oddness of *Orestes* must have been intentional and its failure—if it is adjudged a failure—must be that of today's audience.

Like Wedd, Arrowsmith some fifty years later attempts to legitimize *Orestes'* literary value. But Arrowsmith believes Apollo's entrance at the end of the play underscores the misery of what has transpired on stage. Arrowsmith writes that this final scene

> is a transparent tour de force, an apparent resolution which in fact resolves nothing, the illusion of a *deus ex machina* intervening to stop the terrible momentum of the play by means of a solution so inadequate and so unreal by contrast with the created reality of the play that it is doomed into insignificance. The resolution, that is, is so designed as to be an apparent resolution: if the experience of the play is a real one, what remains after Apollo leaves is not the taste of the happy ending but the image of total disaster. . . . Euripides had deliberately inverted the *deus ex machina* to show precisely that *no* solution was possible; not even a god could halt the momentum of these forces in their sweep towards inevitable disaster. The magician waves his wand, but the nightmare survives the magic; the discord outlasts both the coda and the concert. (p. 190)

For Arrowsmith, Apollo was intended as a means to heighten the havoc on stage.

In a more recent translation of the play, John Peck and Frank Nisetich put Arrowsmith's viewpoint in a more positive light. They write:

> Apollo's appearance at the end of the play, however, seems to have satisfied no one. It has been called "an apparent resolution which in fact resolves nothing" (Arrowsmith) even though, in fact, it resolves everything. . . . Once he (Orestes) has been cast in the role of criminal

psychopath, the god who rescues him loses all claim to respect. Apollo cannot be real.[3]

Arrowsmith and, later, Peck and Nisetich share the conviction that, if the gods do wrong, surely no gods they are. Thus, according to these scholars and translators, the "appearance at the end must have left everyone in the theater depressed by the thought that reality is the chaos in Argos and Argos equals Athens" (Peck and Nisetich, p. 14).

The play is dated to a year before Euripides left Athens in voluntary exile. He had become disillusioned with the Athenian political and military system. Wedd tells us, "Athens was thoroughly exhausted by her previous disasters in the [Peloponnesian] war and by her domestic feuds" (p. xxxiv). We may assume that the poet wished his play to suggest to the people of Athens something of his views about what was wrong and what should be done to improve matters. Indeed, if Arrowsmith, Peck, and Nisetich are correct in thinking that Apollo isn't really divine, my notion is that Euripides himself is appearing in the guise of deity to instruct Athens: "Go your way and praise peace, / because of all the gods, she's the fairest."

Euripides may also have been implying that he didn't hold out much hope for peace, by his elevation of Helen—literally in a preposterous ascent to heaven. At the time of the play's first performance these scenes must have had a profound and shocking effect on the audience. The extraordinary *deus ex machina* was what, in theater parlance, used to be called a "clap trap." A little broader, and only a little bit sillier, the Phrygian slave, Helen, and the god could have been lent out to Aristophanes. The melodrama of the play's basic structure was clearly a crowd pleaser, particularly when the crowd's usual diet was the more restrained and constrained formula of the kind of tragedy Aristotle writes about.

We must ask ourselves, however, whether the play's viability may not be to some extent limited to the particular time and place for which it was created. Arrowsmith argues that "the political climate of the play itself graphically represents the state of affairs in Athens" and that "Apollo is here

---

[3] *Orestes*, trans. John Peck and Frank Nisetich, Greek Tragedy in New Translations, general ed. William Arrowsmith and Herbert Golder (New York: Oxford University Press, 1995), p. 14.

transformed from a cool and infallible Olympian into the interested and suspect god of contemporary Delphian politics, neither impartial nor infallible nor even godlike" (pp. 190, 187). His plea on behalf of the play, and that of Peck and Nisetich, succeed if the play is interpreted as a historical document. But its topicality distorts it and diminishes its lasting literary value.

As Apollo sets Helen aloft in his *machina*, surely present day audiences are left with the feeling that this unlikely end is unpersuasive and more than the play can bear. The end of *Orestes* is perhaps akin to Nahum Tate's rewrite of *King Lear*, in which Cordelia is revived, Lear is restored to his throne, and every character in the play who has made it to the final curtain lives happily ever after.

I wish to thank Katharine Washburn for her help with this translation.

ORESTES, son of Agamemnon, brother of Electra
ELECTRA, daughter of Agamemnon, sister of Orestes
HELEN, wife of Menelaus and sister of Clytemnestra
HERMIONE, daughter of Helen and Menelaus
CHORUS of women of Argos
MENELAUS, brother of Agamemnon, husband of Helen, uncle
　　of Electra and Orestes
TYNDAREUS, father of Helen and Clytemnestra, maternal
　　grandfather of Electra and Orestes
PYLADES, friend of Orestes, betrothed to Electra
MESSENGER, an old servant of Agamemnon
PHRYGIAN SLAVE, slave of Helen
APOLLO, god of prophecy, purification, sunlight, music, and art
NONSPEAKING
　　Attendants of Tyndareus and Menelaus

*(In front of Agamemnon's palace in Argos. Orestes lies unconscious
on a pallet, anxiously watched over by Electra.)*

ELECTRA
　　Human nature has to put up with everything under the sun, not
　　　　　　to speak of the out-of-the-blue terrors that the
　　　　　　gods divvy out.
　　Consider Tantalus, the son of Zeus, said to have been a favorite
　　　　　　of the gods—and I don't mean to mock his
　　　　　　end—as he cowers beneath the rock perpetually
　　　　　　pitched inches above his head. Once he wined
　　　　　　and dined with the gods as one of their own
　　　　　　but then, full of himself, he couldn't control
　　　　　　his tongue, or so the story goes.
　　His son, Pelops, had in his turn two sons, Atreus and Thyestes.
　　　　　　The conniving Fates set bad blood between these
　　　　　　two siblings. But why should I rehash my family's

nightmare once more? Atreus butchered
Thyestes' sons and dished them up to his brother.
It's better I skip the intervening years and cut straight to Atreus'
brace of sons, whom he had by Aerope:
Menelaus and renowned Agamemnon—if
renown is the right word.
Menelaus' wife was Helen herself, whom the gods cast an evil eye
upon. Agamemnon married Clytemnestra in a
marriage that became the scandal of Greece.
He had three daughters: me and my sisters,
Chrysothemis and Iphigenia, along with a son,
Orestes.
We all hailed from that one lady, his wife, who—I can't call her
mother—trapped and murdered her husband. It
doesn't take much to figure out her motive. It
isnt a suitable topic for a chaste woman like me.
And what use is there now in accusing Apollo? Everyone is aware
how he coaxed Orestes into killing his own
mother, though no one condones Orestes' act.
Nevertheless, egged on by the god, he murdered
her, and I helped him as much as any woman
could, along with our friend Pylades.
Afterward Orestes broke down and collapsed here; the guilt
of his mother's blood drove him to this crazed
state. I say "mother's blood" because I dare not
mouth the names of the furies that harass him
relentlessly now.
Six long days ago we dispatched her remains to the pyre. Not
a drop of water has passed his lips since, nor
has he washed. He just lies there, bundled in
blankets.
Whenever his fever lifts and he comes to his senses, he sobs and
then, in a fury, bolts to his feet like a wild colt
fighting loose of its bridle.   10
Meanwhile Argos has condemned us as matricides, outlaws,
forbidding anyone to give us shelter or even utter

a single word to us. Today is the day that's set to
decide whether we are to be executed and, if so,
whether by stoning or by the sword.

But still we have a modicum of hope. Menelaus, our uncle, has
just arrived from Troy, docking at Nauplia. His
ships cram the harbor after their long, stormy
wanderings.

He has sent Helen, the cause of the bloody war, ahead to his
palace under cover of night, for fear all those
who lost sons at Troy would stone her as soon
as they laid eyes on her. She's there this very
minute, keening her sister's demise and our
family's ruination. But she takes some comfort
in her daughter, Hermione, whom Menelaus
brought from Sparta and left in my mother's
care before he set off for Troy.

Now Hermione consoles Helen and helps her forget her lot,
while I'm here, craning to spot Menelaus
approaching along the road. Unless he helps us
now, we're lost. Nothing is more pathetic than a
royal family brought low.

(Helen enters from the palace.)

HELEN

Ah, dearest Electra, Clytemnestra's very own daughter.

What? Are you unmarried still, after all these years? And how
are you? How is your poor brother? What
misfortune, I can't believe it. You must both be
going through such a dreadful time. To murder
one's own mother. How horrible.

I myself see no reason to spurn or blame you, knowing this is
all due to Apollo's scheming. Still, Clytemnestra
was my one and only sister. And to think I
haven't laid eyes on her since I sailed off to Troy,
overcome by some divine fate and madness. Now
she's gone, and I alone grieve for her.

ELECTRA

> Helen, can't you see what's under your nose? There lies the son of
> Agamemnon with hardly a breath left. I haven't
> had a moment's sleep watching over him. I don't
> condescendingly mock and reproach his
> sufferings. Whereas you, smug with success,
> swollen with glory, come here as if to gloat on
> our misfortunes.

HELEN

> How long has he been lying in such a state?

ELECTRA

> Ever since he shed the blood of that woman who bore him.   20

HELEN

> Poor son. Poor mother, to die such a death.

ELECTRA

> He murdered himself murdering her.

HELEN

> Oh, I've been meaning to ask. Would you do me a favor?

ELECTRA

> I will, but it depends on the state of my brother.

HELEN

> Will you, for my sake, visit my sister's grave?

ELECTRA

> What! You can't be serious. You mean my mother's grave? Why?

HELEN

> Just to pour this wine libation and leave a clipping of my hair.

ELECTRA

> Shouldn't you go yourself and pay respects? After all, she's *your*
> sister.

HELEN

> I'm too scared and ashamed to be seen in Argos.

ELECTRA

> It's a bit late for shame. Where are such feelings when you
> ditched your husband and ran off?   30

HELEN

> You speak more with the barb of truth than the balm of
> kindness.

ELECTRA

> So why, exactly, are you ashamed?

HELEN

> I'm terrified of the fathers who lost sons at Troy.

ELECTRA

> As well you should be. Your name is cursed all over Argos.

HELEN

> Please, I beg you, save me from this duty and go on my behalf.

ELECTRA

> No. I just couldn't face my mother's grave.

HELEN

> Please. It wouldn't be right to send a servant in my place.

ELECTRA

> Why don't you send your own daughter, Hermione?

HELEN

An unmarried girl shouldn't be seen alone on the streets.

ELECTRA

But surely it's her duty to pay a visit to the grave of the woman
who brought her up.   40

HELEN

That's true enough, dear. I hadn't thought of it like that. I'll
call her.
(Helen calls into the palace.)
Hermione. Hermione, dearest. Come out here a moment.
(Hermione enters.)
Now darling, do exactly as I bid you. Bring this libation and
offering of my hair to Clytemnestra's grave. Pour
this mixture of nectar, milk, and wine as you
utter this prayer: "Your beloved sister, Helen,
who cannot visit in person for fear of the
Argives, sends you these gifts."
Beseech her not to look harshly on us—my husband, you, myself
and these poor wretched children who were
undone by Apollo. Impress on her that I will
fulfill all the sisterly duties and rites befitting the
dead. Hurry now, dear. Perform this rite and
dash back.
(Hermione quickly exits. Helen retires into the palace.)

ELECTRA

Oh, how despicable can human nature get? Did anyone notice
how she just cut the tip of a lock of her precious
hair, careful not to spoil her looks? Still the same
old Helen. May the gods despise you and shower
you with misfortune for bringing such ruin on
me, Orestes, and on all Hellas.
(Slowly the Chorus enters.)
Oh, here come those women who are on our side. They keep

watch and keen with me, but if they wake him
I'll have to bear seeing him demented once more.
Please, dear friends, do not misunderstand me, but tread lightly
and don't utter a word. I am grateful for your
kindness, but if he wakes I won't be able to
bear it.

CHORUS *(to each other)*
Shhh. Keep it down.

ELECTRA
Back, don't come so close to his bed. Keep your voices down.
Draw carefully closer and whisper why you've
come. Now at last he sleeps in some peace.

CHORUS
How is he?   50

ELECTRA
He's barely breathing.

CHORUS
Poor soul.

ELECTRA
Careful. If he wakes he'll surely die.

CHORUS
How painful. How unfair. He was just Apollo's pawn.

ELECTRA
How unfortunate. It was a crime Apollo himself maneuvered. A
murder for a murder.

CHORUS
Watch. Watch. Look, he stirs.

ELECTRA
> Shush. Yes, your rumpus woke him.

CHORUS
> No. No. he just stirred in his sleep.

ELECTRA
> Move away. Back from us and hush.

CHORUS
> He's still fast asleep.   60

ELECTRA
> Then let him slumber.

CHORUS *(keening quietly)*
> O mother, queen of night,
> who bestows the gift
> of sleep to troubled souls,
> rise now from your darkness
> and fly to Agamemnon's palace,
> for agony and ruin are here
> and we're at our wit's end . . .

ELECTRA
> Shhh. Enough, enough. In heaven's name, be still. No more
> plaintive mourning. My friends, won't you allow
> him sleep in peace?

CHORUS
> But what's going to happen? Where will it all end?   70

ELECTRA
> Death. What else? He won't let a morsel pass his lips.

CHORUS
> He's certain to die so.

ELECTRA

> Yes, Apollo finished us both when he had murder leapfrog
> > murder, murdering our father's murderer, our
> > mother.

CHORUS

> It was indeed a deed of justice.

ELECTRA

> But it was not right. Mother, you killed and were killed.
> When you killed our father, you killed us also, the children of
> > your own flesh and blood. We died by your
> > death. We are the living dead. I live here a mere
> > shade in the mocking sunlit world, haunted by
> > my misspent life, without a child or husband,
> > dragging out dark days in endless misery.

CHORUS

> Electra, check to see if your brother has died while we keened.
> > He lies so still now. His stillness is troubling.

(Orestes suddenly stirs and wakes.)

ORESTES

> O balm of sleep, succor of the infirm, sweetly you descend upon
> > me in my dire need, monarch of forgetting to
> > whom those troubled solicit. Where am I? How
> > did I get here? I can't remember.

ELECTRA

> Orestes, how relieved I was to see you rest. Can I raise your head?
> > Can I help you?

ORESTES

> Yes, give me a hand and wipe the sleep from my eyes and mouth.

80

ELECTRA

> Gladly, I'll tend you with a sister's love.

ORESTES

Sit by my side. Brush back the tangled hair that's blinding me.

ELECTRA

Poor noggin—Look at your hair, so knotted and grimy. It's so
long since you washed.

ORESTES

Please set me back again. Good. After these fits, I haven't a tack
of strength.

ELECTRA

There, now. Lie back. Bed is the place for the sick, frustrating as
it may be.

ORESTES

Prop me up again and turn me. Sorry I'm so helplessly ill and
hard to please. I must be a burden.

ELECTRA

Would you like to chance walking a step or two? A change might
do you good.

ORESTES

I suppose so. It's better to show a face of health, even when
you're far from it.

ELECTRA

Orestes, listen now. I want to tell you something while the Furies
give you a break.

ORESTES

If it's good news, then please tell me; otherwise I'm not able
for it.

90

ELECTRA

> Menelaus, our uncle, is right *here*. His fleet has anchored at
> Nauplia.

ORESTES

> Honestly? There's light at last. Our uncle whom our father did so
> much for is actually *here*?

ELECTRA

> Yes. Helen is proof. He brought her back from Troy.

ORESTES

> I'd envy him more if he were alone. By bringing Helen home he
> brings trouble.

ELECTRA

> Poor Tyndareus. What daughters he sired: infamous throughout
> all of Hellas.

ORESTES

> Mind now that you don't follow *that* pair. I mean in your heart
> as well as in your head.
> *(Orestes darts up, his eyes wide in terror.)*

ELECTRA

> Orestes! Your eyes are crazed again . . . the madness is back and
> only moments ago you were fine.

ORESTES

> No, mother, please. Keep them off, those hags with bloodshot,
> gory eyes and serpent-coiled hair. Help. They're
> lurching at me.
> *(Electra catches him by the arm and tries to lead him back to bed.)*

ELECTRA

> Easy, please lie down now. There is absolutely nothing there,
> nothing. They're all phantoms of your
> imagination.

ORESTES

> O Apollo, help me! They want to kill me, those bitches of
> infernal hell!   100

ELECTRA

> I won't let you go. I'll hold you still by force.
> *(She grabs Orestes and holds him down.)*

ORESTES

> Let go of me! You're one of those Furies, grabbing me, grappling
> to hurl me down to hell!
> *(He bursts loose and springs up.)*

ELECTRA

> What can I do? How can I help? He's beyond saving. The Gods
> are pitched against us.

ORESTES

> Hurry, get the horn-tipped bow that Apollo gave me. I'll ward off
> these bitches.
> *(Electra hands him the bow and quiver and he draws the bow.)*
> Back, you demons! Supernatural you may be, but unless you go,
> this arrow will wound you. Blast it. Can't you see
> this drawn bow? Get going. Fly. Go and pester
> Apollo. Blame him.
> *(He falters, drops his bow, and recovers.)*
> What? What was I uttering? Why am I up and gasping? Wait.
> The storm has past. Such calmness once more.
> *(He sees Electra by his bed sobbing into the veil of her robe.)*
> Electra, why are you weeping? Why cover your face? I'm so
> ashamed you have to suffer me suffering this
> sickness and shame. Please don't weep for me.

Let me take the full brunt. I know you condoned
   the murder, but it was I who spilled the blood
   and not you.
I blame Apollo. He drove me to it without ever lifting a finger
   himself. I'm sure that our dead father if he got
   the chance at the time would have implored us
   not to kill her. That wouldn't bring him back
   to life.
Now I am doomed to these seizures. It all seems hopeless. But
   come, Electra, uncover your face. Don't cry any
   more, even if there's no glimmer of hope. Tend
   me when I'm down. Give me solace and I, in
   my turn, will comfort you with love when you
   despair. I won't let you down. Love is the sole
   solace for the likes of us in times such as these.
Go in. Wash and nourish yourself, rest your tired eyes. If your
   watch exhausts you and you turn ill, then I'm
   done. Everyone else has deserted me. You're my
   only light.   110

ELECTRA

I can't leave you. My place is at your side. I'll live or die with you.
   For you are *my* only light. I'm nothing without
   you, a woman helpless and alone. How could I
   manage?
But since you think it best, I'll go in and rest. First, though, *you*
   must return to bed and rest. Try, more than
   anything, to control the fancy of your terror and
   keep calm. Stay in your bed. Even an imaginary
   sickness plays upon the mind and spirit and
   weakens a body, so don't brood.
(Electra enters the palace and Orestes lies down.)

CHORUS

Goddesses of the terror,
   speeding in the wind,
   you revel together

in your cloud of tears.
Eumenides, your presence
shrouds the very atmosphere
with your vehemence for vengeance.
Avengers of murder,   120
we implore, we beg you
to vouchsafe this lad,
Agamemnon's son,
from the onslaught
of his frenzy.

O miserable Orestes,
we cry mercy, pity
for the crime,
the murder
that Apollo incited   130
you helplessly on to
from his Delphic temple.

O Zeus, is there not a mite
of mercy or hope here?
Poor lad, what is this agony,
this terrible torment
hailing and lashing you?
The whirlwind of furies
blows with retaliation,
unsettling your house,   140
assailing you with gale
after gale of grief,
blood for your mother's blood.
We take your side.
We'll mourn your house
wrecked on fortune's reef.

Happiness sways briefly.
It will not hold.

The heavens toss it
like a frail sailboat.   150
Gusts of anguish
whip down, striking terror.
Waves after swamping waves
of tragedy strike,
capsizing the poor craft.
Happiness goes down
among the flaying and crying.

And yet, surely, no other house
deserves to be lauded
as much as this one, sprung from Tantalus   160
and the marriage of gods?

Look now, here comes the king,
royal Menelaus . . .
(Enter Menelaus with his attendants.)
All hail the king,
the king who launched
a thousand ships to Troy.
He did what he swore to do
with the help of the gods.
Fortune was with him and his crew . . .

MENELAUS

Home from Troy at last. How good it is. Yet I am also saddened,
              never have I witnessed a house more put upon
              by tragedy than this.   170
Approaching Malea I heard the report of Agamemnon's murder
              at the hands of his own wife. Truthful Glaucus,
              the god and prophet of sailors, sprung from
              the sea and before our very eyes exclaimed:
              "Menelaus, your brother lies dead in his bath, the
              last his wife will run for him." We all burst into
              tears at this unbelievable news.

Then, as soon as we reached Nauplia and I sent Helen on
　　　　　ahead of me to the palace, I looked forward to
　　　　　seeing Orestes and his mother again. I thought,
　　　　　of course, they at least were all right. But
　　　　　then a sailor tells me of Clytemnestra's
　　　　　unbelievable end.
Can you guide me to where I might find my nephew Orestes? He
　　　　　was but a babe in his mother's arms when I last
　　　　　laid eyes on him before leaving for Troy. I'd
　　　　　never recognize him now. I'd pass him on the
　　　　　street.

ORESTES

Menelaus, here I am: Orestes himself, the very man you ask for.
　　　　　I'd tell you the whole story of my downfall, but
　　　　　first I drop on my knees and beg you to save me.
　　　　　You've arrived at the nick of time.

MENELAUS

Heavens above. Is this body still really in the land of the living?
　　　　　Has he returned from the dead?

ORESTES

Yes, I'm from hell, my own living hell.

MENELAUS

How dreadful you look, your grimy hair all knotted.

ORESTES

It's not my looks, but my crime, that undoes me.

MENELAUS

Your eyes are burnt holes.

ORESTES

My life is spent, only my name remains. I'm the murderer of my
　　　　　very own mother.　　　　　　　　　　180

MENELAUS

So I've heard, but the less said the better.

ORESTES

I'll spare you, but I wish the gods spared me.

MENELAUS

What ails you? What's brought you to this?

ORESTES

My conscience. The scruples of my mind.

MENELAUS

What exactly do you mean? Speak plainly.

ORESTES

Guilt. I'm steeped in guilt . . .

MENELAUS

A tough one that, but you can recover.

ORESTES

And madness besetting me for killing my mother.

MENELAUS

When did that begin?

ORESTES

The very day we built our mother's tomb.   190

MENELAUS

Where exactly were you when it came on? At home or at
                    the pyre?

ORESTES

It was by the pyre that night as I waited to gather her remains.

MENELAUS
Was there anyone there to take care of you?

ORESTES
Pylades, who helped me murder my mother.

MENELAUS
Can you describe these fits?

ORESTES
I seem to see three women, black as a cloudy night.

MENELAUS
Enough said. I know exactly who they are, but I won't mouth
their names.

ORESTES
You're wise not to. They're too frightful.

MENELAUS
So it's they who harass you for doing away with your mother.

ORESTES
Aye, they hound me. It's agony.   200

MENELAUS
It figures, such suffering follows such deeds.

ORESTES
There is only one way out.

MENELAUS
To kill yourself? There's no sense in that.

ORESTES
No, not that way, but via Apollo. I was the tool to his murderous
cause.

MENELAUS
  You're right. He was unjust.

ORESTES
  We are the lackeys of the gods.

MENELAUS
  And still Apollo won't come to your aid?

ORESTES
  Oh, he will, but the gods are on their own time.

MENELAUS
  How long has it been since your mother died?

ORESTES
  Just six days. The pyre's still warm.   210

MENELAUS
  Just six days? The gods might be slow, but her avengers are quick
    off the mark.

ORESTES
  I may not be wise, but I'm loyal to those close to me.

MENELAUS
  Yes, but where has that got you? Is there any help from your
    father?

ORESTES
  No, nothing. And since there is nothing, there will be nothing.

MENELAUS
  What about the city?

ORESTES
  That's as bad. The city has disowned me.

MENELAUS
Have you, according to custom, washed your hands of the blood?

ORESTES
How can I? Every door is shut on my face.

MENELAUS
Who in all of Argos wants you banished most?

ORESTES
Oeax—he blames my father for the death of his brother,
                Palamedes, at Troy.   220

MENELAUS
I see. He wants revenge.

ORESTES
It wasn't my fault. And there's another source.

MENELAUS
Another? Who? Aegisthus' crowd, probably?

ORESTES
Yes. They've all got the city's ear.

MENELAUS
Will Argos let you hold on to your father's power?

ORESTES
How, when they won't allow me to live?

MENELAUS
What can you be certain of?

ORESTES
Today they are to vote on our fate.

MENELAUS

Have you any idea of the verdict?

ORESTES

Death by stoning.   230

MENELAUS

Why don't you escape?

ORESTES

We're trapped. There are men armed with swords all around us.

MENELAUS

Are they personal enemies or Argive soldiers?

ORESTES

It's as simple as this. Every Argive is on duty. They all want
          my hide.

MENELAUS

You're definitely in a tight spot.

ORESTES

You are my sole chance. Here you are, back on the wave of
          success. I'm your brother's son. Make room for
          us on that wave. Don't exclude us. You owe it to
          our father. True friends remain steadfast in
          rough seas.

CHORUS

Look, here comes the Spartan Tyndareus. In spite of his age, he's
          sprightly. He's shaved his head and wears black in
          mourning for his daughter.

ORESTES

I've had it now. I dread him more that any other man alive. How
          can I look him in the eye after what I've done?

He brought me up. He kissed and hugged me
often when I was just a child. He spoiled me with
affection.
He and Leda cradled me in their arms. They treated me like
Castor and Polydeuces, as if I were their own.
And now look how I return their love. What
black cloud can conceal me from his eyes?

(Enter Tyndareus and his attendants.)

TYNDAREUS

Women, where can I find Menelaus, my daughter's husband?
While I poured libations over Clytemnestra's
grave, I was told he had returned home with
his wife after all this time abroad. I'm anxious
to see and greet the man himself. Can you
direct me?   240

MENELAUS

Hello, Tyndareus, the husband who shared his wife with
mighty Zeus.

TYNDAREUS

Welcome, Menelaus, my son in law—What . . . is that creature
here? The curse of the future is never knowing
what's around the corner. He's right here, the
dark prince of matricide. I can't look at him.
Menelaus, you're not actually speaking to this
thing.

MENELAUS

Why not? He is my brother's son, and I loved my brother.

TYNDAREUS

What? This unnatural thing! The son of Agamemnon?

MENELAUS

Yes, his son. Thus, he must be honored no matter what.

TYNDAREUS

I see you've learned new ways while abroad.

MENELAUS

It's always been a Greek custom to honor your kin.

TYNDAREUS

But not if the law has to be sacrificed.

MENELAUS

Necessity is the boss here. Under the compulsion of the gods, no
man on earth is free.

TYNDAREUS

All right. You can hold to such notions, but I'll have no truck
with them.   250

MENELAUS

Your anger and your age aren't the best combination for sound
thinking.

TYNDAREUS

Sound thinking! You're pushing it a bit in *this* case.
If wrong and right are clear to everyone as night and day, what
man ever acted so unsoundly, senselessly, with
less understanding than this man?
Consider this, not once did he consider taking his cause to the
law courts. When his father was murdered by my
very own daughter—and I admit that was an
abomination that I'll never condone—he ought
to have impeached her at the court with the
murder and made her pay the price: banishment
from her house, an outcast.
As things stand now, he's no better than his mother. No, terrible
as she was, he was twice as bad when he killed her.

Menelaus, look at it this way: supposing this man is murdered by
his wife; then their son in his turn murders her,
and then his son adds to the cycle of murder
with another murder. Tell me, where and when
will the vicious cycle end? Each killer is doomed
to death by the next killer's revenge.
No. Our ancestors managed these matters wisely by banishing
the murderer from sight, forbidding everyone to
meet or speak with the outcast. They avenged the
crime by banishment, not another killing and,
thus, by doing so put an end to the cycle of
killing and vengeance.
Don't get me wrong. I abhor wicked women and, most of all, my
own daughter Clytemnestra, who did away with
her husband. And I feel the same toward your
wife, Helen. I'll never speak with her again as
long as I live. I don't envy you that trip you made
to Troy to fetch the likes of her.
No, it is the law that I am concerned with. I'm bent on enforcing
it to check this vile, unnatural contagion of
murder that corrupts our cities and our country.
(He turns abruptly on Orestes.)
As for you, you devil! What sort of inhuman heart beat in you
when your mother came begging to you for her
life, baring her breast? I wasn't there to witness
it, but the very thought of it is enough to make
me weep.   260
I'm sure of one thing: the Gods despise you. Your fits of frenzy
are the penalty they impose upon you. These fits
are proof indeed of your crime.
Take heed then, Menelaus. Should you assist this man, you are
defying the gods. Let him be stoned to death or
else never dare set foot in Sparta again.
My daughter paid her due by her death. Yet he had no right to
take her life. I'd have been a happy man, but for
my daughters. They were my misfortune.

CHORUS
>   The man whose children bring him happiness in life, rather than
>   shame and calamity, is most fortunate.

ORESTES
>   Grandfather, I'm afraid to open my mouth, knowing anything
>   I say will be wrong. Your gray hair stops my
>   tongue. I admit the murder of my mother was a
>   crime. But in another light, since I was revenging
>   my father, it wasn't.
>   I ask you what else could I have done? I was bound by two
>   contradictory obligations. Granted, I wouldn't be
>   here without my mother, but the same goes for
>   my father. As a matter of fact, my father comes
>   first, since he was the seed. Thus, I figured I must
>   be loyal to him first, rather than my mother.
>   Another reason for taking his side is that your daughter—I can't
>   bear to call her mother—took another man, a
>   lover, wantonly into her bed. It hurts me as
>   much as I hurt her to utter this, but Aegisthus,
>   yes, was her lover. He was her bedroom mate. So
>   I murdered them both out of revenge for my
>   father's murder.
>   For this now I'm to be stoned! But, believe me, my act was on
>   behalf of my country. If wives take my mother's
>   example, and then run to their sons baring their
>   breasts to invoke pity, then the law will be a sham
>   and a husband's murder mean damn all. But my
>   so-called crime has checked this.
>   I, more than anyone, had the right to kill my mother. She
>   betrayed her husband while he carried out his
>   duty as chief of our army at Troy. No sooner was
>   his back turned than she sullied his bed with a
>   lover! And *then*, when she was caught in the act,
>   she hadn't the dignity to see justice through.

Instead, she murdered my father to protect her
own skin: crime coupling crime to save herself.
I should not look to the heavens for justification, but in heaven's
name what other justice was there? And what
would my father have done if I had not acted
thus? He'd have hounded me with the furies of
a father's vengeance.   270
Are there only Furies on my mother's side? Were there none to
avenge my father?
Tyndareus, you are really to blame: *you* destroyed *me*. You sired
the woman who murdered my father and landed
me in this position. Look, Telemachus didn't kill
his mother, but then *she* didn't murder her
husband. No, *she* refused to take a lover. She
remained loyal to Odysseus while he was away
at Troy.
Mark this. Apollo ensconced in his throne at Delphi is the one
God whose oracle is tried and trusted by all
mankind without question. And it was *he* who
commanded me to *murder* my mother. So accuse
him of this crime. Stone *him* to death. He's the
criminal, not I.
What was I supposed to do? Where can I go now, what now can
I do, if the very God who bade me murder my
mother will not or cannot protect me? Let no
one say then that our act was evil, but that we
did what we had to do at our own great cost.
The same is true of marriage. Happy the lives of those whose
marriage is fortunate, but for those whose
marriage is unfortunate, they are unhappy
at home and abroad.

CHORUS
It seems women were created to muck up the lives of men.

TYNDAREUS

    Your brazenness, your smooth talk really gets under my skin.
               Now I'm even more dead set on your death. I
               came here to lay flowers on my daughter's tomb,
               but now you've incensed me to the added
               purpose of instigating your end. I'll go to Argive
               council, whether they like it or not, and whip
               them into stoning you and your sister.
    She deserves to die even more than you. She guided and goaded
               you on with her tall tale, telltale dreams that
               Agamemnon *supposedly* sent her, ratting on your
               mother's infidelity, that affair with Aegisthus
               that she made out had vexed the gods of the
               underworld as much as it angered us here. She
               cunningly fired you up until the whole house was
               ablaze.
    Now, Menelaus, I'm warning you, if you take any stock in
               our kinship, pay heed of my vehemence and
               don't dare shield this wretch from heaven's
               punishment. Let the people stone him. If you
               interfere you'll pay for it: you'll never set foot
               in Sparta again.
    Keep what I've said in mind and don't cast aside law-abiding,
               god-fearing men for the sake of this miscreant.
               Now, my servants, enough, lead me out of here.   280

(Exit Tyndareus and servants.)

ORESTES *(to himself)*

    Good, you crotchety old fool; go, so that I can have the ear of
               Menelaus without you getting in the way.
    Menelaus, why are you pacing back and forth with such a
               furrowed brow?

MENELAUS

    Don't ask. I don't know which way to turn. All right?

ORESTES

> Please, before you come to any decision listen to me and then
>> decide.

MENELAUS

> Okay, fire away. I suppose sometimes it's better to keep your
>> mouth shut, while other times it is better to
>> speak.

ORESTES

> Now is the time to speak. I'll need to talk a bit to get at the whole
>> story. To be honest, Menelaus, I'm not requesting
>> anything from you that is yours. All I'm asking is
>> a return of the favor that you owe my father, your
>> *own* brother. It's not money I'm asking for, but
>> what my father gave you once: not money,
>> but life.
> Yes, yes, I crossed over the line between right and wrong. I
>> admit that. But now I ask you to cross over and
>> transgress to help me. When my own father
>> gathered an army for the siege of Troy he did
>> the same for you. He tried to right your wife's
>> wrongdoing. He did it with the best intentions,
>> out of the goodness of his heart. Return that
>> favor now.
> He would have given his life for you, a true brother. He fought
>> by your side, bracing his shield next to yours in
>> order that you could win your wife back. Return
>> the loyalty he gave you there and stand by my
>> side, not for ten long years, but just a single,
>> lousy day.
> And there is another reason for helping me. I'm not going to
>> look for satisfaction for the death of my sister,
>> Iphigenia, at Aulia. She died on account of you.
>> You needn't touch a hair of Hermione's. Let her

live. My hands are tied with this. I'll make
 allowances.
So for the life my father gave you, then give me and my unwed
 sister life in return. Save our lives. If I die, I leave
 this house without an heir.   290
You'll say it's hopeless, that our hour has come, but surely this is
 the time to help us Menelaus. You are our own
 flesh and blood. Now's the time to show loyalty
 when all seems lost? Who needs help when the
 heavens smile on us and all is well? But now we
 need *your* help.
Everyone is aware how much you love your wife. I'm not trying
 to butter you up, but in her name . . .

(aside)
Oh, look what I've come to, but as they say, beggars can't be
 choosers.

(to Menelaus)
Yes, in *her* name, I appeal to you on behalf of our house.
Oh, my father is hovering over us this minute. He's behind what
 I say. I've made my claim. This is my position.
 I'm begging for my life as naturally as any man
 would.

CHORUS
 We are just women, but we also beg you to help them. Save them.
  You have the power.

MENELAUS
 Honestly, Orestes, I think a great deal of you and would do
  anything to take your side. Duty bids one to help
  a kinsman in such dire straits, even if the cost is
  death fighting the enemy. But oh, I wish the gods
  would give me such power, because I've returned
  weakened.
 I have no allies and hardly a single soldier after my interminable
  wandering that was fraught with hazards. We'd

never be able to overwhelm Argos with a show
of power.
Our only hope is diplomacy and tact. It would be crazy to expect
great things any other way.
When the mob is swept by rage, resistance is only fuel to their
raging fire. It's best to ride out the stormy wave
of their ire. We may have a chance of winning
them over when their own anger runs its course
and they're easy to control. Wait for that change
of wind.   300
I think the best course is for me to lobby Tyndareus and the city
and try to persuade them to calm down. A ship
whose mainsail is drawn too tautly reels and
keels, but once the sail is trimmed and slackened
the craft rights itself again and sails smoothly.
People resent being pushed and badgered in the same way that
the gods do.
You're right, it's my duty to protect you, but this is the way to go
about it and not by force as you think. I've yet
got to exercise my power in either peace or
wartime here, being but the brother of the late
king. I'd never overwhelm the formidable forces
against you right now. Now is the time to be
prudent and solicit fate.
(Exit Menelaus abruptly with his followers.)

ORESTES

Oh, you wimp. You're worthless except when it comes to leading
an army on behalf of bloody women. You're not
worth a damn when it comes to taking care
of you own kin. You turn on your heels and
scram. Have you forgotten everything that
Agamemnon's done? O father, we are without
an ally in our affliction! I haven't a chance. The
Argives are certain to put me to death now. My
one glimmer of hope was this man.

But wait. Here comes beloved Pylades rushing from Phocis!
        What a relief to see him. No sailor welcomed
        calm waters more than I welcome this loyal
        friend.

(Enter Pylades.)

PYLADES

I tore through the streets as soon as I heard about the assembly.
        I saw them with my very own eyes. They've got
        together to kill you and your sister. What are you
        going to do? How are you? You are my friend,
        blood brother and cousin.

ORESTES

Finished. In one word. Kaput.

PYLADES

Then I'm finished too. Friends stay friends through feast or
        famine.

ORESTES

Menelaus, that traitor, has left us in the lurch.

PYLADES

Tell me something new. It's not strange that a betraying woman's
        husband should turn betrayer himself.   310

ORESTES

He might as well not have returned.

PYLADES

So, he *really* has returned?

ORESTES

At long last, but he wasn't so long at ditching his own.

PYLADES
And what about his wife, that slut. Did he ship her back?

ORESTES
Nope. It wasn't he brought her, but she brought him.

PYLADES
Where is she now, that woman who brought about the death of
so many from Argos?

ORESTES
In *my* own very house. If you could call it mine now.

PYLADES
What did you ask Menelaus, your father's brother?

ORESTES
To save us from being put to death.

PYLADES
By the Gods, what was his answer? This I want to know.   320

ORESTES
He was cagey.

PYLADES
But what reasons did he give? They tell a lot.

ORESTES
That father who sired that *lovely* pair of daughters turned up.

PYLADES
You mean Tyndareus? He must really have it in for you, what
with his own daughter's death.

ORESTES
You bet. Menelaus put him before his own flesh and blood.

PYLADES

Surely your uncle offered to give you a helping hand?

ORESTES

He's no hero, though he plays the big guy among the ladies.

PYLADES

You're finished, so death is certain.

ORESTES

That's for Argos to decide when they vote.

PYLADES

Before I get a heart attack, tell me exactly what they are to
vote on.   330

ORESTES

Life or death: such easy words with such scary consequences.

PYLADES

Escape then. High-tail it from the palace with your sister.

ORESTES

Are you blind? We're surrounded by guards.

PYLADES

Yes, yes, you're right. I noticed guards at the end of every street.

ORESTES

We're penned in like a surrounded city.

PYLADES

You never asked me about my situation. Like you, I've had my
problems.

ORESTES

Really? Who heaps more misfortune upon you, upon me?

PYLADES
Strophius, my father, has banished me.

ORESTES
On what charge? Was it between him and you? Or did the courts
expel you?

PYLADES
He bans me for helping you kill your mother, declaring her death
a foul crime.   340

ORESTES
Oh, to think you must suffer for me on top of everything else.

PYLADES
I'm no Menelaus: I can take it. ·

ORESTES
Aren't you afraid the council will condemn you to death also
with us?

PYLADES
They can't. I'm from outside their jurisdiction. I'm Phocian.

ORESTES
I wouldn't be so sure. Cunning, evil men can rouse the mob to
do what they bid.

PYLADES
Yes, but under upright men the mob makes upright decisions.

ORESTES
That's the answer. We'll solicit them ourselves.

PYLADES
But why?

ORESTES

Suppose I went to the council and . . .

PYLADES

And said you were fully justified?   350

ORESTES

Yes, that I avenged my father, their king!

PYLADES

That might backfire and then you've had it.

ORESTES

What should I do—give in and die cowardly without a word?

PYLADES

No! That is only for losers.

ORESTES

What then?

PYLADES

If you wait, is there any chance?

ORESTES

None!

PYLADES

If you go to the council is there any possibility you might be
            saved?

ORESTES

With luck, maybe.

PYLADES

Well, surely that's better than doing nothing?   360

ORESTES
Should I go, then?

PYLADES
Yes, for even if you die, you'll die with dignity.

ORESTES
True. At least they won't be able to brand me a coward . . .

PYLADES
You'll have a better chance than if you stick around here.

ORESTES
And my cause is just, also.

PYLADES
We can only pray that everyone will see it like that.

ORESTES
And if I'm fortunate, some might take pity on me.

PYLADES
And the fact that you're royalty should help.

ORESTES
Not to speak of my understandable outrage at my father's
murder.

PYLADES
Everything is clearer now.   370

ORESTES
The course is set. If I have to die I'll go down like a man!

PYLADES
That's the spirit!

ORESTES
>Should we let Electra know?

PYLADES
>Heavens, no!

ORESTES
>She'd probably weep and wail.

PYLADES
>That wouldn't be good.

ORESTES
>We'd better not say anything.

PYLADES
>That will save some time too. The less we have to deal with the
>>better.

ORESTES
>There's maybe one other stumbling block . . .

PYLADES
>What's that, now?   380

ORESTES
>What if the Furies strike with another bout of madness?

PYLADES
>Now, don't worry. I'll take care of you.

ORESTES
>It's not easy dealing with the sick.

PYLADES
>My friend, when it comes to helping you, it's not difficult for me.

ORESTES
> But watch out, being in such close quarters with the Furies, you
> might be touched by madness too.

PYLADES
> Forget such misgivings.

ORESTES
> So, you're not afraid?

PYLADES
> No. It would be an offense for a friend to shirk danger for a
> friend.

ORESTES
> Then lead on.

PYLADES
> I'll be glad to, my friend.   390

ORESTES
> Take me to my father's grave.

PYLADES
> What! Why there?

ORESTES
> To pray for his help.

PYLADES
> Yes, that's the right thing to do.

ORESTES
> But don't let me catch a glimpse of my mother's grave.

PYLADES

>I know—She wasn't on your side. Hurry, so the council won't
>>condemn you before you even get there. Let me
>>help you. You're so feeble.
>
>I'll bear you through the jeering streets gladly and not care a jot
>>for the rabble. What is friendship worth if I can't
>>prove it now to a friend in need?

ORESTES

>The old maxim is true: "Rely on friends and not kin alone." One
>>good friend, one sole friend, is worth umpteen
>>relatives.

(Exit Orestes and Pylades.)

CHORUS

>The grand posterity,
>the mighty prowess   400
>flowing through Greece,
>and on by the banks of Simois,
>has ebbed again
>and its waters have turned
>bloody,
>>polluted
>from its source
>when the house of Tantalus
>was cursed with a feud over
>a golden fleeced lamb.
>What followed from that   410
>was the most gory banquet:
>a feast of slaughtered princes;
>tragedy after bloody tragedy
>submerging now the heirs of Atreus.
>What had seemed right
>turned dreadfully wrong
>as soon as it was done.
>To slash a mother's throat

and then raise the righteous blade
dripping in the sunlight   420
with her dark blood,
is perverted and anyone
who thinks otherwise is crazy.

At the end, Tyndareus' daughter,
cried out again and again,
terrified of death: "No, my son,
no, if you murder your mother
you'll lose everything.
In revenging your father,
you'll wrap your name   430
in an eternal flame of shame!"

What affliction is more terrible?
What cause for grief
and weeping in any land
could match a son
steeping his hands
in the blood of his *own* mother?
For his crime, the Furies
furiously torment him
and drive him berserk.   440
Agamemnon's very own offspring
is unable to escape.
His eyes roll wildly:
those same eyes that beheld
his mother bare her breast to him
through her gold-embroidered clothes
and he stabbed her there
with his own hand
for the wrong done his father
had wet the brand.   450
(Enter Electra.)

ELECTRA

> What? My heavens, has Orestes gone off somewhere in a flight of
> madness?

CHORUS

> No, no. He's gone to the Argive court
> to appeal his own case and yours.

ELECTRA

> But why? What possessed him?

CHORUS

> Pylades. Look, here comes a messenger who'll probably answer
> your question.

(Enter Messenger.)

MESSENGER

> Child of our war-chief, poor, unlucky daughter of Agamemnon.
> Lady Electra, I come with terrible news.

ELECTRA

> Alas, we're undone. You don't have to tell me. The sentence is
> death.

MESSENGER

> The Argives have decreed that you and your brother are to die.

ELECTRA

> So, what I've dreaded and expected for so long is finally here. Tell
> me about the trial. What speeches ruined us and
> condemned us to death? Tell me, must I die by
> stoning or by the sword?

MESSENGER

> As it happened, I came in from the country to find out how
> Orestes and you were faring—Your family always

took care of me and I always stood by your
  father. I'm just a poor peasant, but I'm loyal. 460
I saw a crowd seated on the very hill where they say Danaus held
  the first public assembly in Argos for the trial of
  Aegyptus. So, seeing the crowd, I went up and
  asked a bystander, "What's going on in Argos?
  Are we being threatened by our enemies?"
And he replied, "Can't you see Orestes down there heading to
  stand trial for his life?"
And then I saw something I never thought I'd see and never want
  to see again: Pylades helping your brother who
  was slumped on his shoulder. Orestes was on
  his last legs. Pylades, afflicted by his friend's
  affliction, nursed him along like a brother.
By then all the seats were full and a herald rose and cried: "Who
  will be the first to speak up? Should Orestes live
  or die?"
Talthybius rose—the same man who helped your father at Troy.
  He spoke, but he was no more than the mealy-
  mouthed courtier you'd expect him to be. Two-
  faced, he paid your father lip service, but damned
  your brother. He intertwined noble sentiments
  with foul ones, the gist being that Orestes' deed
  would not fare well for parents. While all the
  while he threw smug, flattering looks at
  Aegisthus' shower. But that's typical of him,
  always falling in with the in-crowd. He'd sell
  his soul to get in with the swells.
Prince Diomedes spoke after him. He believed that you should be
  exiled and not put to death, out of reverence to
  the gods. There was a murmur of praise for this,
  but others gave it thumbs down.
And then after him rose the kind of loudmouth who would offer
  his own mother to be stoned if he thought it
  would win him advantage, calling himself a
  patriotic Argive, though we all knew he became a

citizen by foul means. But for all his bluster and
coarse speech he was glib and cunning enough to
win over some of the crowd. He exhorted the
people to stone Orestes and you while Tyndareus
cheered, prompted, and egged him on.

Then, at last, someone rose up to speak against him. He wasn't
impressive to look at, but you knew he was a
man. You wouldn't see him strutting around
the marketplace and town. He works the land
himself, a farmer, the kind of man our country
relies on. But he was no fool. He was eager to
take on the loudmouth and spoke his bit
shrewdly.

This neutral man, who never hurt anyone, moved that Orestes
should be crowned because he dared to avenge
his father's murder by killing the evil and godless
wife who was only a burden on the country. This
woman kept men from war. Husbands refused to
leave, fearing that those men left behind would
usurp their beds and destroy their families. He
seemed to win people over, too, at least upright
people.

Then your brother addressed them: "Men of Argos, lords of
Inachus, the land given over to our care by our
fathers, it was for your sake as much as my
father's that I slew my mother. By killing me you
will okay the murder of husbands by their wives,
and then you are all as good as dead—or else
mere slaves to your wives. You will have taken the
wrong path. The woman who betrayed my
father's bed is now dead, but you'll nullify her
death by slaying me. The sooner a man dies the
better, since women will have a free rein on
crimes then and won't be accountable." 470

He spoke well, but the bigmouth who had appealed to the mob
earlier prevailed and a sentence of death was

hailed. The only thing poor Orestes could
persuade them to do was to postpone the
sentence of public stoning by promising that
both of you would take your own lives.
Pylades brought him away crying, followed by a group of friends
who were all weeping and lamenting themselves.
So he comes to you, a pitiable sight. Your time
has come. Neither your royal birth, nor Apollo
on high has helped you. On the contrary, Apollo
has destroyed you both.

CHORUS

O girl weighed down with such burden. You stand speechless,
your eyes downcast. Your lamentation waits to
burst from you, on the verge of tears . . .

ELECTRA

O Pelasgia, let me lead the keening chorus.
My white nails furrow my face.
I hail a rain of blows on my head.
I welcome Persephone, bow to her place
underground, the queen of the dead.
You virgins, let the sharp steel of light
shear you hair in sympathy with those who die,   480
heirs of Hellas' chieftains surrounded by a night
of one-eyed monsters. Oh, cry.

Lost, gone vanished is my house; the race
of Pelops erased, a house once envied for its happiness
has been blasted by heaven off earth's face,
being given the death-blow by the citizens of Argos.

Oh, troubled lives that last but a day,
look how all our hopes flit away.

Sorrows are doled out to everyone
in their turn and nothing is certain.   490

Oh, let me rise
to that shard of Olympus
that hangs high,
swaying in the sky,
from a fragile gilt chain.

Once there I'd howl my grief to
Tantalus, the father of my lineage—
what terrors we have lived through—
who witnessed the first dark stage
when Pelops rode over the sea,   500
hurling the body of Myrtilus
into the deadly surf at Geraestos,
beginning the chain of murderous treachery.

Then the son of Maia, Hermes,
set a lamb with a golden fleece
among the flocks of Atreus,
bringing down the king, Atreus,
the renowned breeder of horses.

That dreadful day
drove even the sun astray.   510
The sun rose in the blood-stained east
and set in the blushing west.
Zeus altered the very course
of the seven sailing Pleiades.
And the stain spread further,
murder cockaloruming murder
from Thyestes' gruesome banquet
and the faithless bed of Aerope of Crete,
until it all careered home
to fulfillment in our doom.   520

CHORUS

Look, here comes your brother,
sentenced to death for your mother.
Pylades helps him along, a true friend
of faltering Orestes, staying to the end.

ELECTRA

Oh, I weep to see you my brother standing before the grave. I
can't bear seeing you now for the last time. My
spirit fails me.

ORESTES

Now, quiet, Electra. Enough of the dramatics. Accept this. It's
dreadful but, nonetheless, we must face our
deaths nobly.

ELECTRA

How can I hush when we'll never see the light of day again?

ORESTES

Oh, you're killing me. Isn't it enough that I have been sentenced
to death? Don't make it worse.

ELECTRA

But you are still so young, Orestes. Such an untimely death. Your
due is life, not death.

ORESTES

O heavens, please don't turn me into a wimp and make me
break down.   530

ELECTRA

We're going to die. What else can I do but lament? That is only
natural.

ORESTES

Now this is our last day. We must choose either the noose or the
sword.

ELECTRA

O my brother, I want you to kill me. It is not fitting that some
lowly Argive put a child of Agamemnon to death.

ORESTES

No. It is enough that I have my mother's blood on my hands.
You must choose your own means, but you must
die by your own hand.

ELECTRA

Okay, okay. I choose the sword, but I want to go first and
not behind you. Let me lay my arms around
your neck.

ORESTES

You can enjoy that vain pleasure, if pleasure is possible to those
just about to die.

ELECTRA

My dearest, my sweet brother. How I love to call your name. We
are one together.

ORESTES

You will break my heart. How can I not take you in my arms?
What on earth can shame me now? Oh your
warm embrace is all we can ever know of
marriage and children.

ELECTRA

Oh, if only the sword could slay us in one stroke, together, and
we be laid in the one cedar coffin.

ORESTES
>   That would be sweet, but who of our family is left to bury us?   540

ELECTRA
>   Didn't Menelaus speak up for you against our deaths? He's such a
>   traitor to our father.

ORESTES
>   He didn't even show his face at the assembly. He is too busy
>   thinking of the throne to risk helping us. But
>   now, come, it is time for us to die nobly and
>   prove our strain, worthy of Agamemnon.
>   I will show the city my high blood by plunging the sword into
>   my own heart. You must follow my example and
>   not flinch.
>   Good Pylades, let you be caretaker of our deaths. Lay out the
>   bodies. See that we are brought to our family
>   grave and buried there.

PYLADES
>   Hold on, please. Orestes, I have one complaint. Do you really
>   expect me to go on living if you die!

ORESTES
>   What? Why should you die as well?

PYLADES
>   How can you honestly ask? My life is worth nothing without your
>   friendship.

ORESTES
>   You haven't killed your mother, as, heavens, I have mine.

PYLADES
>   I shared your deed and now I must share your suffering.

ORESTES

> Go back to your father and make amends. Don't die with me.
>> You have a father's home, a city, and plenty of
>> wealth—unlike me.   550
> You can't marry my sister as I promised you would out of
>> friendship. But there are other fish in the sea;
>> take another bride and raise healthy sons. There
>> is no such tie between you and me.
> And now, my dear companion, farewell, since we in death
>> cannot fare so well.

PYLADES

> How little you understand me, Orestes. If I ever let you down,
>> may the rich earth and the sunlit skies reject my
>> body. I cannot betray you and go free myself. I
>> own that I too took part in the murder. I was the
>> one who planned it, and for this I must suffer the
>> same fate as you and Electra. She was pledged to
>> me and, as far as I'm concerned, that is enough.
>> She is *my* wife already.
> And what fair story would I tell on returning home to Delphi and
>> Phocis? That I was your friend when your luck
>> was in, but now that it's out, I'm not? No way.
>> This task is mine as well as yours.
> But since we must die, let's try to figure out some way to make
>> Menelaus suffer, too, before we go.

ORESTES

> My friend, I'd die easier if we could work that.

PYLADES

> Listen to me and put away the sword for now.

ORESTES

> I'll wait with pleasure, if I can get vengeance.

PYLADES

> Keep it down. I don't trust those women.

ORESTES

> Don't doubt them. They are on our side.   560

PYLADES

> Fine. We could best get Menelaus by getting Helen.

ORESTES

> But how? I'm all for it, if we can pull it off.

PYLADES

> The answer is simple: by the sword. Look, she's taken refuge in
> your house, so she'll be easy to get at.

ORESTES

> Yes, you're right. She's putting her seal on every blessed thing
> we own.

PYLADES

> But not for much longer. Hades is soon going to grab her.

ORESTES

> But how will we manage it, with all her slaves about?

PYLADES

> Slaves! No Trojan stroge will scare me!

ORESTES

> Yes, those plebs of mirrors and perfume!

PYLADES

> She's the pits! Such cheek! Did she really drag those Trojan
> bimbos and baubles home with her?

ORESTES

Oh, Hellas is too straightlaced for this biddy.   570

PYLADES

A slave is no match for a free man.

ORESTES

I'd die twice if we could pull this off.

PYLADES

I would too.

ORESTES

So come on. Tell us the plan.

PYLADES

We'll go into the palace, letting on that we're to kill ourselves.

ORESTES

Okay, go on . . .

PYLADES

We'll weep and wail about our downfall to her.

ORESTES

Of course, she'll pretend to cry on our behalf, but she'll really be
gloating.

PYLADES

Exactly. But we'll really be laughing at her gloating. We'll have the
last laugh.

ORESTES

But then how will we get the chance to kill her?   580

PYLADES

We'll hide our blades beneath our cloaks.

ORESTES

What'll we do about her slaves? Will we have to kill them?

PYLADES

We'll bar them in outside rooms.

ORESTES

And we'll kill any who can't keep silent.

PYLADES

After that, we'll play it by ear.

ORESTES

"Do away with Helen": that will be our catch cry.

PYLADES

That's it in a nutshell. But here's the real beauty of my plan. If we
killed some other, more respectable wife, we'd
definitely be murdered. But everyone will be
delighted with Helen's death—all those who had
their sons killed in action at Troy and every wife
who was made a widow.
There will be hurrahs on the streets, bonfires will be lit to thank
the gods. People will praise us to high heavens
for ridding them of such a nasty piece of work.
They won't be calling you matricide then.
They'll crown you with a better title: Helen's
executioner—Helen, the murderer of the nation.
Menelaus shouldn't be allowed to thrive after your father,
yourself, and your sister have been snuffed out.
Your mother—I won't say anything about that,
needless to say. But it's all wrong that Menelaus

should take over your house after he owes his life
and his wife to your father's bravery.
And if we don't get away with Helen's murder, we'll set the palace
on fire and make it our pyre. We can't lose either
way. We'll either die with honor or come through
with honor.   590

CHORUS

This daughter of Tyndareus, who shamed the name of women,
deserves every woman's disdain.

ORESTES

Ah, there's nothing in this world like a true friend. Money
or power pales next to it. You masterminded
Aegisthus' punishment. You stood by my side
through thick and thin. And now you've come
through again.
But that's enough praise. It can be too much. If we must give up
the ghost, I'll get my enemies. I'll make those
who betrayed me sorry before I go.
I'm Agamemnon's son, right, the son of one held worthy to rule
all of Hellas? He was no tyrant, yet he ruled with
the power of a god. I'll not brook dying like a
slave. I won't let him down. I'll go out a free man
avenging Menelaus. That alone would be enough.
And if we manage to kill Helen and somehow outsmart death
ourselves, well and good. This I pray for. Hope
lifts the heart and costs nothing.

ELECTRA

My brother, I think I see a way to make this wish come true.
Freedom for you, Pylades, and me.

ORESTES

Come on, only the gods can save us now. But excuse me, I know
you are no fool.

ELECTRA
Listen then. Pylades, you pay attention also.

ORESTES
Tell us so. At this stage even an inkling of hope is good to hear.

ELECTRA
Do you know Helen's daughter?—What am I asking?—Of course
        you do.   600

ORESTES
Didn't my own mother raise her since she was a kid?

ELECTRA
Even she's off paying her respects at Clytemnestra's grave.

ORESTES
So what? What does this have to do with our getting away?

ELECTRA
We'll take her as hostage when she returns here.

ORESTES
How will this save us?

ELECTRA
If Menelaus threatens to kill us after we deal with Helen—and
        since the three of us are in this together, he's sure
        to—then you must swear that you will kill
        Hermione. By holding a blade to her throat,
        you hold it to his.
If, seeing Helen lying in her own blood, he at least wants to save
        his daughter by letting us go, then let her go.
But if, out of his mind, he attempts to kill you, then kill the girl.
        My guess is that he'll be all bluster at first, but
        that he'll cool down pretty quickly. He's a coward

really. This plan is the bulwark that will save us.
That's it.

ORESTES

Some woman. You have the spirit of a man within a woman's
    body. More than any other woman you deserve
    to live rather than die! Pylades, this is the woman
    you'll lose if we lose, but if we win you'll be lucky
    enough to have her as a wife.

PYLADES

By heavens, there'd be no one more proud than myself to bring
    her home to Phocis as my bride.   610

ORESTES

But Electra, when is Hermione due to return? I like your plan,
    but when can we take that traitor's cub?

ELECTRA

As it happens, she's due to return any time now.

ORESTES

Good. Electra, you wait outside the house to greet her. Keep an
    eye out for Menelaus or any of his crowd in case
    they foul this up before we even begin. Give us
    some sign: knock on the door or call in to us.
Now, Pylades, let's go into the palace and arm ourselves with
    swords for this latest battle. We are comrades
    in arms as always.
(He prays to invoke the ghost of Agamemnon.)
O my father, dwelling now in the house of night, come now and
    help your son, Orestes, in his direst moment. It
    was for your sake that I suffer, condemned
    wrongfully and betrayed by your own brother,
    though all I sought was justice. Please, father,

help us trap his wife and kill her. We need
your help.

ELECTRA

Father, we call you. Come if you can hear our prayers beneath
the earth. Hear our cry. We die for you.

PYLADES

My uncle, Agamemnon, listen to all our prayers. You can save
your children.

ORESTES

I killed my mother . . .

PYLADES

I helped raise the sword that killed her . . .

ELECTRA

I encouraged you, checking my doubts.   620

ORESTES

Father, I did it for you.

ELECTRA

I didn't abandon you either.

PYLADES

Won't you take their part, take care of your own?

ORESTES

I offer you a libation of tears.

ELECTRA

I offer you my lament.

PYLADES

Enough now, let's act. If prayers like spears can pierce the earth,
he hears you.

Zeus, father of all our fathers, and wielder of justice, please grant
us your blessing and success. The three of us face
this together, one cause, one outcome. Together
we stand or fall!
(Orestes and Pylades exit into the palace.)

ELECTRA
Beloved Women of Mycenae, noblest of Pelasgia's first city . . .

CHORUS
Princess—you still have the right to that title in this city—what
is it you want to say?

ELECTRA
Some of you man the main road here, the rest of you man the
side road over there, guarding the palace.   630

CHORUS
But why do you ask us to do this?

ELECTRA
I'm afraid that someone might spot my brother and Pylades
getting ready to murder and cause our plan to
backfire.
(The chorus breaks into two semichoruses.)

SEMICHORUS I
Hurry, we'll keep our eyes peeled on the road to the east.

SEMICHORUS II
And we'll watch over the road coming from the direction where
the sun sinks.

ELECTRA
Keep a sharp lookout on every side now.

SEMICHORUS I
You don't need to worry on that score.

ELECTRA
> Stay focused.

SEMICHORUS II
> Look out. Be careful. Someone is coming, a peasant. Who could
> it be?

ELECTRA
> Then our number is up. He'll give the game away to our enemies
> on the spot.

SEMICHORUS II
> No, no. Don't fret, it was only a false alarm. There's no one there
> after all.   640

ELECTRA
> And you over there, is the highway clear? If it is, then yell. If not
> then keep quiet.

SEMICHORUS I
> It's all clear on this side. There's not an Argive in sight.

SEMICHORUS II
> The same here. Nothing stirs.

ELECTRA
> Now's the time to signal to them inside:
> What's holding you up? There's not a enemy in sight. When will
> you dye your hand in blood?
> They can't hear a word I say! Has her beauty weakened their
> resolve? Anytime now soldiers will arrive and
> rush to the rescue.
> Watch carefully. This is no time to be slacking off. That group
> returns to keep watch on the east, the other on
> the double, return to the west.

BOTH SEMICHORUSES
> We're watching on every side . . .

HELEN *(from within)*
> Help. They'll murder me!

SEMICHORUS I
> Do you hear? The men steep themselves in blood.   650

SEMICHORUS II
> It's surely Helen screaming.

ELECTRA
> O Zeus, Zeus, eternally all powerful, please help my companions
>   in their supreme moment!

HELEN *(within)*
> I'm dead. Menelaus where are you? You are so near, yet so far!

ELECTRA
> Stab her—kill her—butcher her.
> Raise your sharp swords together
> and gut that creature
> who ditched her husband and father,
> who caused so much murder
> on the banks of the Scamander
> where spears fell like tears.   660

CHORUS
> Quiet now, hush. Listen, footsteps. Someone is coming.

ELECTRA
> O beloved women, it must be Hermione. She enters this cycle
>   of murder right on time. Quit your outcry. She
>   is entering our net. She'll be a grand catch if
>   we nab her. Compose yourselves and return

to your stations. Don't give any hint of what's
happening in there. I won't allow my face to
give anything away.

(Enter Hermione.)

Girl, are you returning from laying wreaths and pouring offerings
on Clytemnestra's grave?

HERMIONE

Yes, I have carried out the rights and won her favor.
But on my return I heard a hair-raising screech coming from the
palace.

ELECTRA

Doesn't our present predicament warrant such a scream?

HERMIONE

Ah, please don't say another word. Don't tell me there's more
bad news.

ELECTRA

Argos has condemned us to death.

HERMIONE

Oh, no . . . you are my own flesh and blood.

ELECTRA

Everything is set. We are standing smack dab under the yoke
of fate.   670

HERMIONE

So that was the reason for the cry.

ELECTRA

Yes, he dropped at Helen's feet in supplication and cried . . .

HERMIONE
But who exactly? I'm in the dark until you tell me.

ELECTRA
Why, Orestes of course, begging for his life and mine.

HERMIONE
So now I get why you cried out like that.

ELECTRA
Why else would I raise such a plaint? But, please, help us. Plead
with your mother, perfection herself, to persuade
Menelaus to put a stop to our executions. O you
who were cradled in my very own mother's arms,
have pity on us and save us. You are our one and
only chance now. I'll escort you there myself.

HERMIONE
Of course, I'll head straight into the palace and do everything I
can to save you.
(Hermione exits into the palace.)

ELECTRA
Hello in there, armed comrades, now's your chance to nab her.

HERMIONE *(within)*
Oh no, help. What's this?

ORESTES
Shut up. You're here to save us and not the other way round.   680

ELECTRA
Grab her, snatch her. Put a sword to her throat and silence
her. Show Menelaus he's dealing with no
Trojan flunkies. We'll back him against
the coward's wall.

(Exit.)

CHORUS
> Hurry sister, raise a hubbub
> to drown out the crime's commotion
> that is sure to alarm the Argives
> and send them rushing to the rescue.
>
> Before they get here, let's make sure
> Helen is lying in a flood
> of her very own blood.
> Let's make certain of her death,
> even if we only hear of it by word of mouth.   690
> We know something terrible has occurred,
> but what exactly we haven't heard.
> God's vengeance has descended on Helen,
> justice has finally landed from heaven
> on the woman who made all of Greece
> weep for the sake of spineless Paris
> who drew the men of Argos
> to fetch Menelaus' wretched wife.
>
> But listen, someone is sliding open the bolts of the royal door.
> > Someone is coming, some slave who can tell us
> > what has happened.

(Enter Phrygian slave.)

PHRYGIAN SLAVE
> I'm ducking de Greeks. I'm scramming from murderers in me
> stockin vamps. I waxed a gaza otta dare over da
> roof. Me heart's in my shaggin mouth. Ladies dis
> is your place, where can I go? Maybe I can fly to
> de land-hugging sea.   700

CHORUS
> What is it? What's wrong?

PHRYGIAN SLAVE

O blessed hills of me cuntry.
You are de berries. I keen for you,
brought down in de wink of an eye.
Dat wan born of a swan put de cawhake on you,
dat septic bitch, Leda's chick: Helen.

CHORUS

Now, now, tell us as clearly as you can all that went on inside.
    Calm down. Tell us one thing at a time. We
    couldn't make out much from what you just
    blurted.

PHRYGIAN SLAVE

Ochón Ochón is the keen of me people.
Let me tell ye de whole story. Gutty boys came into de palace.
    One was de son of General Agamemnon, de
    udder was his pal Pylades who is a right bad
    drop, trouble, a tarry-boy if ever I saw one. He's
    a kind of Odysseus: a chancer, a cheater, dough
    loyal to his comrades and good to have on your
    side in a scrap. I hope dat sneak will be ruined
    for all his behind de scenes trickery.
Dey walked in wit tears in dare eyes and plonked themselves
    on eider side of Helen, de biddy who Paris, de
    archer, ran off wit. She was hemmed in by dese
    tarry boys and dey licked up to her to be saved.   710
When dey grabbed her around her knees we, her slaves, jumped
    up, mumbling to each udder dat someding
    dodgy was up. A few of us taut dat was all
    . baloney, but udders would have no truck wit dat
    and had dose two buckoes taped. Dey twigged
    dat a stroke was going to be pulled on Helen by
    dat snake who did away wit his own Ma.

CHORUS
  And where were you? Had you escaped?

PHRYGIAN SLAVE
  No, no, in fact as it happened I was takin care of Helen, keepin
      her cool. She was spinning yarn dat trailed along
      de floor, sewing de gift of a purple cloth from her
      Trojan spoils to lay on Clytemnestra's grave.
  Den Orestes begged her, "O child of Zeus, please rise up from
      your seat and accompany me to de ancient alter
      of Pelops, our ancestor, to listen to what I've to
      say in dat sacred spot." So she goes along wit
      him, completely green.
  Meanwhile his pal Pylades, his chum in crime, is up to no good,
      herding us slaves outta de way, shouting "Get
      out you Trojan bums." He locked us out in de
      outside rooms and stables . . . separating us from
      our trapped queen.

CHORUS
  And then what awful thing happened?

PHRYGIAN SLAVE
  O blessed Mother! What poxy deeds of outrageous crime I saw
      dare in de royal chambers. From outta de gloom
      of de purple curtain dey came wit dere swords,
      training dare eyes to see if dere was any sign of
      anyone, and den dose higo shytes attacked me,
      lady, like mountain boars screaming "Do away
      wit Helen. You must die because your wimp of a
      husband has let down Orestes, his very nephew,
      allowing him to die dis very day."
  Den she let an unmerciful scream outta her, her white arms
      lacing her chest and her head. She tore at her
      hair and jumped up in her gold sandals and
      made a run for it. Orestes chased after her and

grabbed her and dragged her head back by de
hair so he could gut her . . .

CHORUS

What did you do to help?

PHRYGIAN SLAVE

Oh, we hollered and tried to bate down de doors dat barred us
from de chamber. We ran about de halls to try
and rescue her, some of us wit stones, some wit
spears and udders wit swords. But every way we
turned we were beaten back by de strap Pylades,
who to give him his due, was as feckin fareless as
Hector or Ajax.   720
We clashed blade to blade, but it was soon as clear as day dat
de likes of us were no match for de Greek. One
made a bolt for it, one lay dead, anudder lay
wounded, anudder fell to his knees, de only
shield he had left was prayer. So we vamoosed
outta dare as quick as we could.
Misfortunate Hermione arrived on de scene as her poor mother
fell to de ground. Da two gowls pounced on her
like lions on a kid.
Den dey turned back to de Helen. But—O God! Earth, sun, and
moon!—she had vanished into tin air. I don't
know if it was wizardry, or some udder kinda
magic, or if da Gods had taken her. I skedaddled
out of there so fast I haven't an iota what
happened after dat.
Oh Menelaus, who traveled so far and suffered so much, has got
Helen back for damn all.

CHORUS

Is there any end to it? Out of strangeness strangeness comes.
But look, here comes Orestes wielding his sword.
(Enter Orestes.)

ORESTES

Where is that cur that tried to escape my sword?

PHRYGIAN SLAVE

O me prince, I kiss de ground you walk on. Please spare me.
Even de most reckless prefer to live radar
dan die.

ORESTES

Didn't you just now cry out to Menelaus for help? Admit it, you
eejit.

PHRYGIAN SLAVE

Oh no, no, no. He's nuting next to you. It was to help you I
called out.   730

ORESTES

Answer this: did Tyndareus' daughter deserve to die?

PHRYGIAN SLAVE

Of course she did. And I'd say de same if she had tree troats to
slash.

ORESTES

Cur. You're just pandering to me. In your heart you feel
differently.

PHRYGIAN SLAVE

But didn't she deserve it for killing so many Trojans, not to
mention de ruin of Hellas?

ORESTES

Swear you're not having me on, or I'll gut you.

PHRYGIAN SLAVE

I swear on me own very life, dat's de most sacred oat I know.
(*Orestes holds the blade right at the slave's throat.*)

ORESTES
> Were all the slaves as scared of the sword as you are now?

PHRYGIAN SLAVE
> Oh please, please draw de murderous blade from me troat.

ORESTES
> But why? Are you afraid of turning into a Gorgon's head?

PHRYGIAN SLAVE
> No, no, I'm afraid of turning into a dead man. I know shag all
>> about Gorgons.   740

ORESTES
> Since you're just a slave, wouldn't death be better? I would set
>> you free.

PHRYGIAN SLAVE
> Shur doesn't every man, even a slave, prefer life?

ORESTES
> Well said: you're saved by your wit. Get back now to the palace,
>> quick.

PHRYGIAN SLAVE
> So, ya won't kill me?

ORESTES
> No, this time I'll let you off.

PHRYGIAN SLAVE
> Oh tank you. It's so good of ya . . .

ORESTES
> Get out of here before I change my mind.

PHRYGIAN SLAVE
    Dat wouldn't be good . . .
(The Phrygian slave hurriedly exits.)

ORESTES
    Fool, I wouldn't sully my sword on your likes. Nobody gives a
            hoot about you. All I wanted was to shut you up
            in case your screams would alert the town that
            would rise up in the wink of an eye.
    Mind you I've no fear of Menelaus. Let him come within reach of
            my sword. He's only a nancy boy with those gold
            curls of his.   750
    If he marches in here with his army to avenge Helen's murder by
            trying to murder me and loyal Pylades, then I'll
            murder his daughter too!
(Exit Orestes into the palace, bolting the doors behind him.)

CHORUS
    O heavens, what's happening?
    Once more terror is raining
    down upon the house of Atreus.

    What'll we do? Should we let the city know?
    It's safer to keep our mouths shut.
    Look up there. Smoke signals rise
    from the house, telling us what's happening.
    They've set the palace of Tantalus ablaze.
    They'll stop at nothing.   760
    Yet the gods are sure to kick in
    and fork out whatever they will.
    The power of the gods is mighty.
    The demons, of course, led this house
    into a path of violence and vengeance
    ever since Myrtilus fell from his chariot.
    Ah, we can make out Menelaus hotfooting it here.

He must have got wind of what's going on.
You in there, bolt and bar the gate.
Hurry. Hurry. Orestes, this fellow   770
on his high horse of victory, will stamp
on anyone who is down.
(Enter Menelaus with armed attendants.)

MENELAUS
　　I have been drawn here by the unnatural deeds of two dreadful
　　　　beasts. I can't call them men. Honestly, I've
　　　　heard the unbelievable rumor about my wife.
　　　　How she vanished into thin air and is not dead.
　　That must be the wacky ramblings of a panic-stricken madman.
　　　　Though I'd say myself it's a ruse contrived by the
　　　　murderers and is obviously a farce.
　　You, inside, open the door.
(Nothing happens.)
　　Okay, so lads, break open the door so I can at least save my poor
　　　　child and recover the body of my unlucky wife,
　　　　whose murder I'll personally revenge.
(Orestes appears with Pylades, Hermione, and Electra on the roof.)

ORESTES
　　You down there, don't you lay a finger on the gate.
　　You, Menelaus, you puffed-up, impotent twerp. If you do, I'll
　　　　bring down the ancient parapet upon your head.
　　　　The doors have been purposely barred to lock
　　　　you out. If you think you can rescue anyone,
　　　　then think again.

MENELAUS
　　Ah. What's this? I see torches and look there's people on the
　　　　roof—And, oh, there's my poor daughter with
　　　　a blade to her throat!

ORESTES

Menelaus, do you want to ask questions or to listen to me?   780

MENELAUS

Neither. But it seems I must put up with listening to you.

ORESTES

If you must know, I'm about to do in your daughter.

MENELAUS

What? You killed Helen. Isn't that enough?

ORESTES

I wish I had killed, but heaven snatched her away.

MENELAUS

You only add insult to injury. You killed her.

ORESTES

If only that were true, but I wish . . .

MENELAUS

You wish what? I can't take this . . .

ORESTES

I wish that I *had* hurled Helen to her death.

MENELAUS

Return my wife's body. At least let me bury her.

ORESTES

You have to ask the gods that. But I'll get your daughter.   790

MENELAUS

This mother-murderer adds murder to murder.

ORESTES

I am my father's avenger who was let down by you.

MENELAUS

But wasn't your own mother's death enough for you?
Orestes, I'd never tire of doing away with filthy, unfaithful wives.
And you, Pylades:
are you a party to all this too?

ORESTES

I speak for him. His silence says it all.

MENELAUS

Unless you can sprout wings, I'll get you.

ORESTES

We'll fly from nothing. And now we'll set a torch to the house.

MENELAUS

What? You mean you'll wipe out your own father's house?   800

ORESTES

Anything to keep it from you—and I'll take your daughter
                    with it.

MENELAUS

Kill her and I'll kill you.

ORESTES

So be it.

MENELAUS

Stop. That's not wise.

ORESTES

Shut up. This is your just desert.

MENELAUS
> What? And how just is it that you should live?

ORESTES
> It is right I should live and rule.

MENELAUS
> Rule what?

ORESTES
> Argos, of course.

MENELAUS
> You? Such cheek.   810

ORESTES
> Why not?

MENELAUS
> How could you perform the sacred rights before battle?

ORESTES
> And I suppose it's right for you to!

MENELAUS
> Of course, my hands are clean . . .

ORESTES
> But not your heart.

MENELAUS
> Who in heaven's name would speak to you?

ORESTES
> Those who love their fathers.

MENELAUS
And what about those who love their mothers?

ORESTES
They should be so lucky.

MENELAUS
You're not so lucky.   820

ORESTES
You bet. I can't abide whores.

MENELAUS
Take your sword from my daughter's throat. She's no whore.

ORESTES
If you expect me to spare her, you have another thing coming.
You're rotten to the core.

MENELAUS
You're going to murder my child?

ORESTES
Ah, for once you're believable: that's not a word of a lie.

MENELAUS
What can I do to stop you?

ORESTES
Persuade Argos . . .

MENELAUS
Of what?

ORESTES
To spare our lives.   830

MENELAUS
  Or else you'll kill my daughter?

ORESTES
  Exactly.

MENELAUS
  O unlucky Helen . . .

ORESTES
  And aren't I unlucky?

MENELAUS
  I brought you all the way from Troy to die . . .

ORESTES
  I only wish she had!

MENELAUS
  Through so many hardships.

ORESTES
  And *I* suffered none?

MENELAUS
  And now I'm helpless . . .

ORESTES
  You gave me no help.   840

MENELAUS
  You have trapped me.

ORESTES
  Scoundrel, you have trapped yourself.
  Hello down there. Electra, now's the time

to make a bonfire of this house.
And you, my most loyal friend, Pylades,
set fire to the parapets.

MENELAUS
O land of Danaus, mighty people of Argos,
rise up and run to the rescue.
Look how this man defies your state   850
so he can live, sullied with matricide.
(Apollo appears above the roof.)

APOLLO
Stop, Menelaus. Take it easy.
I'll sort out everything.
I, Apollo, Leto's son, appeal to you,
and to you too, Orestes,
with your sword at that girl's throat.
Helen, who you tried to murder to get back
at Menelaus, is here with me. This is her
wrapped in shining air. I snatched her
from death under orders from Zeus   860
and saved her from your sword. She's immortal,
since she is the daughter of Zeus.
And now she will live beside the Dioscuri,
in folds of air, the guiding star of mariners.

Menelaus, you must marry again,
for Helen's beauty was the means
by which the Gods set the Trojans and Greeks
upon each other, killing so many,
relieving the chockablock world.
But that's enough about Helen.   870

Your fate, Orestes, is to leave this land
and spend a year in Parrhasia,
that is to be called after you,

Orestonia, by the Arcadians and Azanians.
From there you must travel to Athena
and stand trial for your mother's murder,
arraigned by the three Furies. The gods
shall righteously judge you there on Ares' Hill
and acquit you by a holy verdict.
Then you shall marry Hermione,   880
whom you hold a sword to this minute.
Neoptolemus thinks he will marry her,
but he will die when he travels to Delphi
to get justice for his father's death.
Give Electra's hand in marriage to Pylades
as you vowed. Great things are in store for him.

And you, Menelaus, let Orestes rule Argos.
You go and be king of Sparta, the dowry of Helen,
who has given you nothing but grief up to now.
I will reconcile Orestes to the people of Argos,   890
for it was I who commanded his mother's murder.

ORESTES

Hail Apollo for your sacred oracle.
You are never false. Although, to tell the truth,
I thought I heard bad news in your voice.
Yet all's well that ends well. I'll do as you say.
Look, I take my sword from Hermione
and vow to marry her if her father gives his consent.

MENELAUS

Hail and farewell, Helen, child of Zeus.
I count you among the blessed in the happy home of the gods.
Orestes, at Apollo's request, I give you   900
my daughter's hand in marriage. It is fitting
and fair to see royalty wed royalty.
And as I am the giver I too am blessed.

APOLLO

Let each of you now depart as I have decreed.

MENELAUS

We must obey.

ORESTES

Yes, Apollo. I'll make peace with my suffering and abide by your
oracle.

APOLLO

Go your way and praise Peace,
because, of all the gods, she's the fairest.
Helen I'll bear you with me
to Zeus' mansion in the filigreed sky.   910
You'll be seated as goddess beside Hera and Hebe and Heracles.
Men will forever toast you up there
along with your brothers, Tyndareus' sons,
as you watch over mariners,
Queen of the Ocean.

CHORUS

Great and holy victory:
shine upon our lives
and crown us eternally.

Pronouncing Glossary of Names

Stressed syllables are marked. The descriptions below are based primarily on the Oxford Classical Dictionary.

Acamas (a'-ka-mus). Son of Theseus and Phaedra, brother of Demophon.

Achaeans (a-kee'-anz). Race of warlike bronze-age people who, with the Ionians, came into Greece from the north in the second millennium B.C. Homer uses the term as a synonym for Greeks.

Achaeus (a-kee'-us). Eponymous ancestor of the Achaeans; his parentage varies, but in the *Ion* he is son of Xuthus and Creusa.

Achilles (a-kil'-eez). Son of Peleus and Thetis, the best of the Greek warriors at Troy, hero of the *Iliad*.

Aegeus (ee-jee'-us). Son of Pandion and king of Athens. Father of Theseus by Aethra.

Aegicores (ee-ji'-kor-eez). One of the Ionian-Attic tribes of Archaic Athens.

aegis (ee'-jis). Divine garment worn as armor by Athena (and associated in Homer with Zeus); usually represented as displaying the Gorgon's head.

Aegisthus (ee-gis'-thus). Son of Thyestes, therefore a cousin of Agamemnon and Menelaus. Clytemnestra's lover.

Aegyptus (ee-jip'-tus). Son of Belus and Anchinoë, brother of Danaus. He gave his fifty sons in marriage to the fifty daughters of Danaus. These brides murdered their grooms on their wedding night, all except Hypermestra, who spared her husband Lynceus.

Aeolus (ee'-o-lus). In the *Ion*, son of Zeus, father of Xuthus; elsewhere, son of Hellen and brother of Xuthus.

Aerope (aye'-rop-ay). Mother of Agamemnon and Menelaus, wife of Pleisthenes or in some versions of Atreus. In the latter committed adultery with her brother-in-law Thyestes. The twins she bore were served to Atreus as food.

Aethra (eye'-thra). Mother of Theseus by Aegeus.

Aetna (et'-na). Volcano in Sicily.

Agamemnon (ag-a-mem'-non). King of Mycenae, husband of Clytemnestra, and brother of Menelaus, king of Sparta. They were sons of Pleisthenes the son of Atreus (or, in some versions, they were themselves sons of Atreus).

Aglaurus (a-glow'-rus). Daughter of Cecrops.

Ajax (ay'-jaks). Son of Telamon king of Salamis, brother of Teucer. One of the great warriors at Troy.

Alcmene (alk-may'-nay). Daughter of Electryon, wife of Amphitryon, mother of Heracles by Zeus, who impersonated Amphitryon.

Alcyone. See Halcyon

Alpheus (al-fee'-us). River near Zeus' sanctuary at Olympia.

Amazons (a'-ma-zonz). Race of female warriors. The name "a-mazon" has been interpreted as meaning "without breasts," and they were said to cut off a breast to improve their aim as archers.

Amphitryon (am-fit'-tree-on). Alcmene's husband.

Anauros (an-owr'-us). River in Thessaly near the foot of Mount Pelion.

Andromeda (an-drom'-e-da). Daughter of Cepheus, king of Ethiopia, and of Cassiopeia, who boasted that she was fairer than Hera. Poseidon sent a sea monster to ravage the country and Andromeda was offered to it as a sacrifice to appease it. Perseus saved her and married her.

Aphrodite (af-ro-dye'-tee). Latin Venus. Goddess of love.

Apollo (a-pol'-ow). God of music, healing, and prophecy. Son of Zeus and Leto, twin brother of Artemis.

Arcadia (ar-kay'-dee-a). Country in the middle of the Peloponnese celebrated by the poets for its mountains and its rustic charm.

Archelaus (ar-kel-ah'-us). King of Macedonia, patron of Euripides.

Areopagus (a-ree-oh-pay'-gus). "Hill of Ares" in Athens northwest of the Acropolis; the council associated with it.

Ares (air'-eez). Latin Mars. God of war, son of Zeus and Hera.

Argades (ar'-ga-deez). One of the Ionian-Attic tribes of Archaic Athens.

Argos (ar'-gos). Strictly speaking, an ancient city, the capital of Argolis in the Peloponnese. But all the inhabitants of the Peloponnese, and even all the Greeks, are called Argives.

Artemis (ar'-te-mis). Latin Diana. Virgin goddess of hunting, prophecy, and childbirth. Daughter of Zeus and Leto, elder twin sister of Apollo.

Athena (a-thee'-na). Latin Minerva. Born from the head of Zeus. Goddess of wisdom, crafts, and war, patroness of Athens. The olive is sacred to her.

Atlas (at'-las). Titan, son of Iapetus and brother of Prometheus. He held the sky on his shoulders.

Atreus (ay'-tree-us). Son of Pelops, father of Agamemnon and Menelaus, brother of Thyestes, whom he caused to eat the flesh of his own sons. (Or in some versions, he was the father of Pleisthenes and grandfather of Agamemnon and Menelaus.)

Attica (at'-i-ka). Area around Athens.

Aulia (owl'-i-a). District in which Aulis is located.

Aulis (owl'-is). Port in Boeotia where the Greek fleet gathered for the expedition to Troy. The site of the sacrifice of Iphigenia.

Azania (a-zahn'-i-a). Region in Arcadia around Mount Azan.

Bacchantes (bak-kan'-teez). Also called Bacchae, the priestesses of Bacchus.

Bacchus (bak'-us). God of wine and drinking, son of Zeus and Semele. The Bacchanalia were his festivals.

Biblos (bib'-los). Region in Thrace known for its wine.

Boeotia (bee-oh'-sha). District in eastern Greece.

Bromius (broh'-mi-us). Name for Dionysus, meaning "the tumultuous one."

Cadmus (kad'-mus). Son of Agenor king of Phoenicia, brother of Europa and Cilix. He went in search of Europa, whom Zeus had abducted. He established Boeotia and founded the city of Thebes, which he populated with men (Spartoi) who sprang from the teeth of the dragon he had killed, which guarded a fountain sacred to Ares. He married Harmonia, and introduced the alphabet into Greece.

Calchas (kal'-kus). Soothsayer who accompanied the Greeks, and who told Agamemnon at Aulis that he must sacrifice his daughter Iphigenia.

Callichorus (kal-i'-kor-us). Sacred spring at Eleusis in Attica, site of the Eleusinian mystery cult.

Castalia (kas-tal'-ya). Mountain stream near Apollo's temple at Delphi.

Castor (kas'-tor). Son of Leda, brother of Pollux. The two are called the Dioscuri.

Cecrops (see'-krops). Legendary first king of Athens, often portrayed as half man, half snake. Father of Aglaurus.

Centaurs (sen'-torz). Offspring of Centaurus son of Apollo, half human and half horse; lived in Thessaly.

Cephisus (ke'-fis-us). River on the Plain of Athens; the god of that river. Father of Creusa.

Cerberus (ser'-ber-us). Three-headed beast that guarded the gate of Hades.

Chalcodon (kal-koh'-don). Father of Elphenor the leader of the Abantes in the Trojan War.

Charon (kar'-on). Ferryman of dead souls across the river Styx to Hades.

Chrysothemis (kri-so'-the-mis). One of the daughters of Agamemnon and Clytemnestra, sister of Orestes, Electra, and Iphigenia.

Clashing Rocks. See Wandering Rocks.

Clytemnestra (kly-tem-nes'-tra). Daughter of Leda, sister of Helen, wife of Agamemnon, mistress of Aegisthus, and mother of Iphigenia, Orestes, and Electra.

Copreus (kop'-ree-us). Herald to Eurysthius.

Creon (kray'-on). Brother of Jocasta and king of Thebes after the death of Polynices and Eteocles. Father of Megara, Heracles' wife.

Creontiades (kray-on-ti-ah'-deez). Son of Heracles and Megara, brother of Deicoon and Therimachus.

Creusa (cray-oo'-sa). Last surviving daughter of Erechtheus and Praxithea, daughter of Cephisus; wife of Xuthus; mother of Ion.

Cronus (kro'-nus). Latin Saturn. Titan, son of Heaven (Uranus) and Earth (Gaia). He married his sister Rhea; their children included Demeter, Hades, Hera, Hestia, Poseidon, and Zeus, who overthrew him.

Cyclades (sik'-la-deez). Archipelago in the southern Aegean.

Cyclops (sye'-klops) or Cyclopes (sye-klop'-eez). Race of one-eyed giants, most notable of whom was Polyphemus. They were said to have built the walls of Mycenae with the very large stones that are called Cyclopian.

Cycnus (sik'-nus). Son of Ares and either Pyrene or Pelopia. Killed by Heracles.

Cynthus (sin'-thus). Mountain on Delos.

Danaus (da-nah'-us). Son of Belus and Anchinoë and co-ruler of Egypt with his brother Aegyptus. Father of the fifty Danaids, all of whom except Hypermestra murdered their husbands, the sons of Aegyptus. He left Egypt and went to Greece, for which reason the Greeks are sometimes called Danaans.

Deianira (day-a-nye'-ra). Daughter of Oeneus and Althaea, sister of Meleager, wife of Heracles.

Deicoon (day-ik'-oh-on). Son of Heracles and Megara, brother of Creontiades and Therimachus.

Delos (del'-os). Island north of Naxos (one of the Cyclades), said at one time to be floating, where Leto gave birth to Apollo and Artemis.

Delphi (del'-fye). Town on the southwest side of Mount Parnassus where the Pythia gave oracular messages inspired by Apollo.

Demeter (de-meet'-er). Latin Ceres. Earth-mother goddess of grains and harvests, mother of Persephone.

Demophon (dem'-o-fon). Son of Theseus and Phaedra, king of Athens, brother of Acamas.

Diomedes (dye-oh-mee'-deez). King of Thrace, son of Ares and Cyrene, who fed his horses on human flesh. It was one of Heracles' labors to destroy him. Another Diomedes, the son of Tydeus and Deiphyle, was king of Aetolia and one of the bravest of the Greek chieftains at Troy.

Dionysus (dye-o-nee'-sus). Another name for Bacchus. The Dionysia was the wine festival in the god's honor.

Dioscuri (dee-o-skur'-eye). The twins Castor and Pollux. Served as divine messengers.

Dirce (dir'-see). Second wife of Lycus, king of Thebes. He married her after divorcing Antiope. After the divorce, Antiope became pregnant by Zeus, and Dirce, suspecting Lycus was the father, imprisoned and tormented Antiope, who nonetheless escaped and bore Amphion and Zethus on Mount Cithaeron. When they murdered Dirce, she was turned into a spring near Thebes.

Dorus (dor'-us). Son of Xuthus and Creusa, eponymous ancestor of the Dorians. Elsewhere son of Hellen, brother of Xuthus.

Electra (e-lek'-tra). Daughter of Agamemnon and Clytemnestra, sister of Orestes and Iphigenia.

Electryon (el-ek'-tree-on). Son of Perseus and Andromeda, king of Argos, father of Alcmene.

Enceladus (en-sel'-a-dus or en-kel'-a-dus). The most powerful of the giants who conspired against Zeus. He was killed by Athena in the Gigantomachy, the battle between the Olympian gods and the giants who were children of Earth.

Erechtheus (e-rek'-thee-us). King of Athens, son of Erichthonius, father of Creusa and of three other daughters whom he sacrificed to gain a victory in war. Killed by Poseidon in retaliation of having killed Poseidon's son. In cult practice, identified with Poseidon, not always distinguishable from Erichthonius.

Erechtheids (er-rek'-thee-idz). Descendants of Erechtheus; Athenians in general.

Erichthonius (e-rik-thoh'-nee-us). Father or grandfather of Erechtheus. Child born to Earth when Hephaestus' semen fell on the ground after his failed attempt to rape Athena. He was given by Athena to the daughters of Cecrops and Aglaurus to protect; they were forbidden to look at him, but disobeyed, and threw themselves from the Acropolis.

Erinyes (er-in'-yeez). The Furies, the spirits of divine vengeance, who later became the Eumenides.

Euboea (you-bee'-a). Long island northeast of Athens that stretches from the Gulf of Pagasae to Andros, the chief cities of which were Chalcis and Eretria.

Eumenides (you-men'-i-deez). The name for the Erinyes in their benevolent aspect.

Europa (you-roh'-pa). Daughter of Agenor king of Phoenicia. Carried off by Zeus in the form of a bull, mother by him of Minos, Rhadamanthus, and Sarpedon.

Eurystheus (you-ris'-thee-us). King of Mycenae, son of Sthenelus and Nicippe, whose birth Hera hastened so that Heracles would have to be his servant. He was the one who ordered Heracles to perform his famous twelve labors.

Furies. See Erinyes and Eumenides.

Gaia (geye'-a). Ancient personification of the earth.

Geleon (gel'-i-on). Son of Ion, eponymous ancestor and hero of the Geleontes.

Geleontes (gel-i-on′-teez). One of the Ionian-Attic tribes of Archaic Athens.

Geraestos (ger-eyes′-tos). Port town of Euboea.

Geryon (ger′-yon). Monster with three heads, six hands, and three bodies joined at the waist. King of Tartessus, kept cattle that were guarded by Orthrus, a two-headed dog. Killed by Heracles.

Giants. Children of Earth who attacked the gods in the Gigantomachy.

Gorgons (gor′-gonz). Daughters of the sea god Phorcys. Three monstrous sisters with hair entwined with serpents; Medusa, the only mortal one, was killed by Perseus. In the *Ion*, there is one Gorgon, killed by Athena who made the aegis of her skin.

Graces. The three goddesses Aglaia, Euphrosyne, and Thalia, who dispensed charm and beauty.

Hades (hay′-deez). Latin Pluto. God of the underworld (so the name is used for the underworld itself). Son of the Titans Cronus and Rhea, brother of Demeter, Hera, Hestia, Poseidon, and Zeus. Husband of Persephone.

Halai (hal′-eye). Town on the gulf of Euboea, near the modern Thalizos.

Halcyon (hal′-see-on), or Halcyone (hal-see′-o-nay) or Alcyone (al-see′-o-nay). Daughter of Aeolus who was drowned as her husband Ceyx was going to consult an oracle. She threw herself into the sea and she and her husband were changed into birds, the halcyons, who keep the waters calm while they build floating nests that sit on the surface for a week or two.

Hebe (hee′-bee). Daughter of Zeus and Hera, or, as some say, of Hera alone who conceived her after eating lettuce. She was the cup-bearer to the gods and the goddess of youth.

Hebros (heb′-ros). Now the Marissa, a river of Thrace that empties into the Aegean.

Hector (hek′-tor). Son of Priam and Hecuba, husband of Andromache, father of Astyanax, bravest of the Trojan warriors.

Helen (hel′-en). Daughter of Leda, sister of Clytemnestra, wife of Menelaus, taken by Paris to Troy.

Helicon (hel′-i-kon). Boeotian mountain sacred to the Muses.

Hellas (hel′-as). Name originally applied to a territory and a small tribe in southern Thessaly, it later came to include all Greeks.

Hellen (hel′-en). Son of Deucalion and Pyrrha, father of Aeolus, Dorus, and Xuthus, whose descendants are all known as Hellenes.

Hera (her'-a). Latin Juno. Wife and sister of Zeus, and queen of heaven.

Heracles (her'-a-kleez). Latin Hercules. Son of Zeus by Alcmene. He was tormented by Hera and made to perform many arduous labors

Hermes (her'-meez). Latin Mercury. Son of Zeus and Maia. He was the messenger god and patron of messengers and merchants.

Hermione (her-my'-o-nee). Daughter of Menelaus and Helen. She was married to Neoptolemus but had no children by him. Eventually she married Orestes and had a son Tisamenus.

Hestia (hes'-ti-a). Goddess of the hearth.

Hippolyta (hip-ol'-i-ta). Queen of the Amazons, whom Heracles gave in marriage to Theseus.

Hopletes (hop-lee'-teez). One of the Ionian-Attic tribes of Archaic Athens.

Hyades (hye'-a-deez). The five sisters of Hyas who, after he was killed by a wild boar, pined away and died. They became stars after their death. They are generally thought to be daughters of Atlas, but Euripides attributes their paternity to Erechtheus.

Hydra (hye'-dra). Monster associated with Lerna in the Peloponnese, many-headed child of Typhon and Echidna, killed by Heracles.

Hyllus (hil'-us). Son of Heracles and Deianira, husband of Iole.

Inachus (in'-a-kus). River in the Peloponnese, and another name for that region.

Iolaus (ee-o-lay'-us). Traditionally, Heracles' nephew and his charioteer, shieldbearer, and helper in his labors.

Ion (eye'-on). In the *Ion*, son of Creusa and Apollo (elsewhere, son of Xuthus); ancestor of the Ionians.

Iphigenia (if-i-jin-eye'-a). Daughter of Agamemnon and Clytemnestra whom he sacrificed at Aulis.

Iris (eye'-ris, Greek ee'-ris). Messenger of the gods.

Ismenus (is-may'-nus). River near Thebes.

Isthmia (isth'-mee-a). Sanctuary of Poseidon near Corinth.

Jason (jay'-son). Captain of the Argo whose life Medea saved and whom he married and then divorced.

Kore (kor'-ay). Greek word for "maiden"; often used as a name for Athena or Persephone.

Leda (lee'-da). Wife of Tyndarus, king of Sparta. Zeus saw her bathing in the Eurotas and, in the guise of a swan, made love to her. She bore two sets of twins, Pollux and Helen, who were thought to be the children of Zeus, and Castor and Clytemnestra, who were considered to be the children of Tyndarus.

Lerna (ler'-na). Country of Argolis where Heracles killed the Hydra.

Leto (lee'-to). Titaness, daughter of Coeus and Phoebe, loved by Zeus to whom she bore Apollo and Artemis.

Linus (lye'-nus). Son of Apollo and Psammathe who taught Orpheus and Heracles music.

Lion Gate. The gate at the entrance of the royal enclave at Mycenae, so called because of the lion carved into the pediment.

Long Rocks. Cliffs on the northern face of the acropolis of Athens.

Loxias (lok'-see-us). Name for Apollo.

Lycus (lye'-kus). Usurping king of Thebes.

Lyssa (lis'-ah). Goddess of madness.

Maenads (mee'-nadz). The Bacchantes.

Maeotis (my-oh'-tis). Lake now called the Sea of Azov, area where the Amazons lived.

Maia (mye'-a). Daughter of Atlas and one of the Pleiades, mother of Hermes by Zeus.

Makaria (ma-kar'-i-a). Daughter of Heracles.

Malea (ma-lee'-a). Promontory of the island of Lesbos.

Marathon. Town about twenty-three miles northeast of Athens. The plain near Marathon was where the Athenians defeated the Persians in 490 B.C.

Megara (meg-ah'-ra). Daughter of Creon, wife of Heracles.

Menelaus (me-ne-lay'-us). King of Sparta, son of Atreus, brother of Agamemnon, husband of Helen.

Mimas (mye'-mus). One of the giants.

Minos (mye'-nus). King of Crete, son of Zeus and Europa.

Minotaur (min'-o-tor). Monster, half-man and half-bull. Minos had refused to sacrifice a white bull to Poseidon, who was offended and made Pasiphae, Minos' wife, fall in love with the bull. The Minotaur ate young men and girls whom Minos forced Athens to supply until Theseus came and slew it with the help of Minos' daughter Ariadne.

Minyans (min'-yanz) or Minyae (min'-yeye). Descendants of Minyas, king of Boeotia; also the Argonauts and their descendants.

Muses. Goddesses of the arts, daughters of Zeus and Mnemosyne.

Mycenae (my-see'-nee). Town in the Peloponnese where Agamemnon ruled.

Myrtilus (mir'-ti-lus). Son of Hermes and charioteer to Oenomaus, king of Pisa, bribed by Pelops to sabotage the chariot in which Oenomaus was to race against him for Hippodamia's hand. In the wreck, Oenomaus was killed and when Myrtilus claimed his reward—to sleep with Hippodamia—Pelops threw him into the sea where he perished. This was the sin that brought the wrath of the gods on the house of Atreus.

Nauplia (now'-pli-a). Harbor city of the Peloponnese.

Neoptolemus (nee-op-tol'-e-mus). Also known as Pyrrus. Son of Achilles, king of Epirus. He claimed Andromache as his prize after the fall of Troy.

Nereus (nee'-re-us). God of the sea who married Doris and with her had fifty daughters called the Nereids, who included Thetis and Psamanthe.

Nicippe (ni'-si-pee). Wife of Sthenelus, mother of Eurystheus.

Odysseus (o-dis'-yus). Latin Ulysses. King of Ithaca and one of the Greek heroes of the Trojan war.

Oeax (ee'-aks). Brother of Palamedes.

Oedipus (ed'-i-pus). Son of Laius and Jocasta; husband of Jocasta, father of Antigone, Ismene, Polynices, and Eteocles.

Oenomaus (ee-no-mah'-us). King of Pisa (the area around Olympia), father of Hippodamia, whom he promised to whoever could defeat him in a chariot race. Pelops did so by trickery.

Olympus (o-lim'-pus). Mountain of Thessaly so tall that the Greeks believed it touched the heavens; it was therefore the home of the Olympian gods.

Orestes (or-es'-teez). Son of Agamemnon and Clytemnestra, brother of Electra.

Orion (or-eye'-on). Hunter, son of Poseidon, who pursued the Pleiades and was in love with Eos (the Dawn). He was slain by Artemis and transformed into the constellation.

Orpheus (or'-fee-us). Son of Apollo and a Muse (some say Calliope), who was so gifted with the lyre that even rivers stopped to listen to him.

Paean (pee'-an). Healing god who came to be identified with Apollo; also a song addressed to Apollo.

Palamedes (pal-a-mee'-deez). Clever hero, son of Nauplius and Clymene. Falsely accused by Odysseus of betraying the Greeks at Troy.

Pallas (pal'-us). Name for Athena.

Pan. God of shepherds and hunters, often worshiped in sacred caves. He had horns and goat feet and invented the syrinx or reed flute.

Pandion (pan'-dee-on). Son of Erichton and king of Athens. He was the father of Philomela, Procne, Erechtheus, and Butes.

Parnassus (par-nas'-us). Mountain in Phocis, sacred to the Muses. Delphi is on its southern slopes.

Parrhasia (par-a-see'-a). Town in Arcadia founded by Parrhasus, son of Zeus.

Pelasgia (pel-as'-gi-a). Another name for the Peloponnese, from Pelasgus, a son of Earth or, according to some sources, Zeus and Niobe, who once reigned in Sicyon on the Bay of Corinth.

Peleus (pee'-lee-us). Mortal who married the goddess Thetis and became father of Achilles.

Pelion (pee'-li-on). Mountain in Thessaly.

Peloponnese (pel-o-po-neez'). The large peninsula of southern mainland Greece.

Pelops (pee'-lops). Son of Tantalus, who cut him up and served him to the Phrygian gods. Restored to life, he obtained Hippodamia after defeating Oenomaus in a chariot race by trickery. Father of Atreus.

Peneus (pen'-ee-us). River in Thessaly.

Pentheus (pen'-thee-us). Son of Echion and Agave, king of Thebes who refused to acknowledge the divinity of Bacchus.

Persephone (per-sef'-o-nee). Latin Proserpine. Daughter of Demeter and queen of Hades.

Perseus (per'-see-us). Son of Zeus and Danae, slew the Medusa and then rescued Andromeda from the sea monster and married her.

Phineus (fin'-ee-us). King of Thynia, a land near the Bosporus, who was tormented by harpies and saved by Jason and the Argonauts.

Phlegra (fleg'-ra). Region in Thrace, later called Pallene, where the gods fought the giants.

Phocis (foh'-kis). District of Greece next to Boeotia on the Gulf of Corinth.

Phoebus (fee'-bus). Name for Apollo.

Phthia (fthee'-a). Birthplace of Achilles in Thessaly near Mt. Othrys.

Pirithous (pir-i'-thoo-us). Lapith, son of Zeus and Ixion's wife Dia, friend
of Theseus.

Pittheus (pith'-ee-us). King of Troezen in Argolis. Father of Aethra and
grandfather of Theseus.

Pleiades (plee'-a-deez). Daughters of Atlas, of whom Maia was one.

Pollux (pol'-ux). Son of Leda, twin brother of Castor, also called Polydeuces. See Dioscuri.

Polydeuces (pol-ee-doo'-seez). Alternate name for Pollux.

Polydorus (po-li-dor'-us). Youngest son of Priam and Hecuba, killed by his
brother-in-law Polymestor.

Poseidon (po-sye'-don). Latin Neptune. God of the sea, brother of Demeter, Hades, Hera, Hestia, and Zeus.

Procne (prok'-ne). Daughter of Pandion, sister of Philomela. Her husband
Tereus raped Philomela and cut out her tongue to guarantee her
silence, but she wove the story into a piece of cloth and sent it to
Procne. In revenge, Procne killed her son Itys and served him to
Tereus.

Prometheus (pro-mee'-thee-us). Son of the Titan Iapetus and the Oceanid
Clymene, brother of Atlas, Menoetius, and Epimetheus. He stole
fire from the chariot of the sun and brought it down to earth on a
fennel stalk, for which crime he was tied to a rock for 30,000 years
with a vulture feeding on his liver, until freed by Heracles. In the
Ion, he is said to have delivered Athena from Zeus' head (a role
more often ascribed to Hephaestus).

Pylades (pye'-la-deez). Son of Strophius, companion and cousin of Orestes.

Pythia (pith'-ee-a). Oracle of Apollo at Delphi, which was the site of the
Pythian games.

Rhea (ree'-a). Titaness, wife of Cronus and mother of Zeus and his brothers
and sisters.

Rhium (ree'-um). Place on a headland at the mouth of the gulf of Corinth.

Scamander (ska-man'-der). River near Troy.

Sciros (skir'-us). Hillside village in Arcadia.

Simois (sim'-oy-is). River near Troy.

Sown Men. The soldiers who sprang up from the ground after Cadmus had
sown the teeth of the dragon he had slain. He threw a stone into

their midst and they slaughtered one another, all but five who assisted him in building the city that eventually became Thebes.

Sparta (spar'-ta). Greek city-state in the Peloponnese.

Sthenelus (sthen'-e-lus). Son of Perseus and Andromeda, husband of Nicippe, father of Eurystheus.

Strophius (stroh'-fee-us). King of Phocis, brother-in-law of Agamemnon, having married Anaxibia, Agamemnon's sister. Father of Pylades.

Talthybius (tal-thi'-bi-us). Herald of the Greeks.

Tantalus (tan'-ta-lus). King of Phrygia, son of Zeus, father of Pelops and Niobe.

Tartessus (tar-tes'-us). Country in Spain ruled by the monster Geryon.

Tauris (tor'-is). The Tauric peninsula to which Iphigenia was miraculously transported from Aulis.

Thebes (theebz). Capital city of Boeotia, which Cadmus founded and Amphion and Zethus completed.

Therimachus (ther-im'-a-chus). Son of Heracles and Megara, brother of Deicoon and Creontiades.

Theseus (thee'-see-us). Son of Aegeus and Aethra and king of Athens, slayer of the Minotaur.

Thessaly (thes'-a-lee). Territory to the north of Greece proper.

Thetis (thee'-tis). Wife of Peleus, mother of Achilles. Usually thought to be a Nereid, but said by Euripides to be the daughter of Earth.

Thrace (thrays). Area encompassing most of the world north of the Black Sea.

Thoas (thoh'-as). King of the Taurians.

Titans. Legendary predecessors of the Olympian gods.

Trachis (tray'-kis). Town on the bay of Malea, near mount Oeta.

Trophonius (tro-foh'-nee-us). Seer whose oracle was located near Delphi.

Typhaeus (tif-ay'-us), Typhoeus (tif-ee'-us), or Typhon (tye'-fon). Giant who took part in the war against the Olympian gods. Zeus crushed him under mount Aetna.

Uranus (you'-ra-nus, Greek our'-an-us). Ancient personification of the sky, also known as Coelus, the god of heaven. Produced by and then consort of Gaia or Tithea, by whom he had the Titans, overcome by his son Cronus.

Wandering Rocks. Two rugged islands at the entrance of the Black Sea that were thought in ancient times to float and to come crashing together. Also known as the Cyaneae (sye'-ah-nee-eye) and the Symplegades (sim-pleg'-a-deez).

·Xenios (ksen'-yos). Epithet for Zeus calling attention to his special interest in the sacred host-guest relationship.

Xuthus (zoo'-thus). Son of Aeolus (elsewhere, of Hellen); supposed father of Ion and father (with Creusa) of Dorus and Achaeus.

Zeus (zoos). Latin Jupiter. Son of the Titans Cronus and Rhea, brother of Demeter, Hades, Hera (whom he married), Hestia, and Poseidon. After he overthrew Cronus he became the chief Greek god.

About the Translators

J. T. BARBARESE has published two volumes of poetry, *Under the Blue Moon* and *New Science*, and individual poems of his have appeared in many literary periodicals, including *Antioch Review*, *Atlantic Monthly*, *Sewanee Review*, and *Boulevard*. He writes book reviews for the *Journal of Modern Literature*, *Bloomsbury Review*, *Georgia Review*, *Sewanee Review*, and the *Philadelphia Inquirer*. He received his Ph.D. degree from Temple University and has received the Pennsylvania Council on the Arts Poetry Fellowship.

DAVID CURZON has published a book of poetry (*Doychik*), a collection of poetry and prose (*The View from Jacob's Ladder*), and a chapbook (*Midrashim*). He has also edited two poetry anthologies (*Modern Poems on the Bible* and *The Gospels in Our Image*). Individual poems of his have appeared in anthologies and in a range of literary periodicals, including *Sewanee Review*, *Poetry*, *New Republic*, and *Antaeus*, as well as in other periodicals in Australia, the United Kingdom, and Israel. His translation of Goethe's monodrama *Persephone* was produced at the Harold Clurman Theater in New York in 1998. He is chief of the Central Evaluation Unit of the United Nations and lives in New York.

GREG DELANTY'S latest poetry collection is *The Hellbox*; his earlier volumes are *American Wake*, *Southward*, and *Cast in the Fire*. His poems have appeared in the United States, Ireland, England, and Australia in anthologies such as the *Field Day: Anthology of Irish Writing* and the *Norton Introduction to Poetry*, as well as magazines and journals such as *Atlantic Monthly*, *New Statesman*, *Irish Times*, and *Times Literary Supplement*. He edited, with Nuala Ní Dhomhnaill, *Jumping Off Shadows: Selected Contemporary Irish Poetry* and, with Robert Welsh, *The Selected Poems of Patrick Galvin*. His numerous honors include the Patrick Kavanagh Award, the Allen Dowling Poetry Fellowship, the Wolfers-O'Neill Award, the Austin Clark Award, and the Arts Council of Ireland Bursary. Delanty was born in Cork, Ireland, and lives in Burlington, Vermont, where he teaches at St. Michael's College.

C A R O L Y N   K I Z E R is the author of seven volumes of original poetry (most recently *Harping On: Poems 1985–1995*), a volume of translations, and other works of prose (most recently *Picking and Choosing: Essays on Prose*). She was the first director of literary programs of the National Endowment for the Arts, and has taught at the University of North Carolina in Chapel Hill, Washington University in St. Louis, Barnard College, Columbia University, Stanford University, University of Maryland, and Princeton University. In 1996 she was elected Chancellor of the Academy of American Poets. She has won the Pulitzer Prize, the Theodore Roethke Award, the Frost Medal, and the Masefield Prize of the Poetry Society of America, and has been honored for her poetry by the American Academy and Institute of Arts and Letters, among other arts organizations.

D E B O R A H   H .   R O B E R T S has been a member of the Department of Classics at Haverford College since 1977. She has published work on Greek tragedy and on Aristotle's *Poetics* and is coeditor of *Classical Closure: Reading the End in Greek and Latin Literature*. She has taught a variety of courses in Greek and Latin language and literature and in comparative literature. Her interests include ancient literary criticism, the classical tradition, and children's literature.

K A T H A R I N E   W A S H B U R N — a writer, critic, and translator of poetry from classical and modern European languages—is coeditor of the monumental *World Poetry: An Anthology of Verse from Antiquity to Our Time*, translator of *Paul Celan: Last Poems*, author of the forthcoming novel *The Translator's Apology*, and coeditor of *Dumbing Down: Essays on the Strip Mining of American Culture*. She has received a grant from the National Endowment for the Arts and served for four years as an NEA panelist.